# Out of the Third Reich

**Refugee Historians
in Post-War Britain**

edited by
Peter Alter

I.B.TAURIS
LONDON • NEW YORK

The German Historical Institute London

Published in 1998 by
I.B.Tauris & Co. Ltd
Victoria House
Bloomsbury Square
London
WC1B 4DZ


In association with the
German Historical Institute London


In the United States of America
and Canada, distributed by
St Martin's Press
175 Fifth Avenue
New York
NY 10010

A full CIP record of this book is available from
the British Library and the US Library of Congress


ISBN 1 86064 189 X


Typeset and designed by Dexter Haven, London
Printed in Great Britain by WBC Ltd, Bridgend, Mid Glamorgan

# Out of the Third Reich

To

Eva G. Reichmann

the outstanding scholar of German Jewry

for her hundredth birthday

on 16 January 1997

A PUBLICATION OF THE

GERMAN HISTORICAL INSTITUTE LONDON

GENERAL EDITOR: Peter Wende

# Foreword

On 16-17 June 1995 the members of the *Verein zur Förderung des Britisch-Deutschen Historikerkreises*, the British German Historians' Association gathered at the German Historical Institute in London for the last time before the association's dissolution. The *Verein* was meeting at the Institute which owes its establishment to the initiatives and indefatigable activity of this organisation, whose efforts accompanied the work of the Institute for almost twenty years. Within the framework of this conference a symposium was held on the topic 'Problems of British-German Historiography since 1945'. The response to one of the papers, on 'German-Born Historians in Post-War Britain', was so lively among the audience present that its author, Professor Peter Alter, was inspired to undertake the project whose fruits are gathered in this volume. No one could have been more suitable to bring this task to a successful conclusion than Peter Alter. He was practically predestined for the job by his many years working at the German Historical Institute as a Research Fellow and Deputy Director; his preoccupation with the history of science and German emigration to Britain; and, more than anything, his gift for making contacts and cultivating them as a tolerant partner in conversation and discussion who always has something to offer. The GHI therefore willingly accepted the offer to bring out this volume as one of its own publications. This joint effort testifies to a co-operation that has lasted beyond the editor's period of office at the Institute.

Peter Wende
London, October 1996

# Contents

**Peter Alter**

# Introduction

In his magisterial survey of the 'historical profession' in England over the last 400 years, John Kenyon makes an intriguing observation on twentieth-century historiography in Britain. 'The two greatest historians of the post-war era, Elton and Namier, were foreign by birth,' he writes, '... and though they were both passionately devoted to their adopted country, they sought to elucidate its history by a minute study of institutions in the far past'.[1] Not everyone will subscribe, from today's point of view, to Kenyon's assertion and will rightly point out other distinguished historians in post-war Britain and their important work. However, no one would deny the highly significant contribution which historians from continental Europe have made, as never before in the history of British scholarship, to the writing and teaching of history in post-war Britain.

Who were these 'Continental Britons'?[2] What strange fate had brought them to the shores of England? And what lucky circumstances had enabled them to successfully pursue academic careers in a country whose language few of them spoke on arrival?

Sir Lewis B. Namier (1888-1960), born in the then Russian-occupied part of Poland, was a sort of exception to the rule. He had studied in Britain before 1914. In the 1920s he returned to Britain and after the publication of two epoch-making books on British history in the eighteenth century[3] took up, in 1931, the Chair of Modern History at the University of Manchester. This he retained until his retirement in 1953. Namier, without a doubt, had made his home in Britain of his own free will.

Not so Sir Geoffrey Elton. Elton, born in Tübingen in 1921, son of the classical scholar Victor Ehrenberg, was finally Regius

Professor of Modern History at the University of Cambridge from 1983 to 1988. He had come to England shortly before the outbreak of war in 1939 with his parents and brother, one of the hundreds of thousands of refugees from Central Europe who, for racial or political reasons, were forced into exile by the Nazis.[4] This new wave of emigrants in the thirties came from all walks of life; they had to find a livelihood in Britain under most difficult conditions. Many of them succeeded, others did not. Only a few of them had the good fortune to be able to continue working in the field for which they were trained. Many, particularly those from the learned professions, were confronted with the bitter reality that what they had learnt and studied at home, and what had given them a respected position in society, was more or less useless in their new environment.

However, in spite of all the hurdles and problems of assimilation and adaptation to life in Britain, there was undoubtedly a great number of success stories, particularly in the unlikely field of history teaching and history writing. Geoffrey Elton, who was to become the leading historian on Tudor England, was one of them. But there were many more. Among the flourishing historical profession in post-war Britain refugee historians from Central Europe made a remarkable and lasting impact. As they were academic teachers, researchers or freelance writers with very diverse interests and highly individualistic approaches, these refugee historians in post-war Britain never formed a closely-knit network. They also never had the slightest ambition to establish a 'school' of like-minded scholars. Their achievements were based solely on outstanding individual work and ability.

In retrospect, however, it seems to have been their particular background which enabled them to make a significant contribution to historiography in post-war Britain. Also, it is only in retrospect that these historians can be seen as a group of men who, to all intents and purposes, have two things in common. Firstly, they were all born in German-speaking Central Europe before 1933 and had thus personally experienced the Nazis' 'seizure of power' and the consolidation of the Third Reich. And secondly, they had had to flee the Third Reich and its regime of terror and persecution, very often under dramatic and tragic circumstances, before eventually settling in Britain.

When talking about refugee historians from German-speaking Central Europe who worked in post-war Britain, either as academics or freelance writers, one has to distinguish between two relatively easily defined groups. There were, on the one hand, those historians who had completed their university studies in Germany or Austria and had, in some cases, already started working as academics there. On the other hand, there were those refugee historians and historians-to-be who, after fleeing the Third Reich, went to university (and perhaps school as well) in Britain before embarking on careers as professional historians.

The first group, known as the older generation of refugee historians in post-war Britain, faced profound difficulties in continuing their academic careers in Britain. For various reasons British universities had only very limited opportunities to appoint emigrants to appropriate positions, especially as their English was not always good enough for lecturing at university level. However, if one takes into account the small number of British universities and the scarcity of academic positions at the time, the number of temporary or permanent appointments shortly before and then during the war is remarkable. In difficult times, universities and other academic institutions in Britain have shown a much greater openness to 'foreigners' among their teaching and research staff than German or Austrian universities ever did, even in their heyday in the nineteenth century.

The historian Victor Ehrenberg (1891-1975), for example, father of the late Geoffrey Elton, had come to Britain in 1939. He found work in his field as soon as 1940, at first for a brief period as a lecturer in Dublin, then as a classics master in Carlisle, Newcastle-upon-Tyne, and York. From 1946 on, Ehrenberg was a lecturer in ancient history at Bedford College in London. Another example of a successful new start is provided by the medievalist Hans Liebeschütz. He lived in Britain from 1939 until his death in 1978 at the age of 84. After a short period of internment in 1940, Liebeschütz worked as a teacher in Coventry and St Albans. In 1946 he gained a permanent appointment as a lecturer, and subsequently a reader, at the University of Liverpool, a post which he held until 1959. A third example is Eva G. Reichmann (born 1897), who also arrived in Britain in 1939, became the Director of Research at the Wiener Library in London, and one of the very few women who were able to pursue a career in their chosen field after emigration, albeit in an 'émigré' institution.

Many of the older refugee historians were, of course, initially more or less forced to turn to private studies in libraries and archives. But to be able to do this they had to be lucky enough to obtain financial support from some source or other. A statement which Esther Simpson, the then secretary of the Society for the Protection of Science and Learning, made in April 1939 is well known: 'Next to law, history is the most difficult of all categories to place and we have not succeeded in finding a permanent position here for a single historian. We gave one of our research fellowships to one of the most eminent of the displaced German historians as we were confident that if any historian could find a permanent berth he would; now after about five years in this country he is almost exactly where he was in the beginning.'[5]

Esther Simpson was referring to Veit Valentin who, in 1930, had published a major work on the history of the German revolution of 1848/49. Valentin, a man with strong political views, had come to Britain as early as 1933. After more than four years of lecturing at London University and receiving grants from the Society for the Protection of Science and Learning, Valentin left for the United States in 1940. Others followed the same pattern.[6] Among those who stayed in Britain for a shorter or longer period of time and subsequently became famous historians in the United States were Hans Baron (Newberry Library, Chicago), Fritz T. Epstein (Indiana University, Bloomington), Dietrich Gerhard (Washington University, St Louis), Felix Gilbert (Institute for Advanced Study, Princeton), Hajo Holborn (Yale University), Ernst Kantorowicz (Institute for Advanced Study, Princeton), George L. Mosse (University of Wisconsin, Madison), Franz L. Neumann (New School of Social Research and Columbia University, New York), Hans Rosenberg (Brooklyn College, New York, and Berkeley) and Hans Rothfels (University of Chicago).

Others postponed the decision to move on, sometimes until long after the war. Thus Ernest Bramsted (1901-78), who had lived in Britain since 1933, emigrated to Australia in 1952 when he was offered an academic post in Sydney. In Britain he had worked as, among other things, a teacher, then as a monitor of foreign broadcasts for the BBC, before finally working in the Political Intelligence Division of the Foreign Office. Having become a British citizen in 1940, he returned in 1969 to Britain, where he died in 1978. Fritz Moritz Heichelheim (1901-68), an authority on ancient history, who also emigrated to Britain in 1933, went to Canada in 1951 after having worked as an assistant lecturer, and then as a lecturer, at the University of Nottingham from 1942 to 1948.

Those refugee historians of the older generation who decided to stay in Britain permanently were sometimes invited as temporary guest lecturers by universities and colleges. Examples are Erich Eyck (1878-1964), historian of Bismarck, Gladstone and the Weimar Republic, who arrived in Britain in 1937 and lived there until his death in 1964; Gustav Mayer (1871-1948), historian of the German labour movement, who had been in Britain since 1934 and died there in 1948; and the medievalist Wilhelm Levison (1876-1947) who, having come to Britain in 1939 at the age of 63, was invited to be Ford Lecturer in English History at Oxford in the academic year 1942/43. Erich Eyck, who would occasionally lecture in Oxford and London, could lead a comparatively comfortable scholarly life because his wife ran a flourishing boarding house in London.[7]

The other group, the younger generation of refugee historians in post-war Britain, had come to this country as adolescents, often even as children. They received their university education in Britain, and in many cases most of their schooling as well. Among them were Geoffrey Elton (1921-94), Edgar Feuchtwanger (born 1924), John Grenville (born 1928), Peter Hennock (born 1926), Helmut Koenigsberger (born 1918), Karl Leyser (1920-92), Wolf Mendl (born 1927), Werner Mosse (born 1918), Sidney Pollard (born 1925) and Peter Pulzer (born 1929). In a very few cases, it is difficult to draw a clear line between the older and the younger generation. A good example is Francis Carsten (born 1911). He completed his legal training in Geneva, Berlin and Amsterdam. Only as an emigrant did he become a historian when, during an extended stay in Amsterdam from 1935 onwards, he turned his attention to the history of early modern Prussia. In April 1939 he sailed to Britain. By October 1940 he had been accepted by Wadham College, Oxford, to do his doctorate, which, interrupted by internment in 1940, he completed in 1942. He spent the rest of the war at the Political Warfare Executive which had its headquarters at Woburn Abbey. In 1947 Francis Carsten obtained a post as lecturer at Westfield College, London. Thus was launched a distinguished academic career which ultimately, in 1961, took him to the Masaryk Chair of Central European History at the School of Slavonic and East European Studies in London.

At Westfield College one of Carsten's colleagues was Nicolai Rubinstein (born 1911), who incidentally had been with Carsten at the same grammar school in Berlin. Like Carsten, Rubinstein may be considered a link between the older and younger generation of refugee historians in post-war Britain. After having taken his doctorate at the University of Florence in 1935, Rubinstein became one of the world's leading scholars on Renaissance Italy. He was able to support himself after his arrival in Britain in 1939 by teaching at Oxford and Southampton University College before he got a permanent position in London.

The lives and academic careers of the German and Austrian-born historians of the younger generation in post-war Britain reveal some similarities. The fact that they went to school and university in Britain naturally gave them an advantage which had been denied to the older generation of refugee historians: a confident command of the English language. We know, of course, that Geoffrey Elton, at that time still Gottfried Ehrenberg, arrived in Britain at the age of 17 without knowing a word of English. Nevertheless, by 1943 he had obtained his BA. Werner Mosse received his BA in 1939, six years after arriving in Britain, and his PhD in 1950. Helmut Koenigsberger received his BA in 1940 and his PhD in 1949; Sidney Pollard his BSc in 1948, and his PhD in 1951.

Most refugee historians of the younger generation, just like members of the older generation, were either interned for some time during the war (mostly on the Isle of Man), or served in the British Army. A few, such as Helmut Koenigsberger, Werner Mosse and Karl Leyser, who died shortly before the compilation of this volume, had both experiences. Sidney Pollard (formerly Siegfried Pollak) and Geoffrey Elton changed their names when they joined the army. John Grenville was too young to enlist. Grenville (formerly Hans Gubrauer) changed his name for other reasons: 'With my German name I could find no employment in 1945.'[8] Like Grenville and Peter Pulzer, some historians-to-be escaped internment and military service. They were simply too young at the time. In 1944 Grenville, then aged sixteen-and-a-half, worked as a gardener at Peterhouse at Cambridge. He received permission to use the library provided, as he remembers, 'that I would not attempt to enter Cambridge University.'[9] In 1947 he entered Birkbeck College instead, and then later went on to the London School of Economics.

So much for the background of the numerous historians in post-war Britain who had fled the despicable Third Reich and its deadly regime of political and racial persecution. There is no doubt that the older generation had deep roots in the German academic tradition, and in the final analysis, that is the main difference between the generations. The younger generation was brought up in the academic climate of British universities. However, and this is quite remarkable, even the younger generation has retained a strong personal as well as scholarly interest in the history and politics of Central Europe. In many cases this interest is amply reflected in their academic work.

This leads to the question as to what impact refugee historians in post-war Britain had on British, and in no way less importantly, on

German and Austrian historiography. Unfortunately the answer must remain rather vague and inconclusive. After all, there is no adequate or precise yardstick for assessing the significance of a historian or group of historians. If we ask what success and influence the historians being discussed here had in Britain, then the answer must be that in many cases both academic success and influence on students were striking. Given the difficult circumstances of the times, this general statement must perhaps be qualified to some extent in connection with the older generation of historians. They either could not work as teachers at all, or only for a short period. Therefore, the greatest impact the older generation of refugee historians in Britain had (perhaps with the exception of Walter Ullmann at Cambridge) was through their scholarly publications. But even here their influence was often limited. The work of Veit Valentin and Gustav Mayer[10] does not appear to have left a lasting impression in England. Erich Eyck, with his numerous publications on German and British history, seems to have fared somewhat better. His liberal historiography modelled on the British tradition found an audience in his host country.

As university teachers and scholars the younger generation of refugee historians in post-war Britain had a head start. This, of course, raises the more fundamental question of what actually distinguishes them from British-born historians. Do their origins, by now rather distant, have any significance at all for them and their work? We can probably answer 'yes' to this question for one simple reason: with one or two notable exceptions, all the historians of the younger generation have displayed a strong and enduring interest in the history of Central Europe. In Britain they are seen and appreciated as specialists in the history of Central Europe, for example, Francis Carsten, Arnold Paucker, Peter Pulzer and Edgar Feuchtwanger, or Karl Leyser, Helmut Koenigsberger and Werner Mosse. A number of them have worked in British as well as German history. Examples are Edgar Feuchtwanger, Hellmut Pappe and Peter Pulzer, but also Francis Carsten and Peter Hennock.

With other refugee historians in post-war Britain, an interest in German history, or at least in comparative history, seems to have developed at a later stage of their academic careers. Examples are Sidney Pollard and John Grenville. One can accept Christhard Hoffmann's judgement when he writes: 'The younger generation of refugee historians helped to raise the subject of European history in England to a very respectable level'.[11] The same scholar assesses, for example, Francis Carsten's importance as follows: 'With his contributions, Professor Carsten has set new standards in research on German history in Great Britain. Through his long teaching experience, especially the training of graduate students, Carsten has had considerable influence upon the study of Central European history in Great Britain.'[12]

Have the refugee historians thus helped to overcome what E.H. Carr once denounced as 'the parochialism of English history'?[13] One rightly hesitates to go so far. How difficult, and ultimately, how impressionistic, such assessments are becomes clear when Christhard Hoffmann writes, in summing up: 'In comparison with other disciplines, such as psychoanalysis and art history, the impact (refugee) historians had on British academic life was less spectacular and rather heterogeneous'.[14]

The most notable exception to these sweeping generalisations about the teaching and scholarly work of refugee historians was, of course, Geoffrey Elton. His writing focused exclusively on Britain. Elton became *the* authority on early modern English history in post-war Britain and it has been said that his numerous studies revolutionised the traditional view of the Tudor era. No one who reads Elton's books and articles would ever trace his approach, his arguments, or his conclusions back to the author's distant roots in Central Europe. However, is this statement not somewhat super-ficial, even misleading, after all? Reflecting on his work one might go so far as to argue that Elton's concentration on government and state actually puts him into the main tradition of German history writing. His application of the 'German approach' to early modern English history would thus be an essential ingredient of his origi-nality as a British historian. Elton, who had mastered the English language so quickly and so brilliantly, achieved everything that is attainable in British academic life. What he failed to do, however, was to stimulate and influence the post-war historiography of German-speaking Central Europe. Other refugee historians amply provided this sort of stimulus from which modern German and Austrian historiography has greatly benefited.

Much has been written about the careers and influential role of refugee historians in Britain, Germany and Austria during the war and then especially after 1945. They have been the subject of scholarly conferences and symposia. However, hardly ever were the refugee historians asked about their lives, their research work and their teaching as they themselves saw it. What were their motives in becoming historians or, in the case of the older generation, in continuing their work as historians against all the odds? How do they understand and evaluate their role as intellectual mediators between two societies and two cultures? And how did they come to terms with their own history after the defeat of Nazism which had afflicted them with deep personal scars and losses? Could they establish a relationship with the country of their origin and with German and Austrian colleagues after the war?

This volume is intended to make a contribution to redress the balance. It is a collection of 13 autobiographical essays by those refugee historians in Britain who are still alive and well. When asked to reflect on their extraordinary lives and their scholarly work the initial response was a somewhat reluctant one. However, gradually they all graciously forgave the intrusion on their retirement and privacy. Eventually, they listened to the questions of the inquiring editor and put pen to paper in order to tell their story. I am deeply grateful to all of them, not only for their trust, but also for their kindness, hospitality and unfailing support once the project was on its way.

The essay by Walter Ullmann was added to this collection for the simple reason that it addressed most of the questions which I put to all the others. A few years before he died in 1983 Walter Ullmann had given this short account of his life on the occasion of his election as a Corresponding Fellow of the Austrian Academy of Sciences. The Academy generously granted permission for the text of Ullmann's speech to be included in this volume.

Regrettably, one much respected and loved scholar is missing in this collection, Eva G. Reichmann, rightly called 'one of the most imposing intellects German Jewry has produced'.[15] Celebrating her hundredth birthday on 16 January 1997 she was unable to write or be interviewed on her long and productive life. Her great studies on the coexistence between Germans of different religious beliefs as well as her searching investigations into the hidden roots of National Socialist anti-Semitism and the Holocaust have not lost any of their earlier validity.[16] They will last as the testament of a wise scholar and a great humanist who has witnessed in horror what man is able to do to his brother and has herself experienced the mental strains that inevitably accompany exile. Her friends and admirers all over the world salute her with respect and affection.

Finally, I have to mention colleagues and friends who helped in various ways to put this volume together. Professor Ernst Schulin (Freiburg im Breisgau), the eminent expert on modern European historiography, drew my attention to the group of British historians who are represented in this volume. Dr Arnold Paucker, the

Director of the Leo Baeck Institute in London, generously and willingly offered me his advice whenever I needed it. His broad knowledge, varied contacts and effective 'powers of persuasion' eased some slightly awkward situations. The Director of the German Historical Institute in London, Professor Peter Wende, unwaveringly encouraged and supported the project right from the start. The Master and Fellows of Trinity College, Cambridge, gave permission to reproduce the photo of their former fellow Walter Ullmann. For help, discussions and common sense I could always rely on Professor Peter Hennock, Dr Angela Davies, Daniel Kiecol, Konstantin Korda, Antony Paris-Simons, Jane Rafferty, Lothar Reinermann, Ruth Streeter and Hermann-Josef Terörde. My most sincere thanks go to all of them.

## Notes

1   John Kenyon, *The History Men: The Historical Profession in England since the Renaissance* (London, 1983), p 273.

2   Marion Berghahn, *Continental Britons: German-Jewish Refugees from Nazi Germany* (Leamington Spa, 1988).

3   Lewis B. Namier, *The Structure of Politics at the Accession of George III*, 2 volumes (London, 1929); Idem, *England in the Age of the American Revolution* (London, 1930); Julia Namier, *Lewis Namier: A Biography* (London, 1971).

4   There are differing figures for the number of immigrants who came to Britain from Germany, Austria and the Sudetenland. At the beginning of the war there seem to have been about 74,000 refugees from Central Europe in Britain. A year later, 55,000 of them were granted official refugee status. See A.J. Sherman, *Island Refuge: Britain and Refugees from the Third Reich, 1933-1939* (London, 1973), pp 269-271; Gerhard Hirschfeld (ed.), *Exile in Great Britain: Refugees from Hitler's Germany* (Leamington Spa, 1984), p 2; Doron Niederland, 'Areas of Departure from Nazi Germany and the Social Structure of the Emigrants', in Werner E. Mosse et al. (eds), *Second Chance: Two Centuries of German-Speaking Jews in the United Kingdom* (Tübingen, 1991), pp 57-68.

5   Quoted in Christhard Hoffmann, 'The Contribution of German-speaking Jewish Immigrants to British Historiography', in Mosse et al. (eds), *Second Chance*, pp 162-3.

6   See Gerhard Hirschfeld, 'Durchgangsland Grossbritannien?

Die britische "Academic Community" und die wissenschaftliche Emigration aus Deutschland', in Charmian Brinson et al. (eds), *England, aber wo liegt es?' Deutsche und österreichische Emigranten in Grossbritannien 1933-1945* (Munich, 1996), pp 59-70; Idem, '"The defence of learning and science..." Der Academic Assistance Council in Grossbritannien und die wissenschaftliche Emigration aus Nazi-Deutschland', *Exilforschung: Ein Internationales Jahrbuch* 6 (1988), pp 28-43; Hartmut Lehmann and James J. Sheehan (eds), *An Interrupted Past: German-Speaking Refugee Historians in the United States after 1933* (New York, 1991); Klaus Fischer, 'Die Emigration von Wissenschaftlern nach 1933', *Vierteljahrshefte für Zeitgeschichte* 39 (1991), pp 535-549; Catherine Epstein, *A Past Renewed: A Catalog of German-Speaking Refugee Historians in the United States after 1933* (New York, 1993); Georg G. Iggers, 'Die deutschen Historiker in der Emigration', in Bernd Faulenbach (ed.), *Geschichtswissenschaft in Deutschland: Traditionelle Positionen und gegenwärtige Aufgaben* (Munich, 1974), pp 97-111; Claus-Dieter Krohn, *Intellectuals in Exile: Refugee Scholars and the New School of Social Research* (Amherst, Mass., 1993); Mitchell G. Ash and Alfons Söllner (eds), *Forced Migration and Scientific Change: Emigré German-Speaking Scientists and Scholars after 1933* (New York, 1996).

7    On the role of wives and women in the struggle to make a living, hitherto deplorably neglected in the writing on emigration, see Sibylle Quack, 'Everyday Life and Emigration: The Role of Women', in Lehmann and Sheehan (eds), *An Interrupted Past*, pp 102-108, and Ead., *Between Sorrow and Strength: Women Refugees of the Nazi Period* (New York, 1995).

8    Letter to the editor of this volume, 24 April 1995.

9    See below, p 64.

10   Veit Valentin's major works: *Deutschlands Aussenpolitik von Bismarcks Abgang bis zum Ende des Weltkrieges* (Berlin, 1921); *Friedrich der Grosse* (Berlin, 1927); *Geschichte der deutschen Revolution von 1848/49*, 2 volumes (Berlin, 1930/31); *Bismarcks Reichsgründung im Urteil englischer Diplomaten* (Amsterdam, 1937); *The German People* (New York, 1946); Gustav Mayer's major works: *Friedrich Engels: A Biography* (New York, 1936); *Johann Baptist Schweitzer und die Sozialdemokratie: Ein Beitrag zur Geschichte der deutschen Arbeiterbewegung* (Jena, 1909); *Bismarck und Lassalle* (Berlin,

1928); *Arbeiterbewegung und Obrigkeitsstaat* (Bonn-Bad Godesberg, 1972); also see his recollections: Gottfried Niedhart (ed.), *Erinnerungen: Vom Journalisten zum Historiker der deutschen Arbeiterbewegung* (Hildesheim, 1993). The book was first published in 1949.

11    Hoffmann, p 164.

12    Ibid.

13    Edward H. Carr, *What is History? The George Macaulay Trevelyan Lectures delivered in the University of Cambridge January-March 1961* (London, 1961), p 145.

14    Hoffmann, p 172.

15    Arnold Paucker, 'History in Exile: Writing the Story of German Jewry', in Siglinde Bolbecher et al. (eds), *Zwischenwelt 4: Literatur und Kultur des Exils in Grossbritannien* (Vienna, 1995), p 245.

16    Eva G. Reichmann, *Grösse und Verhängnis deutsch-jüdischer Existenz: Zeugnisse einer tragischen Begegnung* (Heidelberg, 1974); Ead., *Hostages of Civilisation: The Social Sources of National Socialist Anti-Semitism* (London, 1950); Ead., 'Diskussionen über die Judenfrage 1930-1932', in W.E. Mosse and A. Paucker (eds), *Entscheidungsjahr 1932: Zur Judenfrage in der Endphase der Weimarer Republik* (Tübingen, 1965), pp 503-531; Ead., 'Der Bewusstseinswandel der deutschen Juden', in W.E. Mosse and A. Paucker (eds), *Deutsches Judentum in Krieg und Revolution* (Tübingen, 1971), pp 511-612.

**Julius Carlebach**

# Journey to the Centre
# of the Periphery

I was born on 28 December 1922 in Hamburg, the son of the then Director of the famous Talmud Torah *Realschule*. My father was later elected Chief Rabbi in Altona, and there I grew up attending a Jewish primary school and later in Hamburg that same Talmud Torah. I emphasise this because in my childhood I had very little contact with the non-Jewish world although it was all around me. I remember, certainly, the great street battles in Altona between Communists and National Socialists, the parades in the 1930s of the Hitler Youth and of the *SA* outside our home. But whatever happened made very little impression upon me. This was most marked perhaps when my father had become the Chief Rabbi of Hamburg. We lived at the edge of the famous Grindel quarter of Hamburg, a very beautiful and comfortable area, only a few minutes walk from the great Bornplatz synagogue, a giant structure which dominated the whole area.

On 10 November 1938 I clearly remember my mother coming into my room at about six o'clock in the morning and saying, 'Come on my boy, get up, the synagogue is on fire'. I do not know how this information registered, but I confess to my shame that I went straight back to sleep and had to be woken again. By then the tension and the trouble were almost visible. I spent most of that day running messages for my father and mother to members of the congregation. I had first gone, as usual, to school at the Talmud Torah where I had already taken what was then called 'das Einjährige', the school certificate which was taken a year earlier under the Nazis. Pupils in the higher grades were assembled in the gym hall of the Talmud Torah on that day and the *Gestapo* came in their classic hats with

3

wide brims, cigarettes dangling from their mouths and with long raincoats in military style. One of them made a speech in which he explained that in Germany there was no room for the likes of us. He advised us to 'Go away' as quickly as we could. There was not much I could do with that information. My parents, of course, went into action and managed to register me and one of my sisters to go with the first 'Kindertransport' to England. I must admit that that period is more like a hazy dream to me than harsh reality.

I remember going in a taxi with my father to the railway station; I remember his last desperate words trying to give me an orientation, a focus in life. I remember getting in the train and the terrible near panic when the train got to the German border between Germany and Holland and the Nazis came in to inspect and control. We were all desperately afraid of what might happen. The train was allowed to cross the frontier and on the other side the Dutch put on what was almost a party with dancing, singing and clapping, which was nice after all the stress we had suffered. I was one of the oldest of the refugee children. I was fifteen at the time, many were much younger: seven, eight, nine. We were abruptly and suddenly torn from our parents, bewildered and not knowing what was going on, what was happening, not even able to show appreciation for this gesture of humanity to the Dutch customs people and border police.

We boarded a boat to Harwich and there again, because I was awake all night, I remember that all the children were terribly sick and they all wanted to die while I was trying to avoid the terrible smell, the crying and desolate whimpering.

When we arrived at Harwich there were masses of photographers wanting to see the refugee children and wanting pictures. I think they were somewhat surprised, even disappointed by the turn-out, by the good clothes we all wore, by the obvious signs of care and attention we had. We were not the usual poor children who in the 1930s were so obviously recognisable. We were mostly children from good, comfortable, middle-class backgrounds. We didn't look like children in trouble. In any event the organisers of the camp in Dover Court Bay, a Butlin's holiday camp, that was used as a reception centre, made a great fuss of all of us. They seemed concerned to reassure me because, as the son of the Chief Rabbi of Hamburg, I think people were very keen to show me, and through me the other children, that they had made the necessary provision for us. I remember how they took us round to huge sheds, absolutely enormous, filled with clothing from Marks & Spencer, again much to everyone's surprise, because clothing was not what we needed. However, it was the generosity and friendliness which made the first pains of separation a bit easier I think. We learned our first English songs: 'Daisy, Daisy give me your answer do', which I thought was very, very English and also 'It's a long way to Tipperary'. I didn't stay in Dover Court Bay for very long, because of my religious background. The organisers, that is the Children's Refugee Committee, were very keen to palm me off as soon as possible into religious hands so that I might be cared for in the manner which my father would have expected. I was sent to a very orthodox rabbi with perhaps, shall we say, more East European traditions than strictly the typically Western German traditions in which I had been reared. He had three children. It was quite interesting that very quickly I was more or less asked not to associate with the children because I made too many jokes. The children in fact had been teaching me English and were by far the best teachers I have ever had, and they laughed a great deal at my many mistakes. I think the rabbi, my host, was a bit put out. He had offered to take a refugee boy and probably had visions of someone small, vulnerable and delicate, instead of which he got a great big hulking adolescent. I remember that the very first thing I said in his study when I introduced myself was 'May I smoke?' He was so taken aback at my request that he agreed, and that, I am sure, he regretted forever after.

I don't want to spend too much time on my refugee adventures. I learned English. I went at first to a Jewish school, Schonfeld School, a big secondary school where I didn't make very much progress. I was rather childish in fact, a first reaction to the separation I had suffered. My academic performance at school was poor. I am sure that that was one of the reasons why the Refugee Committee decided that I would have to leave school because they could not afford to keep me there. At the same time my hosts were preparing to go abroad because they did not want to be in England when war was imminent. So they arranged for me to go to a Yeshivah (Talmudical College) but I refused. I had had some preliminary sessions in a Yeshivah in London at that time, full of military duty shirkers whose interest wasn't really in learning. The whole thing put me off, although later I often regretted deeply that I did not carry on with my Talmudical studies.

When the war broke out I became a refugee in a double sense because I was homeless and without activity. After some painful experiences sleeping in the open and not having anything to eat, which is an upsetting but important experience, I was first given a grant which I had to collect every week from Bloomsbury House in London. Then I was given a job with a furrier where I was supposed to learn a trade: the trade of sorting rabbit furs shipped all the way from Australia and used to make gloves for pilots and that sort of thing. I didn't earn very much and I didn't have very much, but on the whole I was quite contented. I was determined to study medicine as my mother had wished, although I had absolutely no idea how I might go about it. However, as a first step, with one of the first wages I received, I bought a copy of Black's *Medical Dictionary* for £1. That was my flag, that is what I looked at regularly while I dreamed of becoming a doctor. The interest was centred, not really in medicine or in natural science, but more in my grandfather, the famous medical historian Julius Preuss, whose classic work *Biblisch-Talmudische Medizin* I was to meet and use again and again in the course of my adventures.

The furrier job seemed to me a dead end, and was at that time particularly dangerous, as it was right in the heart of the City of London. Air-raids occurred almost nightly, and the escapes I had are too numerous to relate. So I got myself another job with a firm that made heat-resistant bricks for gun emplacements. There I discovered the pains and the joys of physical labour. It was also dangerous, but in a different way. I worked with many 'yobbos', all kinds of society's flotsam that came to look for casual labour. When the planes were over London these navvies often threatened to kill me because I was German. When I made attempts to leave, my employer said that I couldn't, I was in a restricted occupation, essential to the war. So I did the only thing I could do: I joined the Alien Pioneer Corps where at first I was sent to Cattering in the North. When the Alien Pioneer Corps began to disintegrate because many aliens began to transfer into regular service units, we moved to Darlington to the 69th Company. That was a very interesting time, a jolly and some-what unwarlike situation. From there I volunteered for the Royal Navy. The Royal Navy took in a magnificent forty-five refugees and we were used in a so-called 'headache programme'. We intercepted German surface radio telephone messages, de-coded them and passed them directly to the ships' captains, who could then plan their manoeuvres in relation to those of the enemy. Where it worked it was a formidable additional weapon. The trouble was that the Germans were not as active at sea as we were, but my service with the Royal Navy was my first contact with an élite way of life which I thoroughly enjoyed. I was very conscious of the fact that it was the senior service. Normally, people of non-British origin were not accepted in the Royal Navy. The privileged status was reflected in the extra rations we received and the attention we enjoyed because of our uniforms, especially from the young ladies.

We were offered extension of our service in 1945 once the war was over. I was even offered a commission in the Royal Navy because, obviously, my knowledge of German could have been put to good use, but I declined. My dream of medicine swam before me and I left the navy in 1946 as a Petty Officer in Naval Intelligence.

With the return to civilian life, I applied for and received a grant from the Government to study medicine, and met a woman who was an Area Manager for the Refugee Children's Committee. Mrs Greta Birkell of Cambridge, the wife of the Master of Peterhouse, was the first of many women to have a great influence on my life. Her theory was that 'her boys', that is to say those refugee youngsters coming through her hands, should show their mettle by becoming professors. There was no other ambition in life worth pursuing than to become a professor, and I believe that every one of the youngsters she took an interest in did become a professor.

When I met her and explained to her my dream of studying medicine, for her this was, shall we say, a first self-evident step in my career. She hawked me round the homes of various academics and masters of various colleges in Cambridge. In the end it was her husband's college, Peterhouse, which offered me a place on condition that I passed the so-called First MB, but I didn't. I failed miserably. So she took me once again on the rounds in Cambridge, and I was offered a place at Queen's College. Once again I let her down. I couldn't get through the First MB. The time had clearly come for some serious thinking. I had to ask myself why, when I was so keen to study medicine and the world had almost literally offered the whole process on a plate, I couldn't make it.

The first simple conclusion, albeit not immediately apparent, was that I didn't really want to study medicine. I was interested in medicine, as I still am, but not in being a doctor, not in treating patients. What interests me in medicine is precisely that which interested my grandfather. It was an intellectual exercise that moved him, I think, and certainly that moved me. I wanted to study medicine or to deal with medicine theoretically, but it was never really my intention to lay hands on other people in order to deal with them.

By the end of 1948 it had become clear that I was not going to pursue a medical career. I occupied myself by giving lessons. I specialised in training Bar Mitzvah boys who had never gained even an elementary knowledge of Hebrew reading and whose fathers discovered some six months before they were due to be Bar Mitzvah that the boys didn't know anything. I guaranteed to have the boys up to standard within six months. It meant that by teaching one or two days a week, giving private lessons, I could maintain myself and pursue my interests. These were very general. I had no real thought about my future. I started to act as Literary Editor for *The Ex-Serviceman*, the journal of the Non-British Ex-Service Association, and I would write to publishers whenever I saw interesting books announced, and thus had the opportunity to publish a series of reviews. I did this until 1956 or 1957. I also took a short-term job helping Professor Norman Bentwich collect material for his history of the aliens in His Majesty's Forces during the war.

Later in 1948 I received the second fateful phone call of my life. The first one had been a call from the Refugee Committee informing me that I could no longer attend school. This second one was from the Principal of the Jewish Orphanage in West Norwood. This was an invitation to come and work there because the Principal had heard that I didn't mind scrubbing restaurants, which I did every day, and other menial tasks in order to get where I wanted to be. He thought that he had just the job for me, being a Jewish Housefather. A 'housefather' is someone who would carry out a range of menial tasks, but is free during the day, when the children are at school, to pursue his own interests. This sounded very promising and off I went to Norwood. I met the Principal, Mr Lubran, and discovered what a Housefather was. My ignorance can be excused if I mention that at that time one still had to have Ministry of Labour permission to take on jobs, and this one was classified under catering. My task at first was to relieve colleagues, Housefathers, when they had their day off, and to look after their children. Norwood was at that time organised into groups which were later called families. But when I arrived it was very much a traditional barracks-type institution. In the dormitory I looked after no fewer than forty-five boys. After a year or so I, too, was given responsibility for a group of some thirty boys, aged nine to eleven years.

I accepted the challenge and the offer, and moved into Norwood. Norwood became for me what it was for most of the children there: the great maternal breast which provided us with food, shelter and clean clothing every week, a physical security which becomes quite important for those who are emotionally insecure. This I observed in the children, and I observed it also in myself. It allowed me therefore to think about my future. But first I realised that I would have to come to terms, somehow, with what had happened to my family. I came to terms with it by not doing so. This, for those who have had similar experiences, will be more meaningful than for others. The fact that my family did not survive meant that not only would I have to come to terms with this intimate immediate family problem but also that my attitude to religion and religious practice, which had gone by the board in the war years, was going to be very difficult to hold.

Two things happened in Norwood which were critical. The first one was on the religious side. I had become very fond of the children, and recognised above all the extraordinary strength which they appeared to show, not in coping with their problems but in learning to live with them. I think it is a mechanism whereby children, when they are presented with problems which are too great to handle, adopt an attitude, handling the problem of the moment, that can be got hold of, and store the real problems (problems of family, parents or home) to be dealt with in due course. So on my very first Shabbat at Norwood I remember all the 200 children standing clean and in their best clothes around their little family tables, and singing the Kiddush, 'And there was evening and there was morning the sixth day' (opening words of the sanctification of the Shabbat). I confess to having been very deeply moved. At home in Germany we also began the Shabbat with the family singing at the table. These little children were celebrating Shabbat in the knowledge that everything that really belongs to Shabbat they had had to forego: their parents, their siblings, their home. But here they stood and sang, and I very nearly cried. Somewhere, I also formed a resolution that I would do the same. I would deal with the problems that had to be dealt with whilst, at the same time, leaving until the right moment the problem I shall never be able to solve.

The second thing that happened at Norwood was that I began to develop a very real interest in the task before me. Child welfare was an issue and a subject about which I knew nothing, but which was clearly desperately important. The children at Norwood at that time were the real legacy of war. They were children from broken, divorced, deserted and sick homes. Every conceivable form of neglect, cruelty and abandonment had been the experiences of these children, and to try and rear them, to try and help them was a very difficult thing. At the time there was a great debate (after the Curtis Committee Report of 1946 and before the Children Act of 1948) over whether the children would be best reared in small intimate homes, foster homes, or whether it would be better to rear them in institutions, the old Victorian institutions of which the Jewish Orphanage was a classic example. The first thing I did was to try to get myself some kind of background in the field. At that time, although there was *planning* for training for adults to work with children, there was virtually no training. I more or less had to make my own training course. I started all kinds of things. I received permission from the school Medical Officer of Health, who came to look at our children regularly, to sit in at his Toddlers' Clinic, and I got permission to visit Juvenile Courts. Dr Joshua Bierer who ran a child guidance clinic assigned me to his psychologist, who helped me to study the problems in case histories of children. I enrolled as a so-called occasional student at the London School of Economics, where I followed courses by Dr E.J. Anthony of the Maudsley Hospital and the great Claire Winnicott, née Britton. So I began to get some grounding, coupled with my practical experience, which was very important.

Fairly early on, in the early 1950s, I wrote a paper on the problem of relationships in children's homes. My key interest was that it was demonstrable in the children's home that the behaviour of the children, particularly unruly behaviour, was always a product of the interaction with adults. Although the literature talked about maladjusted children or children beyond control, the adult side of the equation was usually left out. This fascinated me. In the paper I set out some of my observations. I offered to take boys into my group in Norwood who were officially classified as 'beyond control' but very often showed not the slightest disciplinary problems whilst they were in the institution.

That paper had a very interesting history. It almost gained me a place at Cambridge – I was one of the last three candidates in a selection process. It caused tremendous excitement amongst a number of psychiatrists. Since I was a very frequent visitor to the Maudsley Hospital, where I took many of the disturbed children we were looking after for treatment, I met Dr Peter Scott, the Home Office psychiatrist. He became a great friend and took a tremendous interest in my work. There was Dr E.J. Anthony who subsequently obtained a Chair in Child Psychiatry in St Louis. He helped me enormously over a number of years as a sort of supervisor and teacher. In fact, when I look through my papers and correspondence there are names like John Bowlby, Edmund Glover, Emanuel Miller, Martin James and Kenneth Cameron, the great psychiatric figures of the 1950s. They showed extraordinary helpfulness and willingness to support, in spite of the fact that all of them, without exception I think, took the view that I would do much better with a regular university course instead of jumping in at the deep end. Being a natural deviant I stayed my course and gained a great deal of satisfaction from this opportunity to relate the practical work I was doing with the children to my theoretical work.

There was another factor. I had long been interested in psycho-analysis and had met Anna Freud early on in England. She was related to me by marriage. I felt that an analysis might help me over-come my intellectual inhibitions. I attended the Institute of Psycho-analysis for three years for a full Freudian analysis, and certainly learned a great deal. I was encouraged to find that I had been assigned to a 'lay analyst'. This helped me to de-medicalise the experience, until I discovered that my analyst was a PhD and a reader at London University. While the analysis was slow and made no great inroads, it proved to be superb in enabling me to relate and analyse – with expert guidance – the problems, difficulties and behaviour disorders of the Norwood children and indeed of the staff.

In 1955 I enrolled at London University and did sociology which I enjoyed very much, but here again it was the unusual that turned out to be most interesting. In order to explain this I should mention that at Norwood, which was established in the early nine-teenth century, there was a magnificent nineteenth-century library which was of no interest to its occupants in my time. I liked to rummage round some of the old books, and found two beautifully produced and bound volumes by Arthur Griffiths, an Inspector of Prisons, *Secrets of the Prison House or Gaol Studies and Sketches*. It had been published in 1894 and covered the whole gamut of penology. But what interested me in particular were the chapters on juvenile crime and its treatment.

London University had a system where one could volunteer over the long vacation to write an essay which would be specially marked and for which one was assigned a special tutor. I thought that here was a marvellous opportunity to re-write the stuff from 1894 to gain myself an easy good mark. When I started reading the material, things changed very quickly. I was assigned a tutor at London University called John Burroughs. He took me to the stacks because that kind of literature, what there was of it, wouldn't be on the shelves. The first thing I picked up was the report by Captain Hall, the Governor of Parkhust Prison, for the year 1853. As I read his report, it struck me that this could just as well have been a report from 1953. The problems which Hall had identified a hundred years earlier were so close to the problems of residential care of adolescents in my own time that I thought I must really look at this in depth, and I did. I embarked on a series of intensive investigations for which I received my very first research grant from the Charles Henry Foyle Trust of Birmingham. I began my studies of Mary Carpenter, Sidney Turner and Joshua Jebb and the history of Parkhurst Prison for boys. A whole new world, and a very exciting one, was opened to me. What there was by way of literature was unreliable and repetitive. Nobody, not even the greatest in the field, had taken the trouble to check the sources, so that faulty information was fed through from Mary Carpenter in 1841 to Cyril Burt in the 1920s. When I wrote the special essay on Parkhurst Prison it caused, once again, quite a stir apparently. The doyen of social and economic history at that time at the University of London was Dr H.L. Beales. He really showed considerable excitement over my manuscript and so did the famous Dr O. McGregor. They wanted me to write articles and attend tutors' seminars, but in the end I decided to turn the whole thing into a book which I did, although considerably later.

My attempt to reconstruct a full image of Parkhurst Prison, the first institution specially for the young in England, in 1838, soon raised many issues in relation to the origins and functions of English reformatory and industrial schools. It also made it necessary to investigate the lives and works of the great pioneers in this field. Here again, I had some good fortune. A Philanthropic Society to help destitute children had been established in London at the end of the eighteenth century. Under the leadership of Sidney Turner, it transferred to Redhill in 1845 and remained an 'approved' school and subsequently community home. In 1957 the then headmaster, Mr J.L. Weldon, allowed me to search the attic of the house in Redhill in which Rev. Sidney Turner had lived. It turned out to be an Aladdin's cave, with documents, ledgers and reports going back to 1788, and all in perfect condition. Then I appealed, through the *Times Literary Supplement* and the *New Statesman* for more information, and received a letter from Dr (now Professor) Terence Morris to say that the London School of Economics had just acquired ten box files of papers belonging to Sir Joshua Jebb, the first Director-General of Prisons. I was the first to gain access to these. Then, when I paid a visit to Mary Carpenter's Red Lodge in Bristol, I again found much original material. The road was clear for a reassessment of an important chapter of the origins and development of institutions for children.

By 1959 I had become a senior figure in the Norwood home, but not as indispensable as I thought I was. At the beginning of the year the Principal, Jack Wagman, brought a young woman, Miss Myrna Landau, to Norwood, and it was not long before we announced our engagement. I had no real ambitions to move beyond Norwood and was quite shattered to discover that the home, which was steadily being restructured into small group homes, had no interest in holding us once we were married. On reflection, Wagman was probably right in not encouraging us to start married life as houseparents, but at the time I took it very much amiss – it was somehow another separation. Instead, I accepted a post as Cultural Director of the Board for Kenya Jewry, even though I had to look up an atlas to find out where Kenya was. Before we left England I had another call to ask if I would be willing to act as rabbi to the Jewish community in Nairobi because their present rabbi had just resigned.

I had never really considered the possibility of becoming a minister or entering the rabbinate, although I had over the years found my way back, with the help of the children of Norwood, to love, learn and teach the faith of my ancestors. So I was very perplexed when the offer came for me to take over the ministry. I consulted with the late Chief Rabbi Sir Israel Brodie, who strongly urged me to do so. I had known him mainly through some research work on refugee children which I had carried out for him some years earlier. He thought it a good idea for me to take over the ministry, and so I did. The Nairobi community was a very compact, cohesive little group, and it was most enjoyable to lead them in the religious sphere. They were very co-operative and appreciative. It was a very small community and left me ample time, first of all to write up my researches on the reformatory schools of England and, secondly, to take a look around in the new world which I had entered.

It is difficult to imagine the difference between a life spent in Europe with a life in Africa. Everything is different. First, the difference of scale. In Africa everything seems to be much larger than in Europe, and also much quicker. The rate of growth of plants and animals is almost unbelievable. Apart from the fact, of course, that when you drive a car and you have road hazard signs which say 'Beware elephant or giraffe passing', you know that you are in a different world. I also saw there, for the first time, the scale of poverty and suffering that goes with it. Children and adults crawled across roads, severely crippled, tied to a sort of skateboard with wheels or carried by their friends. I had not yet learned the lesson from Margaret Mead that in Western Europe we put away the ugly signs of our civilisation.

I met there another one of those great women who furthered my career. This was Liselotte Strauss, the General Secretary of the Child Welfare Society of Kenya. If there was not much training and no great career structure in child care in England, in Africa there was absolutely nothing. So, in a way, one might say that the very dearth of any kind of provision there made me a kind of a king. I was a specialist, I had practical and theoretical knowledge and experience in child welfare. So very quickly I was 'promoted' to President of the Child Welfare Society of Kenya. I established a child study group and started a seminar for young men working with homeless African boys and mobilised all kinds of other programmes. The most effective I think was the programme to deal with long-standing malnutrition, for which a German group called Bread for the World gave me, without any discussion, £10,000, which in 1960 was a great deal of money. We managed with that money to feed over 1,000 children for over a year once a day with a scientifically balanced meal. That project was a great success, so much so that it carried on spontaneously for quite a while after the official programme had come to an end.

I revelled in the possibilities presented in Africa because there one's ideas could almost immediately be put into practice. When we had collected a little money, in a matter of weeks we had built a home for homeless children. We had acquired a van and gone to feed totally deserted children in Nairobi. I made contact through this work with the United Nations, and as these things go I became a consultant on the role of women in urban developments in Africa because of my experience in working with children. Some of the research I took to Makerere College, where a well-known British anthropologist Derek Stenning became a friend and co-worker when I prepared and published a small study on juvenile prostitutes in Nairobi.

With much enjoyment I also revelled in the access I could grant myself to the archives of the Nairobi Hebrew congregation who were celebrating their 50th anniversary while I was there, and whose history I published for that occasion. It was in other ways an unusual and interesting time. My two sons were born in Nairobi. As the minister of the Jewish community I was rated amongst the heads of religious groups in the city, like Protestants, Catholics, Muslims, Hindus and the various other groups. This meant that I was invited to all official functions, and met all the great and famous who came from England or from Israel.

I had signed a contract for four years in Kenya, and was deeply involved in many projects. I was invited to stay on for a further four years. It was a very exciting time because Kenya was about to become independent. Nevertheless, in view of the fact that I had two young children, I thought it would be better if we went back to Europe. So I ended my work there and we left with a sense of gratitude and sadness. We went back to the United Kingdom, where I had accepted an invitation to join the Institute of Criminology at Cambridge. There seemed to be some confusion over whether I should embark straight away on a programme of research for a PhD or whether I should first go into what was then the Graduate Diploma course in Criminology. I chose this second alternative because I thought I could benefit from some systematic research. After I obtained the Diploma in Criminology, Professor Lloyd, the Professor of Education at the time in Cambridge, invited me to join his department. There I finished my book on the reformatories, which I published in response to a Government White Paper under the title *Caring for Children in Trouble* and which I think was reasonably successful. One particular stroke of luck was that the book was published on 8 January 1970. This was a Friday on which the *Times Literary Supplement* was bringing out a special issue on law, and the book had a half-page review. This impressed my university colleagues enormously. It wasn't really any mark of distinction – it was a lucky coincidence – but I made the most of it.

I must admit that the years in Cambridge were exceptional, and in spite of the fact that with two young children and a very small grant it wasn't easy, I had every ambition (if it was at all possible) to remain in Cambridge. Apart from the grant I received notably from my college, Emmanuel, I also managed to earn some money by teaching for Stuart Hall, the extra-mural department of Cambridge University, in conjunction with the Workers Educational Association. In my very first year I was invited to give a course of lectures in Hatfield on juvenile delinquency. The students turned out to be a group of mothers with young children who came once a week to the centre. There were playgroups where they could deposit their children and devote themselves to some outside interests. This group was again very important because it enabled me to continue my basic interest in the question of parent/child relationships. The course was sufficiently successful for the women to ask for continuations over the next two years. It wasn't that my lectures were anything special, but mainly that here were young women who, because of their young children, were almost totally isolated in their homes all day and who relished first of all the opportunity to come out and relax and, secondly and perhaps more important, to compare the experience of their children with other women.

It was really quite surprising to observe the amount of anxiety and worry that many of these women carried with them simply because they had no way of telling whether the development of their children was normal or abnormal. The tendency of course is always to fear that it is abnormal. So the experience of getting to know of problems that other people have, that one is not always the only one whose child is uncontrollable, is very reassuring. I think it was this kind of catharsis that made the course so popular and made them carry on for three years studying juvenile delinquency.

Cambridge, of course, was important in other respects as well. Since I was in the field of the Jewish ministry I participated in ministerial activities in the Jewish community in Cambridge and met a number of people who simply were a pleasure to meet, like the great E.J. Rosenthal, the Oriental studies specialist. He had predicted that I would remain in Cambridge permanently. But it wasn't to be. An offer came from Bristol University where the Professor in the Department of Education, Roger Wilson, had heard of this happy combination of practical and theoretical child welfare studies which I had enjoyed. He was looking for a tutor for a year in his department to organise and run the Home Office-financed course for heads of residential institutions for children who were to get some kind of underpinning training to improve the quality of residential work. I accepted the invitation: I had no choice really because here was a proper university post being offered to me. The course I taught in the Department of Education was very stimulating. It was ruled over by, once again, the famous Claire Winnicott. I greatly appreciated making contact with her again. I think I must have been something of a disappointment to her because as a short-term or yearly renewable appointment, the post made me very insecure and very unsettled. We only stayed in Bristol for two years. But here again I participated in running the synagogue services and in Jewish communal life. I took an interest in Jewish students who at that time, in 1966-68, had particular difficulties because of the Six Days War. Funnily enough, the synagogue in Bristol is right opposite the Mary Carpenter Lodge, so I returned from whence I had come when we were in Bristol.

Shortly after settling in at Bristol, Professor Wilson received an enquiry from the Jewish Agency about a specialist in residential care to look at a movement in Israel, Youth Aliyah. This was an association for the residential care of young people with something like 250 youth villages and 17,000 or so children. The organisation was having some problems, was looking for someone to look detachedly at these problems and suggest some solutions. I was offered this opportunity, and was awarded a Wyndham Deeds fellowship from the Anglo-Israel Association to go, with my family, to Israel for a period of research.

This proved to be extraordinarily interesting, and once again I began by building up a little history of the organisation. I then met in particular the senior staff of the organisation, that is to say the Director-General, Meir Gottesman, the inspectors, the managers and the directors of the different youth villages. Not all, but most of these were former German-Jewish refugees who had come to settle in Israel. Some were great authorities on the principles, theories and problems of education, but there was relatively less expertise on questions of residential care and above all on the problems of the relationship between residential and educational care of children, which was certainly not unique to Israel. I think I made friends with most of the people I met. I was charmed by Meir Gottesman, and a number of the inspectors I met later came to Sussex to do their doctorates.

The work in Bristol had taught me a great deal. It led me to reflect on a key issue in the field of residential social work and that is that although the Home Office was of course right to institute special training for senior personnel, most of these people were professionally untrained. They enjoyed their year at university but, and this is a problem which the course in Bristol could not solve, once people had a certificate from a university they left residential care and went into field work. Field work has always had a higher status, commands better salaries and does not impose the constraints and restrictions which inevitably go with residential work. In a way we were being counter-productive, and I felt a much greater radicalism in the approach to training would have been necessary to make such an experiment work. This I hoped to achieve in Sussex.

Sussex was looking for a new venture to introduce Israeli studies. It was an idea sponsored by the Israeli Government, and it was to be tried in two places, Glasgow and Sussex. As so often happens, they negotiated a financial contribution which by the time I had been appointed was already out of date because a new award had been made in universities and the Israeli Government was not able to meet the extra costs. At the same time I had received another of my curious phone calls, this time from Brighton, where they were going to set up a Hillel House for Jewish students. They wanted to know, since news had got around that I had been appointed to Sussex, if I would run the place. This I agreed to do. At the time it seemed a perfectly normal straightforward step. I had done similar work in Bristol and in Cambridge with Jewish students. What I did not know about, and what certainly hit me at the time, was the great student revolution of 1968, the year we went to Sussex. It was a difficult time, and the dominant ideology was Marxism, especially amongst the students. It so happened that at the same time I was appointed to Sussex as a Lecturer in Sociology and Israeli Studies, the university also appointed the famous Tom Bottomore to the Chair of Sociology. Being curious about the new man whose work I knew but whom I had never met, I went to a bookshop and got myself a book of early writings of Marx, translated and commented by Tom Bottomore. This included Marx's essays on the Jewish question. I had a look at these and was left stunned and bewildered.

I had, of course, dealt with Marx in sociology at the University of London. My tutor had been the well-known philosopher R.S. Peters. But this was political theory and not the kind of polemic that Marx allowed himself in the second essay on the Jewish question. I introduced myself to Tom Bottomore and asked him if he could suggest some reading on this dreadful nonsense that Marx had written. Bottomore said that he knew of no systematic analysis. If I wanted that, I should write it myself.

So I did. I embarked on a project to try and set Marx's writings on the Jews into the intellectual, social and political context of his time. This promised to be a big project, and I obtained some support for it from the Memorial Foundation for Jewish Culture. It certainly occupied all my spare time for a number of years. It was most interesting because it was a field which was relatively unknown to me and, above all, it made it absolutely essential to acquire a proper systematic knowledge of the Jews of Germany. This I did with considerable fascination and admiration for my ancestors and forefathers and their achievements. In view of the size and complexity of the project it was suggested that I might as well use it as a means of obtaining a doctorate. So I registered my project and Tom very kindly acted as my supervisor. Eventually Zev Barbu, a well-known Professor of Sociology, and Sir Isaiah Berlin were my examiners. Although they gave me a fairly rough time I thoroughly enjoyed the process of examination. I had already submitted a somewhat extended manuscript to Routledge & Kegan Paul who had also published my book *Caring for Children in Trouble*. They immediately accepted it and suggested the Littman Library of Jewish Civilisation. I was very pleased and indeed proud to contribute a volume to that series where I was in very flattering company.

At the same time that I was carrying out my full-time teaching in Sussex and acting as Chaplain to the Jewish students I also sat on the managing committee of a voluntary hostel for adolescent girls and two approved schools. Out of the work with the adolescent girls came a research project in which we tried to investigate a curious phenomenon. Most of the girls we looked after were homeless, desperate, destitute, very difficult and awkward-to-handle people. Their lifestyles were pretty horrific but the curious thing was that when we talked to them we always found that their social norms and values were much closer to the somewhat conservative and authoritarian staff who tended to work with these girls than to their own behaviour. In other words, the girls would behave against their own inner convictions. This intrigued us and we investigated it. I worked, in particular, with a woman, Kay Morgan, who had studied with me at Bristol and had shown an outstanding ability to interview adolescent girls. The material I collected I put together in a large manuscript which I called 'Promiscuous Puritans' and in due course submitted to the Department of Health and Social Security who had some critical comments to make but, on the whole, seemed quite positive. But somehow, the manuscript didn't look right and I didn't feel comfortable. With the manuscript of Marx, other preoccupations and my work as acting rabbi in the local community – which had the blessing of four Chief Rabbis – which claimed my attention on and off for over eight years, I just left it as a souvenir, an unprinted piece of work.

The most exciting aspect of Sussex, really, was the nature of the teaching I was involved with. This was of three types. The first was straightforward traditional undergraduate teaching, where my special fields were crime and delinquency and the sociology of medicine. Then there were what was known as the contextual courses, for which Sussex was famous: that is to say, in my case, there were courses related in some way to Africa and Asia because I was in the school of African and Asian Studies. In that context I created some courses which dealt with the problems of social deprivation in Israel, the social role of women in Africa, and their health. I also ran courses on the Judaic tradition. In fact I was able to develop my own courses and in a way the number of students attending every year was a test of their success. The third type of course was the graduate courses. I took a very keen and active interest in graduate work in Sussex, and taught the master's course in the Sociology of Deviance. I also participated in courses for magistrates. After I had been at Sussex for a while, I was asked by the Director of Continuing Education to offer a course on the Sociology of Medicine for young general practitioners. This was a great challenge because these men and women tend to be bright but also very aggressive people who would not automatically accept that sociology has anything to contribute to their study programme. It was a fascinating exercise, and I did this for ten years. I also spent a very interesting time in Jerusalem at the Hadassah Hospital, where I offered the same course to equally vigorous young physicians. But that was fairly late in my Sussex career. I should add that for the whole twenty years in Sussex I also taught a component of the Master of Social Work, with courses on Residential Social Work, which all the students had to take. In that course, which was set up in conjunction with the Home Office, there was the inner discipline and the radicalism necessary to give these young people a new orientation on this very difficult subject.

I should also mention that whilst I was at Sussex, in fact quite early on, in conjunction with my Marx project, I met two men who were to influence me very considerably. They were Dr Robert Weltsch and Dr Hans Liebeschütz. I went to see them at the Leo Baeck Institute in London to get their assistance for some material I wanted. They showed an enormous interest in what I was doing. They generally offered much encouragement, and with the help of Arnold Paucker always at the ready, I was very quickly involved with the Leo Baeck Institute, first as a member of the London Board and then as member of the Executive of the London Board. This has been a very salutary experience.

My physical health began to change. The symptoms of age were manifest. In 1988 I had my first breakdown in health. I reached the age of 65 and was appointed Emeritus Reader in Sociology by my university. I had a computer set up ready to help me to write what I still wanted to write, and to research what I still wanted to investigate. Once again it was still not meant to be, because I had yet another phone call, this time from Professor zu Putlitz who had just relinquished the post of Vice-Chancellor of the University of Heidelberg and who was acting 'Rektor' (Vice-Chancellor) of the *Hochschule für Jüdische Studien* in Heidelberg. I had, of course, heard of that college. In fact when it was first mooted in 1979 I remember a meeting in Jerusalem at which Gershom Scholem emphatically demanded that no one, but no one, in the Jewish world should co-operate with the establishment of this college for Jewish studies. I took no sides in this dispute: for one thing, I knew very little about it and, for another, it seemed too remote for me to cut into the debate. Since then, I had once or twice heard suggestions that I should, after retirement perhaps, go and teach there for one or two semesters, or generally take an interest in the place, but it just didn't register.

But Professor zu Putlitz asked quite emphatically, 'Are you willing to talk about the rectorship of the *Hochschule für Jüdische Studien*?' As always, I told him that I am prepared to *talk* about anything. The next day he presented himself in Brighton. Over lunch he told us the story of the college and its various adventures. He came a second time and invited us to come and visit Heidelberg, which we did. We were spoiled and impressed. I have to be honest: I had not seriously contemplated taking on a post like that. I was aware that many of my friends and colleagues would regard it as peculiar, to say the least, if I went to Germany. While I was in Heidelberg I met with the students to answer (and ask) questions. They asked me what it felt like to come back – and I said to them that whatever happened, I was not coming back. I might be coming to Heidelberg to work but only as a visitor from Britain, not in any other role. This was important to me. I needed to make the distinction, and the fact that people seemed to accept this encouraged me to take the possibility of going there more seriously.

There was another factor. All the people I met who were or are of any consequence pointed out, not explained but pointed out, that the University of Heidelberg had been perhaps the worst in co-operating with the National Socialists. Its authorities were the first to campaign against and dismiss Jewish members of faculty, and their record is a very depressing one. The fact that they not only did not try to hide it but, on the contrary, openly spoke about it, suggested to me that it was a climate in which I might be able to do something. Moreover there was a very personal factor, and perhaps not everybody would see it in quite that way. The college had a small number of Jewish students. There were ten when I got there; there were thirty in 1996, which for the German situation is really quite good. These were young Jewish people who were intending to serve Jewish communities as teachers, administrators, youth workers and so on. In other words, they would have a tremendously important role in maintaining Jewish life in Germany. In a sense, they were another group of young Jews on the margins of social development, the same as the Jewish students in Sussex who were being subjected to the influences of the student revolution of the great anti-religious Marxist movements; the same as the Jewish kids, and indeed as the African kids in Africa who were living in states of uncertainty and insecurity; the same as the hapless children of Norwood who had also been subjected to the pressures and blows of their time and their environment. In each case I felt that at least I was doing something positive in helping to create a climate in which these children could grow up in some kind of peace. It is really the way I have seen my function in life. It seemed to me that if I could contribute something to raising Jewish consciousness in whatever way amongst the Jewish students in Heidelberg then the project would be worthwhile.

Well, of course, it isn't for me to say whether I have succeeded or not. I am not satisfied that I have done the best I could have done. However, I have now served in Heidelberg for eight years. The time has come to change, and I can only hope that I will continue with my researches and my writing. I hope that I will continue to be as fortunate as I was in earlier researches when I found great treasures in the attic of Redhill Community School or had the good fortune to find Karl Marx's notebook in the Institute of Social History in Amsterdam. In the notebook Marx wrote about the Jews of Jerusalem, which turned out to be something he had copied from another author. Many Israeli writers had seen the material as evidence of a Jewish nationalism in Karl Marx. Perhaps it should also be said that when the ubiquitous Arnold Paucker decided to relinquish the editorship of the Leo Baeck Institute's *Year Book*, that masterly flagship of German-Jewish studies in the world, John Grenville became the next editor and he chose me as his associate editor. This association is one that I carry with great satisfaction.

### Selected Writings of Julius Carlebach

Books

*The Jews of Nairobi 1903-1962* (Nairobi, 1962)

*Caring for Children in Trouble* (London, 1970)

*Karl Marx and the Radical Critique of Judaism* (London, 1978)

(ed.), *Wissenschaft des Judentums: Anfänge der Judaistik in Europa* (Darmstadt, 1992) (ed.), *Zur Geschichte der jüdischen Frau in Deutschland* (Berlin, 1993)

(ed.), *Das aschkenasische Rabbinat* (Berlin, 1995)

## Articles

'The Problem of Moses Hess's Influence on the Young Marx', *Leo Baeck Institute Year Book* 18 (1973), pp 27-39

'Deutsche Juden und der Säkularisierungsprozeß in der Erziehung – Kritische Bemerkungen zu einem Problemkreis der jüdischen Emanzipation', in Hans Liebeschütz and Arnold Paucker (eds), *Das Judentum in der Deutschen Umwelt 1800-1850: Studien zur Frühgeschichte der Emanzipation* (Tübingen, 1977), pp 55-93

'The Forgotten Connection: Women and Jews in the Conflict between Enlightenment and Romanticism', *Leo Baeck Institute Year Book* 24 (1979), pp 107-138

with Andreas Braemar, 'Rabbiner in Deutschland: Die ersten Nachkriegsjahre', in *Das aschkenasische Rabbinat* (Berlin, 1995), pp 225-234

'Family Structure and the Position of Jewish Women', in Werner E. Mosse et al. (eds), *Revolution and Evolution: 1848 in German-Jewish History* (Tübingen, 1981), pp 157-187

'Orthodox Jewry in Germany: The Final Stages', in Arnold Paucker (ed.), *The Jews in Nazi Germany 1933-1943* (Tübingen, 1986), pp 75-93

'The Foundations of German-Jewish Orthodoxy: An Interpretation', *Leo Baeck Institute Year Book* 33 (1988), pp 67-106

'The Impact of German Jews on Anglo-Jewry-Orthodoxy, 1850-1950', in Werner E. Mosse et al. (eds), *Second Chance: Two Centuries of German-Speaking Jews in the United Kingdom* (Tübingen, 1991), pp 405-423

with Andreas Braemar, 'Flight into Action as a Method of Repression: American Military Rabbis and the Problem of Jewish Displaced persons in Post-war Germany', *Jewish Studies Quarterly* 2 (1995), pp 59-76

'Hygiene im Judentum', in Nora Goldenburgen et al. (eds), *Hygiene und Judentum* (Dresden, 1995), pp 7-15

**Francis L. Carsten**

# From Revolutionary Socialism
# to German History

Born in Berlin on 25 June 1911, I grew up in a prosperous German-Jewish upper-middle-class family. My father was a well-known opthalmic surgeon and my mother the daughter of a well-to-do banker. Many decades later, some German historians I met were very surprised that my grandmother had owned a palatial villa in the Tiergartenstrasse, 'where only embassies existed'. It was a very grand establishment, with hothouses, a resident gardener, a coachman and stables for the horses – until the First World War. On the site of the villa now stands the *Kunstgewerbemuseum*. As children we played almost daily in the large garden. My father's parents were not that grand. They owned a small department store, 'Die Goldene 110', which is mentioned as newly founded in one of Theodor Fontane's novels.[1] Their two sons studied medicine, and both served as medical officers in the war of 1914. The major part of the family money was lost in the vast inflation of the early 1920s, and a part of the villa was sublet to the Italian Consulate.

From 1920 to 1929 I went to the *Mommsen-Gymnasium* (secondary school) near the Wittenbergplatz. In spite of its name it was a very Prussian school with strict Prussian discipline: after each break the pupils had to march back into the building in class formation, led by the sixth-formers. Most of the teachers were ardent nationalists. They had been officers during the war and, instead of teaching Latin or German, recounted their war experiences and breathed fire and sword against the Treaty of Versailles (pronounced contemptuously 'Versalj'), the French and the Poles (at the time of the battles in Upper Silesia). Latin and Greek were the principal subjects, and in history the emphasis was on ancient and medieval history. As schools go, it was a good school, which means we had to learn a lot, but I disliked it intensely, almost from the beginning. In later years my opposition to German nationalism and Prussianism developed, and I turned sharply to the left. There existed an active socialist group at the school, and at the age of sixteen I joined a Socialist Pupils' Association.

There was a terrible row at home: my parents were completely non-political and conservative, with a picture of William II on the wall. But I persevered, and henceforth spent all my spare time in political meetings and study groups. Marxism attracted me although I knew very little about it, and my socialism was largely emotional and oppositional. From the socialist group which I joined first it seemed only a short step to the youth organisation of the KPD; at first I was totally uncritical, a firm believer.

In 1929 when I left school after another row – this time with the teachers – I decided to read not history, in spite of my growing interest, but law and economics because I was still thinking of a possible political career as a lawyer. Yet the early 1930s were not years suitable for quiet studies, and were punctuated by violent clashes with Nazi students. In May 1933, already under Hitler, I passed the 'Referendar' examination (making me a candidate for the higher civil service) at the *Kammergericht* (superior court of justice) in Berlin with the mark 'satisfactory'. That was the end of my legal career. During the years of the dissolution of the Weimar Republic I began to study seriously the history of the German socialist movement, especially of its split, and began to buy the left-wing pamphlets of earlier years which became the basis of my large collection. This was my first historical study; I began to look for causes of the sad decline of the German labour movement. As a result I became more and more critical of the official party line and recognised that the KPD, through its 'splitting' policy, had become completely ineffective, a party of the unemployed. This was about 1931. I was really in despair, all my earlier illusions gone. From my years as a student in Heidelberg I had close contact with Richard Löwenthal, who had been a prominent Communist but had been expelled from the KPD in 1928 for 'right-wing' deviationism. One day I opened my heart to him and he told me in great secrecy of a new organisation whose aim it was to reunite the split socialist movement by working secretly in the SPD as well as the KPD. Löwenthal himself was not a member of the 'Org.', but some of his friends were, and soon I was recruited too, all by very conspiratorial means.

Early in 1932 I took part in a long introductory course on Marxist theory, the history of Bolshevism and of the socialist movement, bourgeois ideology, the role of the individual in history, to make new members familiar with the conception of the 'Org.'s leader, Walter Loewenheim, known to us as 'Kurt' (another right-winger who had been expelled from the KPD some years before). The members were to become 'professional revolutionaries', with Lenin's 'What is to be done?' as the example. They were told to remain in the existing working-class organisations and to gain prominent positions in them, with the ultimate aim of bridging the gap between them and reuniting the movement, as a precondition for the victory of German socialism. All these hopes, however, were destroyed by the Nazi victory of 1933, which Loewenheim had not foreseen. As the socialist organisations were destroyed and disintegrated, the members of the 'Org.' were withdrawn and it became in effect an underground socialist group, not yet known to the *Gestapo*, and could slowly expand. In the same year the 'Org.' also acquired a name, for Loewenheim expounded his views in a pamphlet *Neu Beginnen! Faschismus oder Sozialismus*, which was rather surprisingly published by the exiled leaders of the SPD in Prague. The pamphlet blamed the bourgeois ideologies of the left-wing parties for the defeat, pleaded for a complete rejuvenation of the movement, which was to be led by socialists inside Germany, and advocated the adoption of a long-term perspective for the defeat of the Nazi régime: a much more realistic attitude than the views held then by the leaders of the SPD and KPD.

In Berlin the 'Org.' continued its activities undiscovered by the *Gestapo* until 1935, with me as a very active member, trying to recruit not only among disenchanted adherents of the former left-wing organisations, but also among the professional classes and intellectuals. It was still very small, at most a few hundred members, and it also recruited outside Berlin, leading to its discovery by the *Gestapo*. In the autumn of 1935 there were mass arrests which continued into 1936, among them some of my closest friends. But I had a valid passport and was lucky enough to get away, after the rather hazardous 'cleaning' of the flat of one of those arrested of all incriminating material which the *Gestapo* had failed to discover (we had to get into the flat at night, and there was a police station opposite). I went to London, and the big question was what I should do in future. I disliked the endless bickering and the personal feuds among the political refugees, but still felt myself a loyal member of 'Neu Beginnen'. After long discussions, in particular with Norbert

Elias, I decided to work on a thesis on early Prussian history and to go to Amsterdam, which had good working conditions (and was much cheaper than London), and where I lived until 1939, loosely connected with the International Institute of Social History and its director, Professor Posthumus. Politically I tried to bring together the feuding émigré socialists in Amsterdam in a large SPD group; after the Moscow trials and the events of the Spanish Civil War, I felt very strongly a Social Democrat and was very critical of the separate groups and factions. I had some success, but it was limited because the adherents of the Prague SPD leaders would not co-operate. I also clashed with Walter Ulbricht about united front tactics when I mentioned the kidnappings which had occurred in Spain. If such methods were used there, I asked, what would happen if the Communists should ever come to power in Germany?

In any case, in my three years in Amsterdam I started serious work as a historian. My research centred around the lands which later formed the Kingdom of Prussia. I wanted to find out what had gone 'wrong' with their history, why *Gutsherrschaft* (the manorial system) and the predominance of the Junkers developed there, in contrast with western and southern Germany and western Europe in general. This finally became my Oxford thesis, 'The Development of the Manorial System – Grundherrschaft and Gutsherrschaft in North-Eastern Germany'. I discovered that the origin of the *Gutsherrschaft* – the ever growing demesnes of the Junkers, farmed with the labour services of servile peasants – was due to the widespread desertion of the thinly inhabited land after the Black Death and other catastrophes, as well as to the decline and subjugation of the comparatively small towns of the area. By contrast, the growing western towns provided markets for the corn exports from the noble estates, which bypassed the eastern towns and thus sealed their decline.

I was very fortunate in that Dr J.G. van Dillen, the editor of the *Tijdschrift voor Geschiedenis*, accepted three of my early efforts for publication (two of them now translated in my collected essays[2]) and Professor Posthumus accepted another one on 'The Peasants' War of 1525 in East Prussia'.[3] This may seem a strange activity in the years before the Second World War, but by that time I considered émigré politics more or less futile and wanted to become a historian, possibly in Holland. But with the Munich crisis and the German occupation of Prague I decided to move to a safer place. In the spring of 1939 I returned to London and continued my researches in the British Museum. Simultaneously I tried to obtain a research scholarship to Oxford or Cambridge. Again I was very fortunate in gaining a Barnett Research Scholarship to Wadham College, Oxford, with the special help of Professor G.N. Clark, who was then the professor of economic history (later Provost of Oriel), of Patrick Gordon Walker of Christ Church (later a Labour MP and minister in the Wilson Government) and F.W.D. Deakin, a Fellow of Wadham (later the first Warden of St Antony's).

Meanwhile the war had started, but I continued to work on my thesis – until I was briefly interned in 1940, together with numerous German professors and academics from Oxford. I had already volunteered for the army and was then put into the Pioneer Corps, but discharged after a severe bout of pneumonia which had affected my lungs. This enabled me to return to Oxford and finally to finish my thesis in 1942, with G.N. Clark and Michael Postan as the examiners. In spite of the war, Oxford was very peaceful. About that time I met my future wife, who throughout her life helped me enormously with all my work. Politically, I was active in the Democratic Socialist Club (which had split off the far-left and anti-war Labour Club) and co-operated closely with Anthony Crosland and Roy Jenkins.

I now had to find a job, and the problem was solved when later in 1942 Duncan Wilson came to see me and offered a post in a secret government department, the Political Warfare Executive (PWE), then housed at Woburn Abbey. My task was to draft, together with Richard Samuel, a handbook on Germany for the information of British officers who were to administer the British Zone of Germany after the German defeat. I was still an 'enemy alien', but for the next two to three years I wrote chapters on German administration, local government, the Nazi organisations and ranks, and German politics in general. But the contribution of A.J.P. Taylor on earlier German history, which he wrote as an out-sider, was so one-sided and partisan that it was rejected on my initiative. When the Basic German Handbook was finished, my work continued on the different parts of the later British Zone, with special small handbooks on Hesse, the Rhine-Ruhr area, North-West Germany and Berlin, each with a detailed historical part. The material came above all from the British Museum and the Wiener Library. I learned an enormous amount of German history, especially on the modern side, which proved very useful for my later work. I also lectured frequently on German affairs to British officers and to German prisoners of war, especially at Wilton Park to selected prisoners of war, later to German civilians brought over from the British Zone.

My first visit to Germany after the war took place in 1947 when I gave lectures on political subjects at a residential college in Rendsburg under the auspices of the British Control Commission. It was a fascinating experience and gave me an opportunity to observe the terrible living conditions in the devastated country, where money had lost its value and everything could be bought for a packet of cigarettes. In the same year I got my first university post, at Westfield College, University of London, which I held until 1961 when I was offered the Chair of Central European History at the School of Slavonic and East European Studies. When I got the post at Westfield, there was no one in London who taught any German history, and very few university teachers outside London did so. I was determined to continue my work on Prussian history; I gave special lectures on the history of the Junkers and published a number of articles, in the *English Historical Review* and elsewhere.[4] In 1954 my first book, *The Origins of Prussia*, was published by the Clarendon Press. The early parts were based on my thesis, and the later ones carried the story to the end of the seventeenth century. The book was well received in Britain, but in Germany there was much criticism from the conservatives, who disliked my stress on social and economic factors. Walther Hubatsch once explained to me why his reviews of my work had been so negative: so as not to make 'my position in England more difficult' – a strange way of reasoning. A German translation of the book had to wait until 1968, until the revival of interest in Prussia in the Federal Republic.

I realised of course that there were other important factors in German history apart from Prussia. To emphasise these, I wrote my second book, *Princes and Parliaments in Germany* (1959), to show that in many parts of Germany the Estates and Diets survived the period of princely absolutism and in certain cases continued to play a very important part in the history of the principality, not only in Württemberg, but also in Bavaria and Saxony. Some German historians were more critical. When I visited Hans Rothfels in Tübingen he said to me: 'Not the main stream of German history'.

At that time, the history of the Estates was not well researched and I had to spend many months in the Bavarian and Württemberg archives to go through the voluminous records of the local Estates. The echo to the new book in England was very positive but in Germany it was mixed. Some of the older generation, such as Fritz Hartung, remained very critical of the role of the Estates and considered the comparison with the English Parliament invalid. But some of the younger generation thought differently, as they told me on several occasions. The book in any case aroused a whole new interest in the history of the Estates in the smaller principalities and led to many publications, but it was not translated into German.

My own interests began to shift to the history of the twentieth century, partly because of my old political interests, partly because the German documents from the Weimar and Nazi periods had become available for research. I had always been interested in the history of the Prussian-German army. I grew up very close to the Bendlerstrasse, and Gordon Craig's *Politics of the Prussian Army* (Oxford, 1955) rekindled my interest. So I spent a period of sabbatical leave in the Federal Archives (*Bundesarchiv*) in Koblenz and in other German archives (Freiburg, Munich, Stuttgart, etc) and interviewed former officers to find out about the activities of the *Reichswehr* and its influence on the history of the Weimar Republic. Its relations with the Red Army interested me particularly, and I found fascinating new evidence. It turned out that, in spite of the losses through bombing of the Potsdam military archives, there was masses of material for a book, more than I could easily cope with, and the result was *The Reichswehr and Politics 1918-1933*, first published in German in 1964 and in a slightly abbreviated form two years later in English by the Clarendon Press. The book made a much greater impact in Germany than in England, and the echo was not always friendly. Again there were sharp criticisms from the conservative side, from former officers and others. The attacks were particularly pointed when I lectured at the *Bundeswehr Schule für Innere Führung* in Koblenz, although my lecture consisted to a large extent of quotations from the documents.

General Hans von Seeckt especially had his ardent admirers. In 1967 Dr Meier-Welcker published a bulky biography of Seeckt to refute my views,[5] but whatever I have seen since has only confirmed my critical opinion. The book also had a large number of favourable reviews, and the *Bundeswehr* bought hundreds of copies for its libraries, in spite of all the criticisms and objections. When later I went through the War Office reports from Berlin I found that the British military attachés in Berlin were extremely well informed about the clandestine (and illegal) activities of the *Reichswehr* in Soviet Russia and elsewhere. Recently the *Militärgeschichtliche Forschungsamt* in Freiburg has sponsored a whole volume on the relations between the two armies, *Reichswehr und Rote Armee 1920-1933* by Manfred Zeidler,[6] which in its subtitle classifies their co-operation as 'unusual':

it was also fateful. It showed how autonomous the *Reichswehr* was, how independent of the civil authorities and of parliament, a tendency which happily came to an end after 1945.

My next book, *The Rise of Fascism* in 1967, was my most popular book, selling in very large numbers, especially in America (as it still does). My aim was to show in a factual way the similarities and the differences between the major fascist movements in the various European countries and, at the same time, to explain why I did not consider certain régimes, such as that of General Franco, fascist, because this term was bandied about in such a loose way in the general literature and even more so in political discussions. In Germany the book was found not sufficiently theoretical and too empirical and descriptive. But after my experience with Marxist theories I much preferred the British tradition of factual narrative, although the last chapter of the book describes the general charac-teristics of the fascist movements. I have never doubted that the Nazi régime was 'fascist' although in many ways very different from the Italian prototype, but even this is still controversial. In a similar way my book on *Fascist Movements in Austria* in 1977 tried to show that the régime of Dollfuss and Schuschnigg, although authoritarian, was not fascist and that their Fatherland Front was not a fascist movement, while the paramilitary organisation of the *Heimwehr* was, as was the Austrian Nazi Party. Indeed, another aim of the book was to describe the Austrian roots of the Nazi movement which went back to Georg Ritter von Schönerer and the pre-1914 German Workers' Party in the Habsburg Empire. The book was welcomed in Austria by academics and the general public and again led to the publication of more detailed studies in the same field.

Meanwhile (in 1961) I had been appointed to the Chair of Central European History at London University, and this focused my interest on a wider field. I wrote *Revolution in Central Europe 1918-1919* (1972) which concentrated on the events in Germany and Austria and tried to show why the revolutionary movements of 1918 did not lead to a 'democratisation' of state and society although democratic constitutions were adopted in both countries, why the old structures in bureaucracy, the judiciary and the army were preserved to a large extent, why the workers' and soldiers' councils faded away so quickly. Among other reasons, I thought, this was due to the widespread fear of Bolshevism or 'chaos' which was very real, especially after the proclamation in March 1919 of the Hungarian Soviet Republic, in which Social Democrats and Communists co-operated. Hunger and fear swept Central Europe after the lost war, and the conditions for the establishment of democracy were certainly not propitious, while the old conservative forces were only weakened for a brief time. They did not accept responsibility for the defeat and were successful in blaming it on the new republican governments and the political Left.

I returned to these questions in *War against War* (1982), a comparison of anti-war movements in Britain and Germany in the First World War, for which British and German archives offered rich material. But in Britain the labour movement remained united, in spite of the anti-war attitude of the Independent Labour Party, and the Communist Party always remained very small. In Germany, by contrast, the pro-war votes of the SPD deputies led to the fatal split, the foundation of the USPD[7] in 1917 and the later emergence, after another split, of a strong Communist Party, which combined with the left wing of the USPD. The deep hostility between the SPD and KPD was of course not alone responsible for the demise of the Weimar Republic, but it was one of the contributory causes of the rise of the Nazi Party. In different ways both these books tried to broaden our understanding of the recent course of German history. So did *Britain and the Weimar Republic* (1984) which was based on the innumerable Foreign Office reports in the Public Record Office. It showed that the British diplomats were very well informed about German developments and often had close personal relations with German ministers, above all with Gustav Stresemann, and many others. The ambassadors also recorded faithfully 'the unexpected successes' of the NSDAP with its 'illogical and confused programme' and its appeal 'to German youth', as well as the growth of anti-Semitism. In general they provided a very realistic picture. *A History of the Prussian Junkers* (1989, first published in German) took up the theme of my thesis, this time over a longer period.

In the 1990s I returned in a way to my roots in the German socialist movement, to which I had been loyal in my younger days. I wrote two biographies, of August Bebel in 1991 and Eduard Bernstein in 1993. They were of course closely connected and published in German. I could write them in London using the voluminous printed sources, as the illness of my wife made it impossible for me to spend long periods in German archives. Yet I found very important material on the early Bebel in Berlin, but was unsuccessful in gaining access to the archives in East Berlin. Somewhat differently, my last book, *The German Workers and the Nazis*, in 1995, is to some extent based on my memories of underground work against Hitler and the history of 'Neu Beginnen'. I found this a fascinating subject, vindicating the German workers and the substantial minority which did resist the Nazis. The book describes the shades of public opinion and the conditions of working-class life in the years of the Third Reich; it is based on the voluminous published sources which have become available. An enlarged German translation was published in 1996. It is a book which is strongly influenced by my own observations.

As has been seen, my choice of subjects and my research were strongly influenced by my experiences at school and in Berlin in the late 1920s and early 1930s. I could almost claim that there was a logical development leading from the one to the other. But one question remained: why did I not follow my youthful inclinations and, after 1945, become a professional politician, and why did I not return to Germany, as I was urged by my friends, such as Fritz Erler and Waldemar von Knoeringen? The question is not easy to answer. When German friends and colleagues asked me I usually replied that I was never offered a chair at a German university, and that was certainly the case. If I had received such an offer I would have considered it seriously at the time when I was still a lecturer. When I became a professor in London the temptation would have been less strong. German history, after all, has to be taught outside Germany too, and in London I had at first almost a monopoly. Now the position has changed completely, but it was quite different when I started. In the end I found an academic career much preferable to a political one in which I could never have exercised much influence. As an academic I could influence my students, and many of my postgraduate students themselves became university teachers. I was very moved when they presented to me, on the occasion of my seventieth birthday, a *Festschrift*.[8] And some of my books reached a much larger public than just university students and academics.

I was always much attracted by academic life in England, with its relaxed and friendly atmosphere. All my teaching was done in small colleges where I knew everybody and felt much at home. Already as a student in Oxford during the war, I received much encouragement from the professors, in particular F.M. Powicke, the Regius Professor, and G.N. Clark, as well as other historians, among them Professor Norman Baynes, a Byzantinist exiled from London, in spite of the war and my insecure status. When I started lecturing in London I found the atmosphere at Westfield College not only friendly but most welcoming. Among several seminars I attended, that of Leonard Schapiro on Russian and Soviet affairs was of outstanding interest. My close friendship with Norbert Elias provided inspiration and new ideas over many years. In 1966 I taught one term at Stanford University in California – the great attraction was the Hoover War Library on the campus – but I turned down the offer of a permanent post there because I wanted to continue my work in London. I preferred England to America, and I did not want to emigrate twice: once was sufficient.

Over many years I have enjoyed close contacts with German historians. I have given lectures at numerous German universities and many German historians have been guests at our house in Hampstead. This began when Hermann Heimpel and Werner Philipp came in the late 1940s, the first German historians after the war to be invited to a conference in Oxford. Later I had to explain to Gerhard Ritter, who was firmly convinced that *the* British historians were anti-German, that they had many, very different opinions on the subject of Germany; but Ritter remained unconvinced. The close relationship with German historians has happily continued over the years. For many years, too, I have been a corresponding member of the *Historische Kommission zu Berlin* and a member of the Council of the Institute of European History in Mainz and have participated in many conferences in both places. Close personal contacts developed with the German Historical Institute in London, the members of its staff and the members of the British-German Historians' Association, to which I belonged from its foundation. As a member of the Advisory Council of the German Historical Institute, I participated very closely in its work. I have always treasured these and many other links, and found them very interesting and valuable. My work in many different German archives was helped by friendly archivists, especially at the *Bundesarchiv* where I worked so frequently. When it came to the *Reichswehr*, however, some difficulties arose when the archivist in question happened to be a former officer who wanted to preserve his secrets, but this was very exceptional.

I feel that I cannot really answer the question about my contribution to German historiography: that others must assess. I hope, however, to have contributed to a better and more critical understanding of Prussian as well as recent German history and to have helped to destroy some legends, such as that of the non-political attitude of the *Reichswehr*. I can truthfully say that I have enjoyed doing my researches and writing books, as well as many contacts with other historians. If they and the students have learned something from my writings and found my books worth reading, so much the better. If some of my books have led to further detailed research in the field in question, that is a source of satisfaction to me. If I have been rather critical of the Prussian Junkers and the *Reichswehr* generals, I have also stressed positive aspects of German history, such as the role of the Estates or that of August Bebel, or quite recently the working-class opposition to the Nazis. After all, the historian has to be critical, he has to weigh the positive and the negative aspects of his subject, and cannot conceal his own views.

## Notes

1   Theodor Fontane, *Die Poggenpuhls*, Ch. 6.
2   'Social Movements in the Pomeranian Towns from the Fourteenth Century to the Reformation', in F.L. Carsten, *Essays in German History* (London and Ronceverte, 1985), pp 51-62; 'The States General and the Estates of Cleves about the Middle of the Seventeenth Century', ibid., pp 81-89.
3   Ibid., pp 63-72.
4   'The Origins of the Junkers', *English Historical Review* 62 (1947), pp145-78; 'The Great Elector and the Foundation of the Hohenzollern Despotism', ibid. 65 (1950), pp 175-202; 'The Resistance of Cleves and Mark to the Despotic Policy of the Great Elector', ibid. 66 (1951), pp 219-241; 'Medieval Democracy in the Brandenburg Towns and its Defeat in the Fifteenth Century', *Transactions of the Royal Historical Society*, fourth series, 25 (1943), pp 73f; 'Prussian Despotism at its Height', *History* 40 (1955), pp 42-67.
5   Hans Meier-Welcker, *Seeckt* (Frankfurt-am-Main, 1967).
6   Manfred Zeidler, *Reichswehr und Rote Armee 1920-1933: Wege und Stationen einer ungewöhnlichen Zusammenarbeit* (Munich, 1993).
7   Unabhängige Sozialdemokratische Partei Deutschlands.
8   Volker R. Berghahn and Martin Kitchen (eds), *Germany in the Age of Total War* (London, 1981).

## Selected Writings of Francis L. Carsten

*The Origins of Prussia* (Oxford, 1954; German edition: Cologne, 1968)

*Princes and Parliaments in Germany: From the 15th to the 18th Century* (Oxford, 1959)

*The Reichswehr and Politics, 1918 to 1933* (Oxford, 1966; German edition: Cologne and Berlin, 1964)

*The Rise of Fascism* (London and Berkeley, California, 1967; German edition: Frankfurt-am-Main, 1968)

*Revolution in Central Europe 1918-1919* (London, 1972; German edition: Cologne, 1973)

*Fascist Movements in Austria: From Schönerer to Hitler* (London, 1977; German edition: Munich, 1977)

*War Against War: British and German Radical Movements in the First World War* (London, 1982)

*Britain and the Weimar Republic: The British Documents* (London, 1984)

*The First Austrian Republic, 1918-1938: A Study Based on British and Austrian Documents* (Aldershot, 1986; German edition: Vienna, 1988)

*A History of the Prussian Junkers* (Aldershot, 1989; German edition: Frankfurt-am-Main, 1988)

*August Bebel und die Organisation der Massen* (Berlin, 1991)

*Eduard Bernstein 1850-1932: Eine politische Biographie* (Munich, 1993)

*The German Workers and the Nazis* (Aldershot, 1995; German edition: Frankfurt-am-Main, 1996)

**Edgar J. Feuchtwanger**

# Recovering from
# Culture Shock

My family background virtually predestined me to become a historian. I was born in Munich in 1924 and my father ran the old-established academic publishing house Duncker & Humblot. He had been a pupil and protégé of Gustav von Schmoller, doyen of *Kathedersozialisten* ('pulpit socialists'). In my father's day Duncker & Humblot were still the publishers of the *Verein für Sozialpolitik* and I recently found a group photograph of the *Verein's* meeting in Zurich in 1928. The only person I could recognise in the photo, apart from my father in the back row and my mother among the wives seated in the front row, was the conspicuous figure of Dr Hjalmar Schacht, then President of the *Reichsbank*. Among my father's authors, who occasionally came to dinner with my parents, I dimly remember Werner Sombart and Carl Schmitt. As was the custom in those days, small children were briefly paraded in front of the assembled guests before dinner and told to shake hands. It was impressed upon me that 'a famous professor' was present and I had to be on my best behaviour.

History was probably the central focus of my father's interests, but he was a polymath and branched into many areas – theology, anthropology, philosophy, sociology – in a way that is unfortunately all too rare in our over-specialised days. He had Jewish interests, but having been brought up in a strictly orthodox family following the Samson Raphael Hirsch amalgam of Judaism and Germanism, with a strong Bavarian admixture, he had rebelled against the rigidities of the religious observances imposed on him in his parental home. The rebellion had broadened into a general distaste for aspects of bourgeois society and organised religion and into mild radical sympathies. A similar development can be perceived in his elder brother, the novelist Lion Feuchtwanger. By the time I became aware of such matters, my father was long past his rebellious phase. From 1930, he edited the *Bayerische Israelitische Gemeindezeitung*, as a sideline and hobby, and wrote much of it himself. It gave him an outlet for his wide-ranging scholarly concerns, and he turned this little parochial news sheet into a highly respected journal. Being brought up in a household so dedicated to academic pursuits did rub off on me, and I remember the great interest I took at the age of seven in the Goethe Centenary Year, 1932.

Then came the Nazis and the Third Reich. We lived, it could be said, at the epicentre of this eventually worldwide hurricane. In late 1929 Hitler had moved into a second-floor nine-room flat in the apartment block Prinzregentenplatz 16, at the bottom of our road and within sight of our window. My earliest memories of the waves made by the tenant of Prinzregentenplatz 16/II probably date back to one of the almost continuous election campaigns of the year 1932. One Sunday our local branch of the *Reichsbanner* (the Republican paramilitaries) mounted a demonstration. Instead of marching past Hitler's apartment block, they turned into a small side street just behind it and as they did so shook their fists in the direction of Hitler's abode. The following Sunday the local *SA* marched past Hitler's flat, saluting it but not evoking, as far as I remember, any response. What impressed itself on my childish mind was the fact that the *Reichsbanner* seemed rather bedraggled and amateurish. They did not keep step and were wearing a variety of shirts which looked as if they had been hastily dragged through some fluid to make them look a muddy green. The *SA*, in contrast, looked fairly well-drilled and uniformly attired in brown shirts, a portent of things to come.

There were other impressions in my worm's eye view of the Third Reich that find an echo in some of the interpretations thrown up by the historiographical debates of our own day. I remember my father using the phrase 'an ordered anarchy' ('geordnete Anarchie') in the thirties. We could, from our proximity, observe Hitler's gradual adaptation to the role of 'the Great Dictator'. In the early days I could still be taken for a walk along the pavement outside his apartment block and study his bell button. The name on the plate attached to it was 'Winter', his housekeeper. I can still see, in my mind's eye, Hitler coming out of the door and getting into his car, dressed in a belted mackintosh, with a trilby hat, which he lifted to the few casual passers-by who gave the Nazi salute. By the middle thirties even the routine and unannounced movements which I witnessed took place in a large motorcade full of *SS* bodyguards. The flat had become a staging post on his incessant toings and froings to Berchtesgaden – the *Autobahn*, one of the earliest to be completed, was entered about a mile away down our road. One got an inkling of the fact that the dictator's rule transcended bureaucracy and that, like Genghis Khan, his court moved with him, in motorcars, rather than on horseback. I still have in my possession the exercise book I used in my elementary school, the *Gebeleschule* in Bogenhausen. It starts on 1 May 1933, Labour Day, with a swastika superimposed upon a hammer. This is followed by the glories of the First World War, a heroic fight against so many enemies, the shame and dishonour of revolution and Versailles and eventually by the rise of a swastika-covered sun, sub-titled 'Germany Awakes', with Hitler disembarking from an aeroplane and being greeted with flowers. Our teacher was an enthusiastic young woman, a 200 per cent Nazi, I suspect, even in May 1933.

'Kristallnacht' ushered in the great change in my life. After *Volksschule* (elementary school) I had from 1935 attended the *Maximiliansgymnasium* (secondary school) in Munich, where I had taken the curriculum usual at a *Humanistisches Gymnasium*. My attendance ended abruptly on the morrow of 'Kristallnacht'. I vividly remember the *Gestapo* officials coming to our flat, taking my father away to Dachau, ransacking his large library and taking much of it away in packing cases. After the war some elements of it were returned, with a label 'Orientalisches Institut Universität Wien, Leihgabe Ahnenerbe'. It seemed a miracle that my father was released from Dachau after six weeks, for it was feared that with his name he would never get out. Efforts to get him released might even prove counterproductive by drawing attention to the name Feuchtwanger. After his release he had to spend at least a week in bed to recover, his face and hands covered with frostbite.

It was time for us to get out as a matter of urgency. In retrospect and with hindsight it seems remarkable that we had not done so before, whatever the formidable moral and material obstacles. It proved possible, since we were lucky enough to have relatives abroad, who had emigrated earlier and were reasonably affluent, to secure what was then called a *Kapitalistenvisum* to enter Britain. A thousand pounds, then a fairly large sum, had to be deposited and was at our disposal. Circumstances had to be truly desperate to make this possible, and this perhaps explains our almost last-minute emigration. I was sent ahead, leaving Germany on 14 February

1939, by train via the Hook of Holland. My father accompanied me as far as the Dutch frontier, and I remember him being admonished by an *SS* borderguard, who examined his passport, that he also should get the hell out of it as soon as may be. My parents in fact did so two-and-a-half months later, in early May 1939. In the meantime, arrangements had been made, through refugee organisations, for me to live with a doctor's family in Cornwall. I was conveyed across London from Liverpool Street Station to Paddington by family friends in a taxi, slightly startled to find it driving on the wrong side of the road, put on the Cornish Riviera Express to Truro and thus started a completely new phase in my life.

I knew only a little English, but fortunately was just young enough to make the switch into another language relatively painlessly. Much of the credit for my linguistic transition was due to the lady of the house, who taught me personally every day and was assiduously concerned for my progress. Even my historical interest was sustained, for the Professor of Scottish History at the University of Glasgow had a holiday cottage in the village. When he and his American wife arrived for the vacation, he dictated to me, into a note book still in my possession, a complete potted history of England from 55 BC to 1939. Thanks again to my hostess, the doctor's wife, it was arranged that I should attend Winchester College from September 1939. The governing body of the school had, bravely in view of the impending outbreak of war, undertaken to offer three or four free places to refugees from Germany. My hostess, skilfully using the networks of English life then unfamiliar to me, secured one of these places for me. Thus, after less than a year's break, I had moved from the increasingly Nazified *Maximiliansgymnasium* into the company of Wykehamists.

It was for me a culture shock, even though I had been warned and told to read *Tom Brown's Schooldays*. No amount of theory could prepare me for the practice, and a public school like Winchester was in those days a structured and regimented environment far beyond what it is now. At Winchester my historical interests were nurtured and sustained, but also diverted into completely different fields. I remember winning, or at any rate sharing, the school history prize, called Vere Herbert Smith Prize, with an extended essay on the Durham Report of 1837, a milestone in the arrival of devolved self-government in the British Empire. Such a theme was light years removed from the ideologically slanted teaching in the German school system of the Third Reich, which had been my diet only a little earlier. Naturally the prevailing orthodoxy at Winchester was a distinctly whiggish view of British imperial destiny, and there was as yet little inkling that it would soon reach its end, or maybe its apotheosis.

Men who were playing important roles in this rapidly moving historical process came to speak to us boys, or men as we were called at Winchester. Wavell, an Old Wykehamist himself, came, on the eve of his departure for India as Viceroy. We did not then know that it was a form of relegation for a man, impressive in himself and commanding great respect for what was seen as the Wiccamical virtue of understatement and self-effacement. It was just through this failure to articulate that he had fallen foul of that great communicator Winston Churchill. Mountbatten came, the very opposite in his breezy flamboyance. He was then Chief of Combined Operations and was soon to preside over the liquidation of British rule in India. Very different again was Montgomery, a master of self-advertisement, but a memorable personality none-theless. He would have been memorable even if he had not arrived at the moment when all eyes were upon him as a national hero. His son was at the school and so he came down to Winchester immedi-ately after making a clean sweep of North Africa in May 1943. Suddenly his black beret, endlessly pictured in the newspapers, was bobbing up and down among the spectators at a cricket match on the green and sunny playing fields. He gave to us schoolboys what must have been the first account of his battles from Alamein to Tunisia. I can see him now, describing the Battle of Mareth only a week or so earlier: 'I pushed three divisions into my left wing' and he rushed to the left of the raised dais from which he was speaking. 'They pushed me back' and he returned to the lectern. We men were impressed, something that did not easily happen to us, for we had never come across anybody who could push three divisions into his left wing. Last but not least among the notable visitors whom I remember lecturing to the school was Jan Masaryk, then Czech Ambassador in London. His was a most attractive personality, full of gentle self-deprecating humour. None could then have anticipated the tragic fate that awaited him.

The teaching at Winchester, particularly in wartime, was not uniformly of high calibre, but at least two of those who regularly taught me helped to foster my historical understanding, and remain engraved in my memory. One was J.D.E. Firth, known as Budge Firth, for every Winchester don had a nickname. He was the son of J.B. Firth, well-known *Daily Telegraph* journalist, and a scion of the Sheffield steel clan. He was also Chaplain of the College and taught the top form on the modern side of the school. I spent at least two years 'up to him' and eventually became what was known as the Patriarch of the div., Winchester word for class. Some of Budge's comments on contemporary events still seem apposite more than half a century later. For example he said of the war then unfolding on the Eastern Front that it was unparalleled in history for ferocity and atrocity. A lot of my modern history was taught to me by Harold Walker, who would not have been out of place teaching at Oxford or Cambridge. It was through him that I ended up at Magdalene College, Cambridge, where I won a scholarship. I went there after a period of war service, mostly spent in Savernake Forest sawing up tree trunks into railway sleepers, to be used in restoring the French railway network after D-Day.

Winchester had, I like to think, made a contribution to my development as a historian apart from the actual teaching. When I eventually settled upon an area of historical research, it was the politics of the later Victorian period, a field that was in the 1950s only beginning to be taken under the microscope with the application of methodologies of research now familiar. It seemed to me that I was able to immerse myself in this subject more easily because my experience had given me a familiarity with the ways of the British establishment. In those days a school like Winchester was still unequivocally a pillar of that establishment, liberal, tolerant, but also very conscious of itself as an élite both social and intellectual. I remember a visit to the school by some Labour MPs, probably to help in the preparation of the party's post-war policy on public schools. It was tending towards abolition and the eventual publication of the Fleming Report. I was among a group of boys showing the MPs round. We got on well, but felt they were visitors from another planet, while they may have been looking at us like animals in a zoo. The inhabitants of the Victorian political world seemed more familiar to me when I came to deal with them. It is a problem for historians, particularly political historians of the modern era, that so much of the time they are dealing with practitioners in an arena which to them as academics is alien territory. Had I been born within the sound of Bow Bells I might have acquired less of the empathy I am, perhaps arrogantly, claiming. Another by-product of my school years that I remember with pleasure was the broadening of my musical taste. Sidney Watson, the Master of Music, later to become at Christ Church one of the pillars of Oxford music, taught me the piano. He was known chiefly as a trainer and conductor of Anglican cathedral and college choirs, but his tastes were much more catholic. Seeing that I was not a budding concert pianist, he used my piano lessons to play me chunks from Wagner and Strauss operas and discuss them with me. For an adolescent like me this was quite a considerable widening of musical horizons, and I acquired an early liking for later romantic German music.

The whole of my three years at Cambridge was spent studying history, completing both parts of the history tripos. Medieval history was one of my main interests, and in my third year I took a special subject on the English Franciscans. It was taught by Dom David Knowles, a memorable teacher. A wide spectrum of subjects was on offer and beyond medieval history I was particularly interested in the history of ideas. It may have been the case that history was being made in the then contemporary world with such intensity and at such a pace that one preferred to be able to cultivate in one's studies greater distance and detachment. The total intellectual stimulus on offer at Cambridge seemed to me intensely exciting. The London School of Economics was evacuated to Cambridge, and one could attend the lectures of people like Harold Laski. One could be present at a debate between Karl Popper and Ludwig Wittgenstein. Once I had lunch with Bertrand Russell and his then wife, in the presence of their young son Conrad, now a distinguished historian and public figure. Sometimes I now like to tease my students by saying that I am so old that I had lunch with the grandson of the introducer of the first Reform Bill. I had many friends reading English and at only one remove one learnt about the controversies surrounding Leavis. Raymond Williams and John Heath-Stubbs were among the undergraduates who commanded attention, at any rate in my vicinity.

My politics moved strongly to the left, though my historical sense made me chary of embracing the Marxist orthodoxy hook, line and sinker, as so many around me did. Religion was at least as live an issue as politics, and in my circle there were conversions to various schools of Anglicanism from evangelical to High Church and to Roman Catholicism. In all of this I was intellectually and even emotionally involved, but in the last resort, in spite of my prolonged sojourn in Anglican establishments, I never shifted from my vague liberal humanism, nor did I ever formally cast aside the Judaism of my birth. Much of my experience of Cambridge life came through my college, Magdalene. Still one of the smaller colleges, it had probably less than 150 inhabitants in the immediate post-war period. Many of the dons were bachelors, lived in college and shared in the social life of the undergraduates.

It was the kind of Oxbridge experience which, it is said, is now much diluted.

When the time came for me to leave Cambridge, circumstances pushed me towards a career in adult education. It was very much within the ethos of the times, and a great expansion of popular education was foreseen. The Workers' Educational Association (WEA) had played a great role in the trade union movement and the Labour Party. Many who now held office in the Labour Government had received most of their education through the WEA. The experience of fascism, which the world had just endured, seemed to give mass education and enlightenment even greater urgency. I remember the secretary of the WEA based in Cambridge, Reginald Jacques, declaring with great fervour that adult education was the only hope of avoiding a repetition of the mass delusion of Nazism. My tutor at Magdalene, Frank Salter, was one of the university stalwarts of adult education and was Chairman of the University Board of Extra-Mural Studies. And so I became an adult education tutor at the University College, soon to become the University of Southampton. One of my Cambridge contemporaries and nodding acquaintances who took the same route was E.P. Thompson.

I was probably never very convinced of the more exalted missionary claims that were made for my calling, but I soon found that the popularisation and dissemination of academic knowledge suited me very well. I was eager to share what I thought were my insights and enthusiasms with others. The whole lifestyle suited me. Much of the work took place in the evening. One could spend most of the day reading round the subject, distilling one's essential insights and testing one's conclusions, psyching oneself up, as it were, to deliver the message at the end of the day. Too much specialisation was not possible, and subjects had to be made relevant to the concerns of the adult students who were the audience. Having had a strong interest in the Middle Ages as a student, I was now inevitably sucked into contemporary history and politics. It did not really go against my inclinations, for my interest in contemporary national and international issues was intense. One could not possibly have lived through Nazism and the war in the way it had affected me without acquiring a deep instinct that it was impossible to contract out of such matters; and further, that it was one's duty to spread the truth as widely as possible, if one had the chance to do so. It was only with the end of the cold war in the late 1980s, long after I ceased to be an adult educationalist, except occasionally, that this urgency left me.

When I now look back on this phase of my career I think it has had a considerable impact on my work as a historian. Much of what I have published consists of synthesis for the reasonably well-informed student or reader, and my training as an adult educator has helped me in this. It also helped me as a teacher, I would like to think. The first commandment when confronting an audience that has come to listen of its own free will and can always absent itself again is to make things interesting and relevant, to entertain as well as to instruct. Otherwise there is the ever-present threat of an empty room the week after. It is a valuable discipline and has stood me in good stead in teaching university students, who are under a greater though by no means absolute compulsion to attend one's effusions regularly.

The call of pure history and genuine research remained strong, and as a member of a university staff it was not too difficult to follow. In casting around for a subject, the Victorian period in English history held strong attractions. It was a field in which much had been taught to me at Winchester and Cambridge and in which I had had to immerse myself as an adult education tutor. It was undoubtedly part of my acclimatisation to English life. By now this had gone a long way, though it never went the whole hog, nor was there ever any inclination to forget, let alone cover up, my background. It seemed to be a bonus to have access to two cultures. My father had died in 1947 and thereby a link with the German sphere was removed. Had he lived longer I might have been drawn to work on a German theme earlier, for I remember discussing with him a few years earlier the possibility of working on a subject connected with Wilhelm von Humboldt. As it was, such ideas slipped almost entirely out of my mental horizons for a while. Victorian political history and work on the private papers of politicians of that era proved more naturally attractive to me. It was a source as yet not fully exploited beyond the usual somewhat hagiographical double-decker biographies commissioned soon after the subject's death. Even the treatment of major figures was only beginning to move beyond these confines. I was also interested in the workings of the British parliamentary machinery, and the development of parties was a live historiographical issue. I had one interview with Sir Lewis Namier, reigning then over the history of Parliament.

The immediate suggestion for what was to become the theme of my doctorate and my first book came from Norman Gash, still a good friend. He suggested there was a gap to be filled in investigating urban conservatism in the later Victorian period, the basis for the phenomenon of the Tory working man and for the ideological concept of Tory democracy. Such a subject may seem a far cry from the unoriginal left-wing outlook of my student days and from the ethos of the adult education world in which I worked, but then I was never particularly dogmatic, always a liberal, and certainly accepted unquestioningly the validity of open-ended historical research. In the early 1950s the *Zeitgeist* was rapidly changing, and from this no one, whatever they may say, claim or feel, can escape. There were also the logistics of the case. As a part-time researcher, private papers deposited in country houses in the South of England, as well as all the resources of the British Museum and the Public Record Office, were within my reach. Thus I became committed to Victorian political history. My work was very much in the British or Anglo-Saxon tradition of empirical, pragmatic historiography, influenced by the Namierite preoccupation with party as the central strand in the development of parliamentary government in England. I do not think my German background had much relevance here. My research was fuelled by the perception that extra-parliamentary organisation, made necessary by a widening electorate, was the key factor in bringing about the more cohesive modern parties, with all this implied for the whole political system. If there was a continental influence it was Moisei Ostrogorski. I might have thought of Robert Michels, but he was less immediately relevant. I distinctly remembered him from my parental home, largely because a fingerstall he wore seemed to me as a child slightly sinister.

There was a return to German history with my book on Prussia, written in the late 1960s and published in 1970. The initiative came from Oswald Wolff, but he died soon after I embarked upon the project and it was his widow Ilse, herself a major figure in refugee and exile affairs, who saw it through. One of Wolff's motives in commissioning such a book was to bring it home to an English-speaking readership that Prussia's role in German history was more complex than the stereotypical villain of the piece perpetuated by the Allied dissolution order of 1947. Although Francis Carsten had already published his *Origins of Prussia* (see p 32) the teaching of the modern history of Prussia in schools was usually still based on *The Evolution of Prussia*, by J.A.R. Marriott and C.G. Robertson, published in 1915. Presenting the profile of a whole country in a slim volume, the task I was taking on, seemed to me to necessitate in large part an excursion into the history of ideas. In this I was certainly influenced by my reading of German historiography. Friedrich Meinecke's *Weltbürgertum und Nationalstaat* (1907), an archetypal example of historiography dominated by the primacy of ideas, with which I had been familiar since my undergraduate days, was one of the works that made me feel that an enterprise such as my Prussia book was a feasible mode of approach. Meinecke's influence and that of other German historians of the older generation, for example Otto Hintze, is probably very evident in what I wrote. The great change in the German intellectual scene that took place in the 1960s had hardly yet made an impact upon me, though it was about to do so.

In 1968 I took the initiative in arranging a visit by a group of my colleagues to the University of Frankfurt. We could hardly have chosen a better moment or a better place for plunging into the thick of the German academic ferment. For us visitors from the sceptred isle the heat and dust of the student revolt and all its peripheral manifestations proved entirely fascinating. What we had to offer our German hosts was less clear but, since more of them tended to the liberal rather than the radical side of the debate, perhaps there was some faint reassurance that the centre might after all still hold. The fascination of our initial contact with Frankfurt ensured that the link between the Universities of Frankfurt and Southampton continued year after year and became institutionalised. Since it is not often one's luck to start something positive that goes on for over a quarter of a century, I take some satisfaction in my role in this project. Our contacts in Frankfurt have been mainly with social scientists rather than historians, but I was myself privileged to spend a semester with the Frankfurt historians in 1980-81. The philosophical and ideological depth of German intellectual discourse has over the years never failed to impress and stimulate my British colleagues and myself, and has continued to reverberate among us long after the meetings were over.

From the late 1960s I had thus become, as far as my published work went, a 'twin-track' historian, with a specialisation both in British and German history. In my writings on German history I have seen myself more as an interpreter and transmitter for an English-speaking readership, rather than as an innovative researcher. Private and professional commitments would have made prolonged forays into German archives very difficult. I did not feel I could really compete with the tremendously thorough and intellectually differentiated work done in Germany. On the other hand there may be virtue in the kind of synthesis I have produced, for example on the Weimar Republic, with a certain amount of distance, perhaps even in the blessed absence of any vestige of guilt. The 'twin track' has been for me a positive experience, even if it has limited my ability to be original as a historian. It is perhaps arrogant to say 'je ne regrette rien', but I do not have many regrets.

## Selected Writings of Edgar J. Feuchtwanger

*Disraeli, Democracy and the Tory Party: Conservative Leadership and Organisation after the Second Reform Bill* (Oxford, 1968)

*Prussia. Myth and Reality: The Role of Prussia in German History* (London and Chicago, 1970; German edition: Frankfurt-am-Main, 1972)

(ed.), *Upheaval and Continuity: A Century of German History* (London, 1973; German edition: Munich, 1973)

*Gladstone: A Political Biography* (London and New York, 1975)

with Richard Bessel (eds), *Social Change and Political Development in Weimar Germany* (London and Totowa, NJ, 1981)

*Democracy and Empire: Britain 1865-1914* (London, 1985)

*From Weimar to Hitler: Germany, 1918-33* (London and New York, 1993)

*Germany 1916-1941* (Bedford, 1997)

**J.A.S. Grenville**

# From Gardener
# to Professor

The educational opportunities for those children and young people who escaped from Germany and Austria and reached the safe shores of Britain before the outbreak of the Second World War were not all alike. But we can roughly categorise them. The first arrivals, in the early thirties, generally came with their parents to support them. These families were often relatively well-to-do immigrants who were able to transfer a proportion of their wealth with them. More fortunate also were the children with well-to-do relations in Britain who were ready to assist. The psychological shock was great, but their education did not suffer once they had adapted, which most of them were quickly able to do. Indeed, in some respects they were really advantaged, since the education in the best of the British public schools was better than anything on offer in Nazi Germany. From these élite schools there was a natural progression to Oxford and Cambridge.

Age, too, was a deciding factor. The very young soon assimilated completely. The seventeen- and eighteen-year-olds could volunteer for the army. After the war, and rightly so, they were treated with generosity and awarded university grants on the same basis as British-born ex-servicemen. The majority of the under-eighteens came to Britain only after the November pogrom of 1938, usually on the 'Kindertransporte'. Most came without possessions, with just the one regulation suitcase, worst of all without parents, destined to be orphaned. Their ages ranged from eighteen down to the babies in the arms of Jewish social workers accompanying the transports. Their 'guarantors' were often involved only financially, and desired no personal contact with the children. Their care was handed to the

Jewish welfare organisation set up for the purpose in Bloomsbury House, London. Some wealthy people saved hundreds of children in this way and could not be expected to personalise the rescue. My own guarantors, each with a 'half share', were a member of the Rothschild family and, I believe, a Jewish committee in Portsmouth. I never met either, though I did write a letter of thanks after the war.

In the last resort much depended on the innate talent, character and perseverance of each immigrant. These qualities determined the outcome of such opportunities as came their way by chance or management. The majority of children and young people belonged to the pauper group, with no parents or other connections in Britain. Relatively little study of these thousands has been possible: their records may not have survived and only few traces remain. Most came from professional and middle-class German and Austrian backgrounds. However, their development, personal expectations and aims in life would have been influenced by their background only if they had had a long enough experience of family life; probably they would have needed to be at least eight years old before being torn from their homes. From such studies as have been undertaken, it is reasonably safe to generalise that for the great majority of refugee children the possibility of a professional life and higher social status was barred by their lack of suitable educational opportunities in Britain.

Why was this? Why were their talents not given the chance to develop to the full? It has to be remembered that it was war-time, and that they were dependent on charity and, later, government support. Was it reasonable that they should be supported more than a British child from a poor family? The school-leaving age was fourteen (it was not raised to fifteen until after the war). Furthermore, the professions were closed to foreigners, with some limited exceptions such as the medical profession. There was no expectation that this would change after the war was over. There was not even a guarantee that the children would be allowed to remain in Britain, let alone be able to acquire British nationality. It therefore seemed only common sense to those who took collective charge of the upbringing of Jewish child refugees, the British Jewish Welfare organisation, that they should try to obliterate the hopes of fulfilling middle-class family expectations from former times which seemed to have no relevance to the children's future. If and when these children eventually re-emigrated, it would be best for them to be equipped with practical skills that would enable them to earn a living. Was another consideration the fear of anti-Semitism, a 'lesson' learnt from Germany, where 'too many' Jews had distinguished themselves in the professions? It was understandable that the well-established Anglo-Jewish community would pay some regard to its own position, as every older-established immigrant community does when faced with unassimilated and impoverished newcomers.

Against this background of somewhat dim prospects for the great majority of refugee children, my own experiences become intelligible. It is not in order to point an accusing finger, but rather to help understanding of those times during the war that this brief general background has been sketched in.

◆━━◆

My family belonged to the professional middle class; my father had risen by the age of forty to a higher judicial position as 'Landgerichtsdirektor' (a judge in the higher court) in Berlin. His father, too, had been honoured with the title 'Justizrat' and was very well-to-do. My mother was descended on the maternal side from an old-established and wealthy Jewish family in Berlin, the Misch family. My maternal grandfather was also a 'Justizrat', beloved by the gypsies whom he defended free of charge or in exchange for a basketful of food. (One sailor without means gave him a parrot, still with us when I left Berlin. Lore, the parrot, displayed the eagerness to conform that is a tendency of many Germans, and liked to cause a commotion: before 1914 she used to call from the balcony 'Der Kaiser kommt,' which had everyone scurrying about and excited; by 1938 she could perfectly mimic 'Heil Hitler,' which had unfortunate passers-by raising their hands to a phantom companion.) My father's and mother's immediate family lost their wealth during the First World War by patriotically subscribing to both the Kaiser's and the Hungarian 'Kriegsanleihen' (war loans). By the 1920s, after the inflation, our family was dependent on a precarious income; and from 1933 to 1939, after my father's dismissal, on his curtailed pension. So I grew up in a household where my mother managed the finances by placing different expenditures each in a separate envelope. One envelope, 'summer holidays', was of special importance. Until 1938 we all escaped from Nazism by taking a holiday outside Germany. I recall one holiday in Denmark. After arriving at our hotel in Copenhagen and being taken to our bedroom, we found ourselves situated opposite the German Embassy with its huge swastika flag. Perhaps the hotelier wanted to please us. When we explained that we were Jewish, he immediately changed our rooms.

Until November 1938 my memories of Germany were happy. I loved Berlin and to wander through the busy streets of a lively metropolis. My first years in the *Volksschule* (elementary school) were uneventful. I experienced no anti-Semitism before 1938. My class teacher, Herr Kuhnert, showed no disfavour and readily excused my attendance on the Jewish high holidays on receipt of a letter from my mother. I considered myself fortunate to get days off school for both Jewish and Christian festivities. The policeman who saw me across the busy Hohenzollerndamm was kind, and appreciative of the box of cigars he received from my father every Christmas. Blond and blue-eyed (in those days), nothing distinguished me from a desirable Aryan, and my particular childish form of 'resistance' was to elicit a 'Heil Hitler' from every passing *SS* man.

At the age of ten, I passed into the *Gymnasium* (secondary school). My parents in 1938 wanted me to enter a German rather than a Jewish *Gymnasium*. It was difficult to find one ready to accept a Jewish boy, but the headmaster of one on the other side of town, near the Spittelmarkt, took me. Here there was a much more determined anti-Semitic influence from above. Although I was more isolated, I still made plenty of friends – only to be expelled in November 1938. That very day I had stood on my desk denouncing the obvious untruths in the textbook on race, with its depictions of Jews, to the great jollification of the class. I did not clamber down in time when Herr Abel, my class teacher, came in with his 'Parteiabzeichen' (party badge) in his lapel. I had to leave the school within the hour, but as this was at the height of the pogrom, on 10 November, I would have had to go anyway. The pogrom remains a frightening memory, with my father arrested and taken to a concentration camp. Flats were broken into and people beaten up. We sought safety in the waiting room at the *Bahnhof Zoo* until midnight. Two non-Jewish friends of the family, my German violin teacher and our Belgian French teacher, offered to shelter us, but my mother – dead-tired – decided to return home with us, her three children. A few weeks followed in a relaxed Jewish school. My father was released from the concentration camp, with severe physical damage, on receiving a visa to enter Britain temporarily, and in March 1939 we were assigned to a 'Kindertransport'. My mother took us to the station; we were never to see her again.

My family experiences had a decisive influence on the rest of my life. Aged eleven when I left Germany, my family background and all the circumstances and cruelties of the Nazi years shaped my outlook and expectations of the future.

The special train left Berlin with a cheerful band of children who were glad to leave Germany, and raised a cheer when crossing the Dutch frontier. We continued by steamer to Harwich. The pain and homesickness came later. We were in touch with our parents and loved ones only until the outbreak of war a few months later. In completely unfamiliar surroundings, and unable to speak a single word of English, I was separated from my two elder brothers and stood, a label round my neck, with two other refugee boys in the waiting room at Harwich railway station. A tall, haggard-looking Englishman turned up; he spoke not a word of German and could only communicate with us by sign language. He drove us in an ancient car to the boarding school, Mistley Place, where he was headmaster. Mr Jackson was honest and hardworking, a headmaster typical of the best establishments where well-off English boys were educated from the age of seven. It was a spartan place; discipline was very strict, the cane in frequent use. Today those beatings would no longer be allowed. Then, they were part of the accepted school code; we were perfectly happy and excellently well-taught.

I enjoyed the advantage of the best possible education, but it lasted only just over two years, until I was thirteen. The school fees were paid by a lady whose name I could never discover in order to thank her. My father had come to England as well; and after internment he worked as a factory worker, making bombs. He could not take care of me, but wrote weekly, so I did not feel abandoned. I saw him a few times during the war. After some weeks of misery, I quickly adjusted. The difference between the English boys at school and many German boys was striking. The fact that we were not like them, could not speak their language or understand their codes of behaviour and so could scarcely communicate, did not lead to taunts or persecution. On the contrary, the English boys went out of their way to help such unfortunates; they had been told that we had fled from our homes and responded with kindness. I made some life-long friends.

The basis of my education was laid at the boarding school. I learnt English, Latin, maths and other subjects to a high standard. I spent the holidays with the farming family of a boy at school, the Lyons. Michael was younger than I, and wanted to learn the violin. Later to become a talented doctor, as a child he had rather short fingers and no great musical talent – but this was more than made up for by character and determination. We struggled, and in the end he could play some Christmas carols. He (aged eight) wrote in a letter home that there was a boy at school who could not go home for Christmas, because of a bad Mr Hitler. Andrew and Margaret Lyon rang the school to find out if this was true, and were told it was. The family's farm became a second home. Mr and Mrs Lyon were not Jews and had no experience of foreigners but, like so many English people, responded simply and effectively to human needs, just as before the war, when thousands had sent their pennies and pounds to the collections for the Lord Balfour Fund, which helped to finance the escape of Jewish children. This is the paradox of England: it shared every common prejudice of the time, including anti-Semitism, yet when it came to helping the needy and desperate a sense of common humanity prevailed. And so it was to prove throughout my career.

At school we were taught that everyone was good at something and valued for that. I played the violin at school prayers, but was miserable at sport. This I was determined to remedy. Short-sighted – but undiagnosed – and slightly asthmatic, I could neither run nor see a ball soon enough! I practised for hours, however, to become a bowler at cricket. Eventually I could pitch the ball at perfect length and spin it left or right: in short I became an excellent slow left-arm bowler, much admired and indispensable to the first eleven. Later I played for the university staff and once even against an embassy team in Washington. I left the boarding school inculcated with the attitudes of an English upper-class boy, full of self-confidence, with a scholarship for a public school virtually arranged. Then my life changed abruptly.

My legal sponsors required me to learn a trade. I was to be apprenticed to a tailor in Leeds. My father intervened, saying he would pay from his meagre income as a factory worker so that I would be allowed to remain at school. A compromise was reached. I would be allowed two years of technical education in Cambridge, where I would live in a hostel with other boys. This was for working boys, but kindly run, later on by Dr and Mrs Fritz Ball. He was a very talented cellist and deepened my love for music. But as far as education in an academic sense was concerned, that had been ended for me at the age of thirteen.

I looked around the technical school and its various departments, and discovered it included an art school. I liked drawing, so I enrolled and drew vases and – when I was lucky – from life. A carefree and blissful three weeks were followed by a reprimand from the children's refugee committee, which had not had this in mind for me. I was transferred to the building department at the Cambridgeshire Technical School. Standards were high and I did well in theoretical subjects, technical drawing and elementary science, but badly in the practical subjects, plumbing, carpentry and metal work. My teachers did their best and I got through the exams. But I made up my mind that I wanted to go to a grammar school to continue an academic education. I wrote to the headmaster of the best school in Cambridge, the Perse School, explaining my plight. A few days later he came to the hostel to meet me and told me I could go to his school without having to pay fees. It did not happen. The committee would not allow it.

There was another way. London University had a wonderful institution: external examinations which could be taken by anyone without having to attend a school or university. I registered, then took a correspondence course which my father paid for. When the committee discovered this, they rang the headmaster of the technical school, as I was breaking school rules. He called me into his study and told me I had to stop. Aged fourteen and small for my age, I breathed defiance: he should expel me so I could do what I wanted. His reply, 'Keep your shirt on,' meant 'Don't get ready to fight – the teachers here will help you'. And they did, with extra lessons.

I chose chemistry and physics as my subjects for eventual university study. Meantime, I borrowed books from the library for refugees and uncritically but voraciously read all the German classics. I know of no one else who read the whole of *Wilhelm Meister*, *Faust* and Gottfried Keller's *Der grüne Heinrich* at the age of fifteen. My thirst was as unquenchable as my understanding was limited. As I had to earn my living, I secured a job as a laboratory assistant in Cambridge in a plant which manufactured insecticides.

My school education had ended when I was only fifteen, but an exciting career began. I studied hard as well, and reached first-year degree standard in the sciences. But I found chemistry boring, especially industrial chemistry. I was further disillusioned when a member of the research team who had a PhD left the company, and the head of research promoted me to take over his work! What then was the point of all this study? Without it I was perfectly well able to do all the routine titrations for testing the purity of compounds and even to make DDT, which was too expensive to buy from ICI at the time. I also got into trouble. As a lab assistant I learnt simple glass-blowing, and blew lots of lovely round balls one Christmas as decorations and gifts for friends. But my compound for silvering them proved unstable, and one night there was an explosion in the lab when the compound turned into a mini-bomb. Clearly I had not the makings of a terrorist. I escaped with a telling-off.

The danger of imminent poisoning made me give up the chemical position, on the advice of a doctor who saw me with green hair and yellowed skin. To regain my health I needed a new job in the fresh air. I became assistant gardener at a Cambridge college, Peterhouse. The next two years were spent gardening, which I had always enjoyed, and studying in my spare time. My request for permission to use the Peterhouse library caused consternation. I was finally given permission, but only on condition that I would not attempt to enter Cambridge University as a student: such was the class snobbery still prevalent among some people even immediately after the war. Actually, I was fortunate in receiving some excellent tutoring from Professor Hersch Lauterpacht, the famous international lawyer, and from the Master of Peterhouse, for whose garden I was responsible once a week. When I appeared, he brought cocoa, two chairs and a table, and we talked. My education from fifteen to nineteen was unstructured, but its width proved a great benefit. By now history was the subject which really caught my imagination.

On my eighteenth birthday I left Peterhouse, having been accepted as an evening student at Birkbeck College, University of London. The Bursar at Peterhouse had asked me to reconsider, telling me the Fellows were impressed by my work as a college servant, and that – to use his words – I had 'the makings of a Head Porter'. Readers acquainted with Tom Sharpe's hilarious book *Porterhouse Blue* will recognise that this was an exalted position which involved wearing a top hat. At this crossroads of my career, I opted for the life of a poor student. I taught in a London preparatory school during the day, and at night attended Birkbeck College, where Eric Hobsbawm was one of the history lecturers. In 1948, after a stimulating year at Birkbeck, I gained entry to the London School of Economics with a London County Council grant, and was a full-time student at last. I could hardly believe my good fortune.

Three years of excellent lectures and tuition during the golden years of the London School of Economics have left a permanent impression. The great teachers I was fortunate to have included Harold Laski and Sir Charles Webster. After gaining first-class honours and a research scholarship, I joined Sir Charles Webster's seminar and prepared for a PhD. He was a formative influence, with his insistence on deep archival investigation and examining foreign policy from the point of view of other countries. Multi-archival study was essential. His work on Castlereagh, the Congress of Vienna and Palmerston was a model of meticulous scholarship. My interest, too, lay in British foreign policy and its domination by the third Marquess of Salisbury at the close of the nineteenth century.

A feature of British academic history writing from Macaulay to Trevelyan and A.J.P. Taylor is to make it accessible to the general reader. I worked hard to improve my style, especially as diplomatic history – the analysis of what foreign offices said to each other – can be rather dry. From early on I felt that historical study would be more creative and interesting if one combined at least two approaches. My previous study of the sciences undoubtedly influenced me in thinking that the combination of two 'pure' subject areas would lead to new creative questions. Examples that sprang to mind, examined only at a very elementary level, were physics and chemistry, mathematics and physics, biology and chemistry. My first combination, as it turned out, was geography and history. In collaboration with a geographer, Dr Joan Fuller, I worked on a history of European exploration and settlement from the fifteenth to the eighteenth century, looking at development from both the geographer's and the historian's viewpoint. A further consideration was to write the history from the 'receiving' perspective, not simply from the perspective of European expansion. The work was published in a series for secondary schools in Africa and the West Indies.[1] It was evidently widely used there, as over ten years more than 100,000 copies were sold, but it passed largely unnoticed among my colleagues in Britain. It sought to convey a non-colonialist attitude at a time when the empire was coming to an end.

The major study on which my academic reputation rested was *Lord Salisbury and Foreign Policy: The Close of the Nineteenth Century* (1964). As the result of more than ten years of intensive archival study in Britain and abroad, it was modelled on the exhaustive approach of my mentor, Sir Charles Webster: to consider all available evidence, to set out what had actually occurred and what were the principles and motives of the decision-makers, and to examine how policies came to be formulated. What I added was the attempt to represent Salisbury, the ambassadors and the foreign actors as real people; in other words, to bring the art of biography to the study of diplomatic history. The book was so well received that I quickly advanced to a readership at Nottingham University, and in 1966, at the tender age of thirty-eight, to a full professorship of International History at the University of Leeds.

Before that, an academic idea and personal circumstances had launched me in a new direction. The personal circumstance was my desire to find a wife; in this endeavour I had so far been singularly unsuccessful. I felt then that I wanted to marry a Jewish girl. Against the background of the murder of millions of Jews, I believed – although I was secular in outlook – that this was the right thing to do. Contacts which might have helped me were non-existent, so I resolved to search for my happiness in the United States. But how to get there? A decision to study US foreign policy combined with a fellowship held at Yale University as a Harkness Commonwealth Fund Fellow in 1959 provided ample opportunity for both endeavours. I met, fell in love with and married Betty Anne, a native of Manhattan. Simultaneously, my research focused on the links between naval war planning and US foreign policy.

Besides my good fortune in finding a wife, the second blessing of my year in the States was the opportunity to get to know the most distinguished of all the American diplomatic historians of the day, Samuel Flagg Bemis. I was able to examine war plans hitherto closed to historians, and the preliminary results impressed Professor Bemis. After my return to England, I received a letter from him telling me that one of his former students, George B. Young, then executive president of Marshall Field of Chicago, had written an excellent thesis on the influence of politics on foreign policy during the years I had covered. It ought to be published; would I like to revise and publish it, financed by a fellowship at Yale? I proposed that my own research on the strategic influences on foreign policy could be added. As a postgraduate fellow at Yale while simultaneously a lecturer at Nottingham University, frequent visits to the US enabled me to continue archival research, and eventually our jointly authored book, *Politics, Strategy, and American Diplomacy: Studies in Foreign Policy, 1873-1917*, was published by Yale University Press in 1969. Its main thrust was to show that the economic explanation for US imperialism was only a minor consideration when compared with the increasing concerns for American security and safety in an age of global conflict. By now I was receiving a number of offers of very well-paid professorships in Australia, Canada and the United States. The rapid expansion of higher education in the 1960s opened opportunities that have not been equalled since, so the large number of offers was not simply due to merit. But I chose to stay in England and went to a professorship at Leeds University in 1966.

Although my stay at Leeds was relatively short, two new academic developments were initiated while I was there. Firstly, a degree in international studies with what, at that time, was a progressive syllabus combining theories of international relations, economic development studies and history. It has proved very popular up to the present day. The second innovation was the use of film, especially news film, as historical evidence. Historical documentaries were, and still are, under the control of their producers for television, with the historian in a purely secondary role. For serious historical work it should be the other way round. Furthermore, from an educational point of view, university teachers are in the business of encouraging students to think critically. Traditionally we have made a good job of this in connection with written history and the academic presentation of history in lectures; I felt we now needed to equip students so they could think critically about the enormous audio-visual output on television. In collaboration with a talented colleague, Nicholas Pronay, a Hungarian refugee from the 1956 uprising, then a lecturer in medieval history and with a background of work in television, we produced a film study of propaganda, 'The Munich Crisis, 1938'. We also founded a consortium of some ten like-minded university departments to produce historical studies in film. We were pioneers, but were soon followed by other like-minded colleagues in the United States. Some three decades later, with many films behind it, the British Universities History Film Consortium is stronger than ever. Professor Pronay went on to found his own well-known Institute of Communications Studies at the University of Leeds, a pioneer in its field and very successful. After making a second film for the Consortium with Pronay, 'The End of Illusions: From Munich to Dunkirk', I eventually worked with commercial television, having been 'discovered' by Dieter Frank, a successful producer for ZDF (*Zweites Deutsches Fernsehen*). Our collaboration proved fruitful and enjoyable, as Dieter Frank brought a sensitivity to the role of historian rare among producers. The first 13-part series we worked on was 'The World of the Thirties'; it was spectacularly successful, as is evidenced by the more than fifty countries and television stations where it has been shown. This was followed by 'The Mid-Century World', and a third series dealing with the early years of the century is currently being broadcast.

I left Leeds in 1969 to take over the headship of the modern history department at the University of Birmingham. Previous experience led to the introduction of some new courses, such as the innovative 'History as presented on television'. My recent colleague in this, Scott Lucas, is now developing such studies to postgraduate level. Then personal tragedy struck. After a long terminal illness, borne with incredible courage and with thoughts only for our family, my wife died in 1974. Throughout the devastation of her illness I sought out work to keep me occupied, but it could only be of a 'routine' nature. I undertook to put together a reference work on the major international treaties of the twentieth century, a history and guide with edited texts of the world's treaties. International lawyers had up to then arranged treaties in a legal framework, distinguishing between bilateral and unilateral treaties. Their historical context had been largely ignored. The work was published in Britain and the United States in 1974. My agent found it very difficult to place in the States, but this was essential, as it was extremely costly to produce. In the end, after many rejections, a then small publisher of non-academic books, Stein and Day, took it on. I told them I expected it to sell about 1,000 copies. To everyone's delight it was listed as one of the best reference books of the year by the American Library Association, and sold very well. A third edition is now in preparation, in collaboration with Professor Bernard Wasserstein.

In 1975 happiness returned with my second marriage, to Patricia Carnie. My wife took firm hold of a household overrun with mice, three orphaned boys needing a mother, and a husband needing love and comfort as well as the time free from (most) domestic chores which would enable him to research and write. A year later *Europe Reshaped 1848-1878* appeared, a book commissioned by Professor J.H. Plumb, the distinguished editor of the *Fontana History of Europe*. I have always alternated between writing more general syntheses for students and originally researched books. *Europe Reshaped* has gone through many editions.

The year 1980 marked another new direction in my academic work. In the previous year I had accompanied a British delegation to the International Schoolbook Institute in Brunswick. There I met Professor Bernd-Jürgen Wendt, who arranged for me to come as a visiting professor to the University of Hamburg. This was my first extended stay in Germany since my departure 41 years earlier. My reception was very warm and understanding. The Wendt family became close friends, as did other colleagues at Hamburg, especially Professor Werner Jochmann, then Director of the Hamburg Research Centre for the Study of National Socialism, and Dr Ursula Büttner, for a long time his principal assistant. Close friendships and academic research intertwined. Beginning with the modest aim of some biographical studies during the National-Socialist period, my interests and research have expanded over the sixteen years since first going to Hamburg into a deeply researched investigation of the relations between Jews and their German neighbours in Hamburg, and the wider issue of racial persecution. The book based on this research, initially jointly undertaken with Werner Jochmann, will – I hope – see the light of day in two or three years.

Research was possible only in vacation periods. In term-time, I read up on a subject which our students were expected to cover, but which none of their teachers could – World History. The time needed to write it, as well as the subject itself, proved longer than I expected. A first part was published by Collins in 1980. Eventually I completed it, and *The History of the World in the Twentieth Century* was published in 1994 by HarperCollins in Britain and Harvard University Press in the United States. It proved to have a wide appeal, and with the help of book clubs its sales and circulation exceeded the wildest imaginings of even an optimistic academic. But research has taken me back to some of my Jewish roots in advancing years. I became a board member of the Leo Baeck Institute and since 1992 editor of the respected *Year Book* as successor to Arnold Paucker.

Looking back over forty years of academic life, is there any consistent pattern? The obvious road to fame is not to change from subject to subject or from one discipline to another, and on the face of it I have made many changes. Personal needs and the accidents of a full life have intersected in unpredictable ways with academic development. But the influence of great teachers, Webster and Bemis as scholars, A.J.P. Taylor as communicator, has accompanied all my teaching and writing. A non-British background made me look at national history from the point of view of an insider as well as from that of an outsider with an acute sense that the individuality of any country is only revealed by comparison. The enforced ability to be bi-lingual, and learning other languages, pointed me towards the study of foreign policy and international history. Later I realised that in the twentieth century foreign policy cannot be fully understood without giving ideology its due weight.

During the current period of my academic work, the last quarter of my career, I have returned to a field which for decades I avoided and distanced myself from: German-Jewish history. It has been possible for me only after forty years to study this period with proper scholarly detachment. I was now not simply drawn to understand and communicate an understanding of what happened in the 1930s and 1940s, I also felt a sense of duty to do so. How many historians had the combination of a training in the British school of history, pragmatic, not obsessed by theories, not monocausal or taking polarised positions, and the ability to read the German documents as speedily as a German? I set out to focus my study on one large city, renowned historically for being liberal and progressive, the 'Freie und Hansestadt Hamburg'. Here, in searching the archives for all clues relevant to the relations between Germans and Jews, I hope to be able to contribute something to the appreciation of how fragile civilisation really is.

Finally, coming back to the question with which I began, has there been any common underlying theme in my studies? With hindsight my answer would be: an interest in people and in how individuals, though inextricably bound to the times in which they live, still have a choice of action and influence, and the ways in which they can make a difference to the lives of others.

## Note

1      J.A.S. Grenville and J.G. Fuller, *The Coming of the Europeans* (London, 1962 and subsequent impressions).

## Selected Writings of J.A.S. Grenville

Books

with J.G. Fuller, *The Coming of the Europeans* (London, 1962)

*Lord Salisbury and Foreign Policy: The Close of the Nineteenth Century* (London, 1964)

with G.B. Young, *Politics, Strategy, and American Diplomacy: Studies in Foreign Policy, 1873-1917* (New Haven and London, 1966 and 1970)

*The Major International Treaties 1914-1973: A History and Guide* (London and New York, 1974); with Bernard Wasserstein, second updated edition in two volumes (London, 1984); with Bernard Wasserstein, third updated edition in one volume (London, forthcoming)

*Europe Reshaped 1848-1878* (Hassocks, 1976)

*A World History of the Twentieth Century: Western Dominance 1900-1945* (London, 1980)

*A History of the World in the Twentieth Century* (London and Cambridge, Mass., 1994, new edition, 1997; Russian edition forthcoming)

## Articles and Contributions to Books

'Lansdowne's Abortive Project of 12 March 1901 for a Secret Agreement with Germany', *Bulletin of the Institute of Historical Research* 27 (1954), pp 201-213

'Great Britain and the Isthmian Canal, 1898-1901', *American Historical Review* 61 (1955), pp 48-69

'Goluchowski. Salisbury and the Mediterranean Agreements, 1895-97', *Slavonic and East European Review* 36 (1958), pp 340-369

'Diplomacy and War Plans in the United States, 1890-1917', *Transactions of the Royal Historical Society* 11 (1961), pp 1-21, reprinted in Paul Kennedy (ed.), *The War Plans of the Great Powers 1880-1914* (London, 1979 and 1985)

'The United States' Decision for War, 1917: Excerpts from the Manuscript Diary of Robert Lansing', *Renaissance and Modern Studies* 4 (1960), pp 59-81

'American Naval Preparations for War with Spain, 1896-98', *American Studies* 2 (1968), pp 33-47

'National Prejudice and International History', Inaugural Lecture (Leeds University Press, 1968)

'Film as History', Inaugural Lecture (University of Birmingham, 1971)

'The historian as film-maker', in Paul Smith (ed.), *The Historian and Film* (Cambridge, 1976), pp 132-141

'Contemporary trends in the study of the British "appeasement" policies of the 1930s', *Internationales Jahrbuch für Geschichts- und Geographieunterricht* 17 (1976), pp 236-247

'Foreign Policy and the Coming of War', in Donald Read (ed.), *Edwardian England* (London, 1982), pp 162-180

'Die Errichtung der nationalsozialistischen Herrschaft in Deutschland aus der Sicht der europäischen Nachbarstaaten', in Ursula Büttner and Werner Jochmann (eds), *Zwischen Demokratie und Diktatur* (Hamburg, 1984), pp 115-139

'Die "Endlösung" und die Judenmischlinge im Dritten Reich', in

Ursula Büttner (ed.), *Das Unrechtsregime*, volume 2 (Hamburg, 1986), pp 91-121

'Der Ausbruch des Zweiten Weltkrieges aus britischer Sicht', in Walter Leimgruber (ed.), *1939: Europäer erinnern sich an den Zweiten Weltkrieg* (Zurich, 1990), pp 245-259

'Imperial Germany and Britain: From Cooperation to War', in A.M. Birke and Marie-Luise Recker (eds), *Das gestörte Gleichgewicht/ Upsetting the Balance* (Munich, 1990), pp 81-95

'Juden, "Nichtarier" und "Deutsche Ärzte": Die Anpassung der Ärzte im Dritten Reich', in Ursula Büttner (ed.), *Die Deutschen und die Judenverfolgung im Dritten Reich* (Hamburg, 1992), pp 191-206

'Die Geschichtsschreibung der Bundesrepublik über die deutschen Juden', in Ursula Beitz, Irene Kaufmann and Barbara Maurer (eds), *Studien zur jüdischen Geschichte und Soziologie* (Heidelberg, 1992), pp 195-205

'Neglected Holocaust Victims: The Mischlinge, the Jüdischver-sippten and the Gypsies' (in a volume to be published by the United States Holocaust Memorial Museum, Washington)

Documentary Films

with Nicholas Pronay, 'The Munich Crisis, 1938' (for the British Universities History Film Consortium and Yorkshire Television, 1968)

with Nicholas Pronay, 'The End of Illusions: From Munich to Dunkirk' (for the British Universities History Film Consortium, 1970)

**E.P. Hennock**

Myself as

Historian

I was originally called Ernst Peter Henoch and was born in Berlin in 1926. In fact I have always been called Peter; Ernst was my god-father's name. My parents, who were assimilated Jews with no religious profession of any kind, had me baptised into the Protestant Church. In Germany, where there was hardly an official document that did not contain a question about religion, that would have seemed to them the obvious next step in the process of full assimilation. By the time of the Nuremberg Laws of 1935 that must have appeared an utterly futile gesture, but it was not. My baptism was to prove highly significant, for it was as a 'non-Aryan Christian' that I was brought to England early in 1939 by a church in the South Coast town of Worthing. Worthing was in the diocese of George Bell, Bishop of Chichester, whose concern for non-Aryans in Germany – who would not be looked after by any Jewish organisations – the congregation of St Matthew's Church, Worthing had come to share. They undertook to provide the money needed to bring me to England and to look after me. They felt that they were saving a child's life, and they were right.

I was twelve years old, and less than two weeks after my arrival I was in an English boarding school. My brother, who had come to England with me, left the following year for the USA. Apart from brief visits to London during part of the school holidays, I spoke no German for the next five years. Eighteen months after my arrival in England I won a scholarship and went as a boarder to Ardingly College, a public school in Sussex. There I was fortunate to find a talented teacher of history who awakened my interest in the subject. In 1944 I won a scholarship to Peterhouse, Cambridge.

This success was made possible by the people in Worthing who maintained me at school and allowed me to remain long enough to sit the Cambridge scholarship examination. Long before then the house of one of them, Miss Mary Maynard, had become my home. Until her death at an advanced age in 1982 our relationship was like that of mother and son.

The process of becoming as much like an English schoolboy as my accent would allow, a process essential for survival under the conditions of a boarding school in war-time, was greatly encouraged by those among whom I moved in Worthing. My father had the misfortune to emigrate to Riga and did not long survive the capture of that city by the German army. My mother had died when I was still a child; my only brother was in the USA. My connections with the German-Jewish refugee circles in London were of the slightest. Mine was an extreme case of uprooting and anglicisation, a process with which I was happy to co-operate.

This is the background to my career as a historian. In a school with a teaching staff decimated by military conscription history was the one subject that was really well taught. It was my history master who taught me how to think, and in particular how to think in a structured, analytical and critical way. That I learnt these skills through the study of history was little more than an accident. In a school with a wider range of talent some other subject might have fired my imagination. For mine was not a particularly historical imagination. I was neither then nor at any other time a romantic historian who thrilled at the thought of standing where some famous figure of the past had stood. Nor did I go in for imaginative reconstruction of the past by means of word-painting. But the material of history is as good a body of material on which to sharpen one's intellectual teeth as any other. The love of history that I soon developed was the love of analysis and argument. That emphasis has remained with me throughout the later years.

I was seventeen when I discovered that my origins barred me from a career in the higher, ie 'administrative' grades of the civil service. I had neither the connections nor the money for the law and I rightly believed that I would meet less prejudice against foreigners in universities than in the world of business. I decided to become what was then known as a University don. In this decision I was influenced by the example of a man whom I have never met. Professor J.L. Morison, Miss Maynard's uncle by marriage, was a graduate of the University of Glasgow who became Professor of History at what is now the University of Newcastle. Long before I ever met my first university historian I had heard about him and decided to follow his example.

Before going to Cambridge, I volunteered for the army and was trained as a signaller in the Royal Artillery. The war with Germany was still in full swing, and like many others in my situation I was advised by the army authorities to anglicise my name to avoid attracting attention in the eventuality of capture. I changed Ernst Peter Henoch to Ernest Peter Hennock. As it happened, I was still undergoing training when the war in Europe came to an end, and I also narrowly escaped the war in Burma. I spent the next two years in Wales as an interpreter in a labour camp for German prisoners of war. That experience transformed my childhood German into something resembling the German spoken by an adult. On demobilisation I qualified for an ex-serviceman's grant to finance my studies at Cambridge and so solved a problem that had seemed insuperable in 1944. The scholarship that I had then won would have been quite inadequate.

In January 1948, a week after leaving the army, I was an undergraduate at Peterhouse, a college with a strong reputation in history. The first class honours in Part 2 of the Cambridge historical tripos, with which I graduated in June 1950, qualified me for a grant to become a research student and register for a PhD.

The only way to explain why I became the kind of historian that I am is by a narrative of what was more like a journey of adventure than a series of strategic choices. Only then shall I be able to give a coherent answer, for the coherence emerged in retrospect. Cambridge had introduced me to a broad range of history, and the requirement of a weekly essay discussed in an individual tutorial had been a good training of the mind. But it had done little to introduce me to the ways of historical research. In theory that was the function of the special subject, based as that was on documents. But the Professor of Ecclesiastical History, whose special subject on the Elizabethan church I had chosen, left us to read the documents on our own, while he lectured twice a week, handing down *ex cathedra* the truth as he understood it. To me, who could see that the documents lent themselves to other interpretations less flattering to his hero, Archbishop Whitgift, this was frustrating. I did once attempt to argue the case with him, but in vain. Interesting though the subject was, it did nothing to introduce me to the methods of historical research, a matter of which I was profoundly ignorant when I became a research student.

The most interesting part of the historical tripos had been the history of political thought, brilliantly expounded in Michael

Oakeshott's lectures, but interesting in any case. I discovered that the simple majority principle had not always been regarded as the most obvious way to make decisions, and I decided to find out how it had acquired its subsequent legitimacy. The limited literature on this was in Italian; the crucial setting of the process appeared to have been the Italian cities of the later Middle Ages. On graduating, I set out to learn Italian in preparation for my research and to do so in the one example of an Italian city state still extant, the Republic of San Marino. An article on San Marino that I wrote on my return for the *Contemporary Review* was my first publication.

I had not given much thought to the technical aspect of the study of medieval history. On my return to Cambridge a session with Walter Ullmann, an Austrian refugee of great erudition (see pp 247-260), who had recently come to teach in Cambridge, convinced me, probably quite wrongly, that I was not cut out to be a medievalist. I transferred my interest in egalitarian ideas to the period of the French Revolution, and Noel Annan was accordingly appointed as my supervisor. As Lord Annan he was subsequently to be Vice-Chancellor of the University of London and at this time was a Fellow of Kings College, Cambridge, and a member of the Faculty of Economics and Politics. I believe that I was his first history research student, and a very difficult one I proved to be. A deeply committed Christian, who had recently discovered Kierkegaard, Martin Buber and Paul Tillich, I rapidly found the thought of the Enlightenment profoundly unsympathetic, and discovered that there is no point in pursuing historical research on material that is uncongenial.

I decided to find a subject that mattered to me, and began to explore the history of the church in the nineteenth century. There were at that time no seminars for research students: we were expected to pick up our knowledge from our supervisor or else, as in my case, on our own. I discovered Charles Booth's survey of religious influences in London[1] and embarked on researching the role of nonconformist churches as social organisations in nineteenth-century English cities. I had picked a small sample and was deep in the records of certain prominent London chapels, when Noel Annan, rightly feeling that this was far removed from what he had expected when he agreed to become my supervisor, announced his resignation. The degree committee of the History Faculty Board looked at my project with consternation, and its members threw up their hands in horror at what had been allowed to happen. Herbert Butterfield, Professor of Modern History and a Fellow of my college, agreed to take responsibility for me and to return me to the proper ways of historical research.

He explained to me that my chosen subject suffered from two fatal flaws: it was too diffuse and in any case it was not history. Was there not some limited matter of political significance that I could take up? In a clerical biography I had read about a reform movement in Birmingham local government, that, it was claimed, had been the work of the nonconformist churches. I suggested this as a suitably limited subject.

'Ah, if it is Birmingham,' said Butterfield, 'you had better go and talk to Mr Briggs at Oxford. If he thinks it is all right you can do it.'

That is how I met Asa Briggs. 'I am just completing a history of Birmingham in the second half of the nineteenth century,' he explained to me. 'I have only said the obvious things about your subject. Go and see what more you can discover.'

So I did, and four terms into my three years as a research student I embarked on my study of the role of religious dissent in the municipal reform of Birmingham between 1865 and 1876. My own commitment to an active role for the church in modern secular society made me willing to extend to nineteenth-century sermons a sympathy that I had withheld from eighteenth-century philosophical pamphlets. I set off for Birmingham where I spent much of my time in the Victorian reading room of the reference library, turning the pages of the local press, and just occasionally wishing that I were in Lucca or Siena, as I might so easily have been. By the summer of 1953, when my grant expired, I had collected a great deal of material, but I was far from making sense of it.

That set off a crisis of confidence in my chosen career. After three years of work I did not know where I was going. University vacancies were few and with my work nowhere near completion there seemed no chance of getting a job. For the first time I began to doubt whether I was really cut out for a highly competitive academic career. I wondered whether I had been too quick to assume that there would have been no niche for me in the legal profession.

My assessment of my talents was apparently not shared by my supervisor, to judge from the responses to his references. I was short-listed though failed to get a lectureship in politics at the University College of East Africa in Makerere, a failure for which I was to be profoundly grateful when, a few years later, Uganda was engulfed in one of its many political crises. In the United Kingdom there were only three posts in my field. I came second to John Grenville (see pp 55-72) at Nottingham, but was appointed soon after to an assistant lectureship shared between the Departments of History and Political Institutions at the University College of North Staffordshire.

It was only when I began to read widely in preparation for teaching that I hit on the ideas that made sense of what I had been studying in Birmingham. It was Philip Magnus's biography of Gladstone that provided me with the organising principle of my PhD thesis.[2] He had presented Gladstone as responding to the nineteenth-century changes in the relation between church and state by transforming his original notion of himself as the Christian statesman in the service of the church into a new highly charged view of popular politics as a religious vocation. I argued that the 'municipal gospel' preached by the Birmingham reformers was similarly a response to the assumption by local government of duties previously associated with the work of the churches. This enabled me to make sense of the highly charged moralistic view of local government that was the peculiar product of the Birmingham reform movement associated with Joseph Chamberlain, and to explain the appeal of Town Council service to the businessmen associated with certain nonconformist churches in the town.

I submitted the thesis early in 1956. Asa Briggs, whose own *History of Birmingham* had appeared in 1952, was the external examiner. He liked my work enough to suggest that it should be published as part of a series of studies in religious history under his general editorship. When he subsequently wrote that he could find no publisher to take up the project, I took that to be proof that the work was unpublishable in the climate of the time. At that stage I should have turned the thesis into articles, but I decided to let it lie for the moment and turned to other things. My first academic article, published in 1957, was in fact concerned to defend S.E. Finer, my head of department, from criticism of his book on Edwin Chadwick.[3] The criticism was not merely ill-judged but ran demonstrably counter to the evidence. That evidence was available in Manchester and easy to consult from Keele, but apparently too far from Oxford to have been consulted by the author of an article with whom I took issue in the pages of the *Economic History Review*. It was my first experience of professional debate.

The University College of North Staffordshire, soon to become the University of Keele, was the only new university foundation in the 1950s. Its innovative four-year degree course and its emphasis on the educational benefits of a residential university, a mixture of Scottish and Oxford traditions, made it unique among British universities. There were not many places where young assistant lecturers and lecturers had as much responsibility thrust upon them as we had. It was a good place at which to learn to teach, but in those early days there was not much of a research environment. In 1957 I obtained a lectureship in history and severed my links with the Department of Political Institutions.

1962 was important in my professional life. Convinced that my thesis could only be published as part of a bigger project, I obtained a research grant from the Leverhulme Trust to expand my Birmingham study into a study of the social composition of town councils in the English provincial cities in the nineteenth century. With the help of a research assistant I began by applying the prosopographical methods that had been part of my thesis to the whole period 1838-1914. I then chose Leeds to be the next city to be investigated.

Determined to clear my desk before embarking on the longer study, I published 'Finance and Politics in Urban Local Government in England 1835-1900', an article that dealt with the problems of nineteenth-century local government finance in the expanding towns. Presenting the results of my study of Birmingham I argued that successful municipal government required, among other things, a marked flair for business. I went on to suggest that such qualities were more likely to be found where the Town Council was at least partly recruited from the more successful businessmen in the community. Not much was known of the social composition of town councils; hence the research on which I had recently embarked. That left the other aspect of the thesis, the religious and ideological dimension of the Birmingham reform movement, still to be published.

I had sent the article in typescript to Asa Briggs for his comments and in return he asked me to look at the proofs of his forthcoming book *Victorian Cities*. It contained a chapter on Birmingham called 'Birmingham, the Making of a Civic Gospel', and the many quotations from nonconformist clergy and from Joseph Chamberlain were only too familiar. The book was published in 1963, unfortunately without footnotes but with a preface and a bibliographical note containing handsome acknowledgments of his debt to my thesis. It was not quite the way I would have wished my work to see the light of day, but it was my own fault for having left it unpublished for so long.

1961 had seen the foundation of the University of Sussex near Brighton. The plans for it had preceded the publication of the Robbins Report, but it greatly benefited from the report's recommendation of a policy of university expansion on innovative lines.

For the University of Keele, the Government's acceptance of the Robbins recommendations was bad news. For the rapid expansion of student numbers the four-year degree course pioneered by Keele in the 1950s was too expensive to be contemplated, and Keele was to be sidelined in the university expansion that now followed. Several of us used the opportunity presented by university expansion to move elsewhere. I had personal reasons for wanting to be near Worthing, and in 1963 I was appointed Lecturer in History at Sussex under Asa Briggs as Professor and Dean of the School of Social Studies.

There is no room here to do justice to the experience of being one of the founding generation of the University of Sussex. I regard myself fortunate to have had that experience, fortunate in the opportunity for innovative and imaginative teaching, in the quality of my students and above all in the quality of my colleagues. One result of my move was that I concentrated even more than I had done at Keele on the teaching of British history. The new kinds of history that we began to teach, 'The Late-Victorian Revolt in Literature and Society' for the School of English and American Studies, 'The Development of Modern Britain' for the School of Social Studies, soon to be called the School of Social Sciences, and 'Images of Childhood' for the School of Educational Studies, ensured that this was far from being a narrowing experience. On the contrary, it continually forced me into new reading and the formulation of new concepts. But it meant that after 1963 I ceased to study much European history.

I replaced the special subject on 'Gladstone's Leadership of the Liberal Party' that I had taught at Keele by one called 'Poverty as a Problem of Social Policy 1880-1914', which I taught for many years. At first there was hardly any good secondary literature and most of the teaching was from the texts. Gradually it became a subject on which important books were published: Bentley Gilbert on *The Evolution of National Insurance in Great Britain* (1966), Gareth Stedman Jones on *Outcast London* (1971), José Harris on *Unemployment and Politics* (1972) and Roy Hay on *The Origins of the Liberal Welfare Reforms* (1975), to name but a few of the best.

Unfortunately Brighton seemed a long way from Leeds. I had devised my research project on the assumption that, living near Crewe, the major provincial cities were easily accessible. Hardly had I committed myself to the study of Leeds than I moved to the South Coast. After each teaching term I would reluctantly travel up to Leeds. In 1966-67 a year's study leave as visiting Fellow at All Souls

College, Oxford, enabled me to concentrate on the work and to reflect on where it was leading. When I returned to Sussex there was still much to be done. The teaching load at a university that prided itself on its commitment to innovative teaching slowed down progress on the book, and it gradually became a burden. The type-script was finally despatched late in 1971.

The book came out in 1973 as *Fit and Proper Persons: Ideal and Reality in Nineteenth-Century Urban Government*, and was well received. I had tried my hand at quantitative history, accumulating in those pre-computer days a formidable set of punch-cards, but the experience taught me that my talents lay elsewhere. Despite these longitudinal studies with their apparatus of tables and graphs, the book was primarily concerned with the dynamics and the programme of two municipal reform movements, one in the Birmingham of the late 1860s and 1870s, the other in Leeds two decades later. The Birmingham study was my thesis of 1956 and it was the best part of the book. After *Victorian Cities* it could hardly have been published in its own right. It now appeared at last, serving as a case-study within the broader framework.

The book's favourable reception owed much to the changes that had come over the study of history. In choosing to study Birmingham civic life, as I did in the early 1950s, I had been eccentric and wilful, following what I considered interesting, not the advice of any mentor. Professor Butterfield constantly felt he ought to warn me against the danger of writing 'parish pump history', and frequently expressed his reservations about the significance of my subject. When I obtained my degree he congratulated me and then strongly urged me to start work on some central theme of history – 'something like Bismarck'. In a way I did what he suggested, except that it was Gladstone on whom I chose to work next. However, in 1961 I took up the urban government theme once more. Within a few years I found myself in the van of fashion, the fashion for urban history, which to my great delight H.J. Dyos was energetically promulgating. I gave a paper at the international conference on urban history that he organised in Leicester in 1966. The proceedings of that conference, published in 1968 as *The Study of Urban History*, became the manifesto of the new breed of urban historians. The annual meetings of the Urban History Group provided me with intellectual stimulus and encouragement. When *Fit and Proper Persons* finally appeared, it was as second in the series 'Studies in Urban History' under Dyos's editorship. The book was fortunate in the reception it received, but also in the trouble that Dyos had taken to ensure a beautiful piece of book production, and to provide the series with constant publicity. Nor am I the only one who owes much to Jim Dyos. There is no doubt in my mind that he killed himself with overwork, the victim of the international success for which he had striven so hard.

While writing *Fit and Proper Persons* I had hardly ever used my on-going research in my teaching. That was a mistake, and I was determined that it should not happen again. The special subject on poverty had given me many ideas that I was at last free to pursue. One result was an article 'Poverty and Social Theory: The Experience of the 1880s' in 1976. It was intended as a criticism of Helen Lynd's book *England in the Eighteen-Eighties*, which was then the most widely accepted view of the significance of that decade.[4] She had portrayed the 1880s as witnessing an economic depression that undermined faith in *laissez-faire* and replaced it with a belief in collectivism. I did not regard the period as one of theoretical innovation but as one that saw the restatement in a firmer and more systematic manner of ideas first promulgated in the 1860s. I therefore suggested a different relationship between periods of perceived crisis and periods of theoretical innovation. As I was finishing the work, Gareth Stedman Jones published his *Outcast London* and I thought that I detected enough similarities between his views and those of Helen Lynd to rewrite the article and to include a section in which I took issue with his views. In 1984 when Stedman Jones produced a new edition of his highly successful book, he responded to the various criticisms that it had received and convinced me that I had partly misunderstood his argument. He then re-phrased it in ways that made it a great deal clearer. It was a courteous reply and one that I regard as a model of how disagreements should be dealt with.

Historians benefit from having to re-phrase their views in response to questions or objections. It is one of the ways in which we can help each other, provided it is done constructively and with courtesy. I am a firm believer in the value of work-in-progress seminars, not only for research students but for all those engaged in research of whatever seniority. It was largely on my suggestion that the historians at Keele began to meet and talk about their research, and at Sussex I organised a highly successful research seminar, which became a regular institution and still exists. Such seminars can be used for aggressive point-scoring. I like to think that we avoided that pitfall most of the time and created the right atmosphere of searching but courteous questioning and constructive suggestion.

A section of the article on the 1880s dealt with Charles Booth's survey of poverty in London, a work then often cited but rarely read with the necessary care.[5] Booth had interested me while a research student in Cambridge, and his poverty survey, together with those of Rowntree and Bowley, was a set text for my special subject students.[6] I developed an abiding interest in the history of social investigation, and have repeatedly written on aspects of the poverty surveys. It was part of my interest in social theory. To me the surveys are more than sources of statistical information: they are attempts to articulate the structure of society. Indeed I have always found the categories more important than the figures. Moreover the methods employed to arrive at the figures are indispensable knowledge for anybody who wants to use them. The object of an investigation, the methods available to the investigator and the relation between the two, which as often as not was one of mismatch, have provided me with my particular approach to the history of social investigation.

That was not the only way in which my special subject teaching influenced my research. Even before I had completed *Fit and Proper Persons* I had decided that my next book would deal with the attitude of British reformers to German institutions in the period circa 1880-1914. I was constantly coming across references to what could be learnt from the Germans. My Leeds Councillors went off to Berlin to look at gas-works, the Birmingham ones to Frankfurt to look at town planning, and Bentley Gilbert's book on *The Evolution of National Insurance* was full of references to Germany. I decided to look at this phenomenon, not because I was interested in Germany but because it seemed to me to signal an important change in the Britain of that period.

This may be the moment to explain what I think my work as a historian owes to my origins. First and foremost they probably account for my concentration on English history. I just found English history so much more interesting and at the same time so much more congenial than anything else. Had I been born in England I might have taken it for granted and turned elsewhere to find matters that intrigued me. As an immigrant I never could take it for granted, and I have been both fascinated and intrigued by British and in particular by English history. There was much that related to my own experience, and I admired it and wanted to examine and to understand it. It is not at all unusual for immigrants to be pre-occupied with the country of their adoption. As historians they have sometimes felt that they could recognise the crucial elements in their adopted country more clearly than native historians. Like any other historian they may be wrong. Posterity has been harsh on Sir Lewis Namier; it may yet be harsh on Sir Geoffrey Elton, but there can be no doubt that both have been immensely influential in their time.

My work on English history has had its own particular emphasis: on religion as socially active, on the role of voluntary associations in shaping English society, on the Liberal belief in progress as a strenuous process of reform, on local rather than central government as initiator, and subsequently on the relation between the two in a country where the monarchy had been deprived in the late seventeenth century of the instruments of central government control. These were matters that appear to me to be crucial to an understanding of nineteenth-century England. I have emphasised them in teaching and research precisely because they were so different from the England that we know.

From that perspective, something new and important seemed to have occurred in the generation prior to 1914, a re-assessment of the nature of the Liberal state, of which the interest in German methods was the symptom. Germany stood for compulsion linked to nation-wide coverage as against a belief in on-going dynamic processes, which would ultimately include those at present still outside. It stood for organisation as something imposed by expert policy makers from above as against the association of men who shared a common purpose, ie for bureaucracy as against the reliance on voluntary institutions.

I decided to investigate the attitude of British reformers to German methods in three fields where German influence was prominent: social insurance, technical education and town planning. I was particularly interested in the extent to which they realised that what attracted them was part of a political system very different from their own, and how they envisaged the process of borrowing from abroad. The early 1970s when I chose this project were years when people in Britain were conscious of the challenge that membership of the EEC was about to pose to the characteristic institutions of this country, but without the paranoia that has marked more recent responses in the Conservative Party. I thought of my project not only as stemming from my personal interest in what I increasingly thought of as the Englishness of English history, to adapt the title of one of Sir Nikolaus Pevsner's books on English art, but also as timely in the age of the EEC.[7]

In 1972 I obtained study leave and decided to spend it at a German university. Although my new project was not about German insurance, but about what British policy makers thought of it, I decided to acquire at least some knowledge of the German literature. I obtained a grant from the British Academy and spent a semester at Tübingen, working at the Institute of Economic History, where Karl Erich Born had assembled a team to publish documents on the social policy of the German Empire.

That was not my first contact with German historians. In 1959, when I was still at Keele, the History Department had received a visit from Werner Conze, sponsored by the British Council. It was his first visit to Britain. He was badly handicapped by his poor English, and I looked after him and spoke German to him. I was probably the only one in the department who had any inkling how important a historian he actually was. In return he invited me to Heidelberg for a fortnight in 1960, and also arranged for me to visit Theodor Schieder's institute in Cologne and the Friedrich-Meinecke Institute under Hans Herzfeld in Berlin. It was obvious that he wanted to show me the best in nineteenth-century history that the German Federal Republic then possessed.

Apart from a few days in 1950 this was my first visit to post-war Germany. On that earlier occasion I had found Germany in post-war trauma most disagreeable, and I prepared for this one with some apprehension. In actual fact I greatly enjoyed it. In Heidelberg, where I was looked after by Professor Conze's assistant Reinhart Koselleck, I was impressed by the good relations between Conze and the students of his 'Oberseminar' (graduate seminar). They had arranged an excursion through the Odenwald, together with Conze and his staff, which I was invited to join and which culminated in a cheerful supper in a country inn. I found the sight of Koselleck and one of the women students dancing a sort of fantastic impromptu, half Scottish reel, half rock, to the music of the traditional military marches on the jukebox of the inn in every way most reassuring. I was also impressed by a lecture that Conze gave to a group of school teachers on the place of the Nazi period in German history. It was a *tour de force* and at question-time he handled difficult political matters with great candour.

I developed both then and subsequently a great respect for Werner Conze, as a historian prepared to tackle the important questions, and as a Liberal influence in the university, and he had my sympathy when as 'Rektor' (Vice-Chancellor) in 1971 he became the special target of student radicals. I, who had valued the good staff-student relations at Keele and in the early years at Sussex, was to find the confrontations that occurred in Sussex after 1968 deeply disillusioning. But I knew enough about events in

Heidelberg and elsewhere to realise that things could have been much worse.

In Cologne I was looked after by Professor Schieder's assistant, Wolfgang Mommsen, who showed me the recently restored Romanesque churches. Cologne proved an important part of my wider education. In Berlin, then still without a wall, the Free University exuded the idealism of its founding period. There I met Wolfgang Hofmann, whose research project, subsequently published as *Die Bielefelder Stadtverordneten* (Lübeck, 1964), bore an uncanny resemblance to my work on Birmingham. I also visited in Wuppertal Wolfgang Köllmann, whose book on Barmen I had recently reviewed. Of all the historians I met in 1960 it was the connection with these urban specialists that proved of lasting significance. I remained in touch with them on my return to England, and was later to include a brief section on German urban local government in *Fit and Proper Persons*.

I was surprised that Germany had proved as agreeable as it had. Only once during my visit did I come up against views unpleasantly reminiscent of the Nazi past. I realized that Conze had probably been careful whom I met, and most people had known enough about my background to exercise tact. To test whether this had been an exceptional experience and in order to see more of Germany, I undertook a lecture tour for the British Council in the summer of 1965. Since this was during the university vacations I found myself talking to non-academic audiences, but the tour included a session with the planning group for the projected university at Bochum, who wanted to know about the new British universities.

I felt that the experiment had been a success. I knew of people who could not bear the thought of visiting Germany, and I was profoundly grateful that I did not feel that way. I did not much analyse the reasons. Basically I felt too British to feel threatened even by the Nazi views which I occasionally met in conversation. The far more common complaints about how badly the Germans had been treated, complaints about the partition of the country, the Oder-Neisse line, expulsions from Eastern Europe or the bombing of German cities, I met with the obvious answer. If anyone asked how I had acquired my fluent German I told them. If they were embarrassed, as they occasionally were, that was their problem not mine. Despite the death of my father, about whose circumstances I am still in the dark, I carry no deep-seated personal pain. I feel I have been remarkably lucky; I vastly prefer being British to being German.

On this basis I continued to pay occasional visits to Germany. Professor Conze invited me to the 'Historikertag' (biennial meeting of German historians) in Brunswick in 1974, over which he presided. There I attended the session on urban history, and I remember being lectured at length by Helmut Croon on the difference between 'lokale Behörde' and 'kommunale Selbstverwaltung'. 'Lokale Behörde', although literally 'local authority', is a term applied to the local office of a central government department, for example a local pension office in Britain. The German term for representative local government, which is what we mean when we speak of a local authority, is 'kommunale Selbstverwaltung'. It is a distinction with which I was quite familiar; I had merely on the spur of the moment translated 'local authority' too literally. That served as a reminder of my limitations as a German linguist. I met some of the younger urban historians such as Jürgen Reulecke and Dieter Rebentisch, but much of the time felt out of place as a specialist on British history at an assembly of German historians.

The visit to Tübingen had also provided the occasion for lectures in Cologne, Bochum, Düsseldorf and Berlin on my work and its relation to the wider themes of British history. Then in 1978 I contributed to the Anglo-German conference on the Emergence of the Welfare State in Britain and Germany, organised by Wolfgang Mommsen in Berlin. I was probably luckier than most of the British contributors in that I was able to correct the German translation of my paper before the publication of the proceedings in both languages two years later, and so ensured that it did justice to what I had been trying to say. On the other hand the few occasions when I have actually written an article in German have convinced me that that is a bad idea. Although usually good enough for conversation or correspondence, my German is not up to the rigours of academic writing. Even the preparation of lectures or papers for oral delivery is an exacting task for which I need the help of a real German-speaker. That is, however, something that I feel I can do, knowing that my clumsy anglicisms will vanish with the spoken word and that any ambiguities can be overcome by means of gesture or be cleared up at question-time.

In 1982 I asked Professors Ritter and Wehler whether I might try out the section of my book that dealt with accident insurance at their respective research seminars. They both agreed. At Bielefeld I raised the question of publishing the paper in *Geschichte und Gesellschaft* and Wehler sent the typescript to several readers for advice. The response was positive except for one matter. There was general agreement among them that it would be easier to retranslate the original English version than to correct my German. I know just what they meant! Unfortunately there was no original English version. I never translate; I had written it in German in the first place. What they had taken for a stilted translation of an English text was actually my very best German. That incident just about sums up my command of what is strictly speaking my mother tongue.

My colleagues at the University of Sussex included John Röhl and Hartmut Pogge von Strandmann. They turned the university into a centre of excellence in German history and attracted able research students. Any German nineteenth- or twentieth-century specialist visiting Britain for any length of time would sooner or later come to Sussex. That is how during the course of the sixties and seventies I gradually acquired some knowledge of modern German history and a wide circle of acquaintances among its practitioners in the Federal Republic. I had no contact with historians in the German Democratic Republic until much later. My first and only professional visit there was to East Berlin in 1988.

After moving to a chair in Liverpool I tried whenever possible to invite historians visiting the German Historical Institute in London to come up to Liverpool. Hans-Ulrich Wehler, Thomas Nipperdey and several others gave outstanding lectures or seminar papers in Liverpool on that basis.

The completion of my book was delayed by the move to Liverpool in 1976. As in 1963, I had hardly embarked on a research project when I was whisked away to the other end of the country from where the relevant archives were located. From Brighton, day-trips to the Public Records Office in outer London had been no problem; not so from Liverpool. In addition I now carried new responsibilities as head of the Department of Modern History. Indeed it was 1987 before the book was published as *British Social Reform and German Precedents: The Case of Social Insurance 1880-1914*. Long before then I had discovered that the three different branches of German social insurance had provoked very different reactions in Britain, presenting me in fact not with one but with three subjects. The original intention to balance the work on social insurance with similar studies of technical education and town planning was reluctantly replaced by a much briefer treatment of these themes in the introduction of what had become a book on the British reception of German social insurance. However, in 1990 I published an article on the reception of the German *Technische Hochschule*, using ideas and material that would have exceeded the bounds of what was appropriate for the introduction.

The book was based on the view that the dominant British Liberal political tradition, whether in its conservative or its radical form, owed little to foreign influence. It set out to identify the conditions, exceptional as these were, under which foreign, and in this case German, models acquired a rare importance. It expounded therefore a deeply insular interpretation of British history by the very manner in which it defined the problem to be dealt with. Even so, one reviewer criticised it for not being insular enough and suggested that the introduction of British national insurance needed no explanation in terms of borrowing from abroad, but that was not the usual reaction. Most reviewers accepted that there was a problem that required explanation and commented on my carefully circumscribed presentation of the impact of the German precedent.

The most considered statement of my view of British history in the later nineteenth and early twentieth centuries was written after the publication of the book, as I continued to reflect on the implications of my work and tried to make it more explicit. Called 'Borrowing Institutions from Abroad', it was written as a lecture for use in America, and has so far not been published, containing as it does little that has not already been said by me in a different form. It has also been useful in Britain.

Despite differences of subject matter, and despite focusing on central rather than local government, the book *British Social Reform and German Precedents* has much in common with *Fit and Proper Persons*. Both were written from the radical perspective. The nonconformist clergy behind the movement in Birmingham, Joseph Chamberlain and Lloyd George were all radical reformers, and both books were about reform. In my teaching I have also paid much attention to reformers, including conservative ones like Peel and Gladstone. Reformers have always interested me, people who were not prepared to accept a situation as given, but wished to change it. 'Poverty as a Social Problem', the subject I taught for many years, was about the difference between accepting something as just a social phenomenon and identifying it as a social problem. It was about regarding poverty, or certain kinds of poverty, as an 'intolerable evil', to use the question-begging term first applied in this context by Oliver MacDonagh.[8] I am well aware that this preoccupation stems from my attitude to the people who brought me to England for no other reason than that they found the German treatment of the so-called non-Aryans intolerable. They had been a minority in a country largely preoccupied with unemployment at home and not at all inclined to welcome immigrants. It is their attitude that I have never been able to take for granted.

By the time that *British Social Reform and German Precedents* was published, much had changed in British universities. The Thatcher years were the era when the iron entered our souls. In one respect I was fortunate, for the headship of what, after the merger of the medievalists with the modernists, became the Department of History was during that time held by my professorial colleagues. The sudden withdrawal of money in 1981, followed by a policy of long-term erosion of funding, inflicted major damage on the department. In 1984 the university required it to shed five members of staff from a total of 25, all of whom had guaranteed tenure, and only one of whom was willing to take voluntary retirement. Personally I felt that for senior people to take retirement at this juncture, when there was no prospect of a replacement, was to solve the financial problems of the university at the expense of our discipline and to leave the department weakened in teaching and research, as well as on Senate. That was not a course I was prepared to take, and my senior colleagues took a similar view. But the effect on the morale of the department was dire. Something like planning blight afflicted it for many years before the necessary savings were finally brought about by methods so ingenious that they actually damaged the study of history at Liverpool very little.

Freed from the administrative burden, I set about encouraging the study of my kind of history wherever it was to be found. No one in my department shared my interest in the history of social policy, and there was no prospect of making any appointments, but the Departments of Architecture, Civic Design, Sociology, Politics and Education all contained historians with an interest in policy-making. In 1985 we decided to establish a cross-departmental Centre for the History of Social Policies, with myself as director. It became a forum for the discussion of common problems and the basis of a research seminar for ourselves and our graduate students, to which we also invited historians from elsewhere in Britain and abroad to speak about their research. For several years we ran a degree course for an MA in Social Policy History with options in the history of health policy, social security, town planning, housing and educational policy. However, in a period of shrinking research funding the centre never became the focus of collective research projects; each of us continued to work in our own field. The whole venture deliberately ran counter to the departmental structure of the

University, but as the University responded to the financial stringency by making each department responsible for its own budget, the members of the Centre increasingly felt the pull of departmental priorities. It became obvious that I would have no successor able or willing to devote time to running the Centre and in 1992, a year before my retirement, we decided to wind it up. It had potential that it never quite fulfilled.

During the last five years before retirement I was heavily involved in decision-making at the highest academic level of the University. In the process I learnt a great deal about the constraints under which universities were obliged to work, and that knowledge did much to save me from the alienation so widespread among my professorial colleagues at the time. As a historian I knew that we were not the only generation to have formed its expectations in one set of circumstances, only to discover that the world had changed around them. Those who specialise in studying social and political change in the past ought not to complain too much when they too are caught up in one of those uncomfortable processes. We judge historical characters by how they coped with change; we should be prepared to judge ourselves by the same standard.

After 1990 I was once more head of my department. Again I was fortunate in the timing. The difficult decisions on staffing had by then been taken, and that had at last enabled us to grasp the nettle of syllabus reform. I took over when the new system was still untried, and had to ensure that it worked. That was a task I found congenial, and the following three years saw the department recover its morale and its financial health. We were able to appoint new colleagues and thereby rejuvenate an ageing department. In 1993 when I reached full retirement age I had the satisfaction of handing over a department that had been rated '4' for its research (the top rating '5' having been achieved by only five History departments in the country) and was in the process of being rated 'excellent' in teaching. I had done the paper-work that set out our claim; the inspection that confirmed it took place in the following term. It was a good note on which to leave, exactly forty years after my first university appointment.

My retirement put an end to teaching and administration and left me free to undertake research. That has provided an opportunity to do something big. On T.S. Eliot's principle that old men should be explorers, I decided not long after the publication of *British Social Reform and German Precedents* that I would write a comparative history of social policy in Britain and Germany, starting around the mid-nineteenth century and ending with the oil-price crisis of the early 1970s. That would present me with the challenge of something quite new, the history of social policy in Germany, while building on what I had studied and taught all my professional life, the history of social policy in Britain.

In the process of writing the previous book I had found that some of the best ideas came to me when I drew on my limited knowledge of the history of the German system to ask comparative questions. Comparative history proved to be illuminating even for a mere study of Britain. When many of the reviewers expressed regret that I had not told them more about German social insurance, I was already more than half prepared to accede to the request.

I knew that there was a distinguished German literature, not just on social insurance but on many aspects of social policy, largely unknown in Britain and never likely to be translated. Far more interesting than a mere translation would be to make it accessible as a commentary on the history of social policy in Britain. Such a project required a reading knowledge of German and a familiarity with the British literature, and I was probably the only one to combine the two. In this way the idea was born of a comparative history, not as an archival project but primarily as a confrontation of two historiographies. That way of conceiving the project would make it possible to tackle a long time-span, in contrast to the necessarily limited scope of archival research. This appealed to me strongly. I knew that there were some interesting contrasts in the period after the Second World War and that these had long historical roots. I wanted to tackle the nineteenth century, but I wanted to tackle the twentieth century even more.

Although apparently a radical departure, this decision to tackle German history is a direct development of my interest in the Englishness of English history. I had begun to be aware how untested my assumptions were about what was peculiarly English. French history had begun to look less centralised than when I had last studied it. I had also discovered that there had been, if anything, more reliance on local initiative in municipal matters in Germany than in England, while Thomas Nipperdey had made me aware of the importance of voluntary associations in the Germany of the nineteenth century. I began to suspect that I knew less about my subject than I had thought, and re-discovered the truth contained in Kipling's line 'What should they know of England who only England know!'

If I wished to remedy that blinkered view, my facility in the language made a comparison with Germany the obvious one to undertake. Even so, it would not have been the obvious course some years earlier. My concentration on British history, while the expression of an interest that was absolutely genuine, had also fitted in with a preferred emphasis on my Englishness and a reluctance to proclaim my German origins whenever that could be avoided. That attitude is understandable in the light of the influence of those in Worthing who dearly wished to bring me up as an Englishman, and of my boarding-school education in war-time Britain. It was not until the seventies that I began to reflect on the price that had been paid in psychological terms for that agenda, and not until much later that I began to wish to come to terms with those aspects of my experience that had tended to be hidden. It was only because of a fundamental change in attitude that I was now willing to make the study of German history a prominent element in my life.

Even then I did not take the matter lightly. The project that I had in mind would necessarily include the racially dominated social policy of Nazi Germany. Only after exposing myself to some of the most harrowing literature on the Holocaust did I decide that I probably had the stomach for the task. Then on the principle that the best way to learn a subject is to teach it, I put on a course, 'Towards the Welfare State in Britain and Germany 1850s-1960s', at Liverpool and taught it for three years before my retirement. That involved writing 22 lectures and compiling English-language reading-lists for numerous seminars. By 1993 I therefore had an admittedly somewhat superficial outline of the subject. In other words, I roughly knew how ignorant I was and what had to be done, now that I had the time.

That would require time spent in German libraries. In the summer of 1991 I had undertaken a preliminary exploration in the libraries in Berlin, which seemed well suited to my purpose. With the support of a two-year emeritus fellowship from the Leverhulme Trust I began to work partly in Berlin, partly in London and Liverpool. I have been most fortunate to find accommodation with the *Historische Kommission zu Berlin*, and a desk, computer and much encouragement at the Free University in Professor Kocka's *Arbeitsstelle für vergleichende Gesellschaftsgeschichte*. The rest is up to me.

## Notes

1   Charles Booth, *Life and Labour of the People in London*, Third Series: *Religious Influences*, seven volumes (London, 1902).

2   Sir Philip Magnus, *Gladstone: A Biography* (London, 1954).

3   S.E. Finer, *The Life and Times of Sir Edwin Chadwick* (London, 1952).

4   Helen Lynd, *England in the Eighteen-Eighties* (New York, 1945).

5   Charles Booth, *Labour and Life of the People*, two volumes (London, 1889-1891). The second edition in four volumes was called *Life and Labour of the People in London* (London, 1892-3).

6   B.S. Rowntree, *Poverty: A Study of Town Life* (London, 1901, revised edition London, 1902); A.L. Bowley and A.R. Burnett-Hurst, *Livelihood and Poverty* (London, 1915).

7   N. Pevsner, *The Englishness of English Art* (London, 1956).

8   Oliver MacDonagh, 'The Nineteenth Century Revolution in Government: A Re-appraisal', *Historical Journal* 1 (1958), p 58.

## Selected Writings of E.P. Hennock

### Books

*Fit and Proper Persons: Ideal and Reality in Nineteenth Century Urban Government* (London, 1973)

*British Social Reform and German Precedents: The Case of Social Insurance 1880-1914* (Oxford, 1987)

### Articles

'Urban Sanitary Reform a Generation before Chadwick?', *Economic History Review*, second series, 10 (1957), pp 113-20

'Finance and Politics in Urban Local Government in England, 1835-1900', *Historical Journal* 6 (1963), pp 212-25

'The Social Composition of Borough Councils in Two Large Cities', in H.J. Dyos (ed.), *The Study of Urban History* (London, 1968), pp 315-36

'Poverty and Social Theory: The Experience of the 1880s', *Social History* 1 (1976), pp 67-91

'The Origins of British National Insurance and the German Precedent 1880-1914', in W. J. Mommsen (ed.), *The Emergence of the Welfare State in Britain and Germany 1850-1950* (London, 1981), pp 84-106

Translated as 'Die Ursprünge der staatlichen Sozialversicherung in Grossbritannien und das deutsche Beispiel 1880-1914', in W. J. Mommsen (ed.), *Die Entstehung des Wohlfahrtsstaates in Grossbritannien und Deutschland 1850-1950* (Stuttgart, 1982), pp 92-114

'Central/Local Government Relations in England: An Outline 1800-1950', *Urban History Yearbook*, 1982, pp 38-49

'The Creation of an Urban Local Government System in England and Wales', in H. Naunin (ed.), *Städteordnungen des 19. Jahrhunderts* (Cologne/Vienna, 1984), pp 19-32

'Arbeiterunfallentschädigung und Arbeiterunfallversicherung: Die britische Sozialreform und das Beispiel Bismarcks', *Geschichte und Gesellschaft* 11 (1985), pp 19-36

'The Measurement of Urban Poverty: From the Metropolis to the Nation 1880-1920', *Economic History Review*, second series, 40 (1987), pp 208-27

'Technological Education in England 1850-1926: The Uses of a German Model', *History of Education* 19 (1990), pp 299-331

'Public Provision for Old Age. Britain and Germany 1880-1914', *Archiv für Sozialgeschichte* 30 (1990), pp 81-103

'Concepts of Poverty in the British Social Surveys, from Charles Booth to Arthur Bowley', in M. Bulmer, K. Bales and K.K. Sklar (eds), *The Social Survey in Historical Perspective 1880-1940* (Cambridge, 1991), pp 189-216

'Lessons from England: Lujo Brentano on British Trade Unionism', *German History* 11 (1993), pp 141-60

'Poverty and Social Reform', in Paul Johnson (ed.), *Twentieth Century Britain: Economic, Social and Cultural Change* (London, 1994), pp 79-93

**Helmut Koenigsberger**

# Fragments of an
# Unwritten Biography

It has been said that history started as myth and mythology. It certainly did so for me. When I was about five, my father told me the story of the Trojan War and of the Odyssey, as a series of successive bedtime stories. He was an architect who had received a classical education at a *Humanistisches Gymnasium* and he was an excellent story teller who at times reinforced this ability by making semi-humorous or ironical drawings while I sat on his lap.[1] No doubt, the irony passed over my head at the time; but I thought the stories were the most wonderful stories I had ever heard and now, when I read Homer again (although, alas, only in translation) I find that I have not really changed my mind.

A year or two later my grandfather died and left me an eight-volume illustrated world history.[2] It had wonderful nineteenth-century romantic-realistic illustrations on practically every page: 'Epaminondas saves the life of Pelopidas', 'Hannibal crosses the Alps', with one of his elephants falling over a cliff, 'Marius on the ruins of Carthage', glowering revenge at his enemies in Rome. It was irresistible. One could dip into these volumes for any age and for any country, although I now realise that the word *Weltgeschichte* meant, in good nineteenth-century fashion, the history of Europe, except perhaps for the ancient Egyptians and Persians. But one would always come up with a good story. For all its nationalistic pre-conceptions, it taught me the equality of all human experience and, gradually, an overview over the course of European history. Perhaps equally important, it taught me that reading history should be fun.

Of course, there was also 'History' at school, taught with enthu-siasm by my successive form masters, from *Sexta* to *Untersekunda*.

They were not primarily historians, but they also had an eye for a good story and at least some idea of the *Problematik* of history. I have fond memories of them, at least until 1933. For me history was an effortless subject. I don't believe I have ever sat down to learn a date the way one swotted French or Latin irregular verbs or even the rivers and mountain ranges of different countries. By the time I was eleven or twelve I had made up my mind that I wanted to be a historian.

My family was not pleased. 'Do you want to become a school teacher, then?'

'No I don't like that idea at all. Perhaps teach it in a university.'

'That's very difficult to get into. You can't rely on it. Anyway, history is "eine brotlose Kunst". Can't you think of something useful?'

So, there it was. History is entertaining. My father loved it – as entertainment. But he himself had chosen an eminently useful profession and my elder brother had followed in his footsteps. 'Perhaps I too should become an architect?'

'Oh no, you shouldn't. Two in a family is quite enough and, anyway, you can't draw.'

The view of the 'uselessness of history' has never gone away, even if now it is put more politely to an elderly professor of the subject. 'Oh yes. History (pause), I always liked it at school.' Or, alternatively, 'I was never any good at it at school'. Both pronouncements imply 'Well, it doesn't really matter, does it? Why didn't you choose something more worthwhile for the real world?' The trouble with this attitude is that it has at least a grain of justification in it. Very few of us professional historians have made more than a moderately decent living from it; and how many of us, when faced with an astronomical plumber's bill, have not felt at least a momentary twinge that we have missed our profession?

My father died in 1932. Less than a year later Hitler came to power. The certainties of life had suddenly disappeared. But my generation, thirteen to fourteen, became politically sophisticated almost overnight. The Nazi experience, with uniformed schoolboys marching and saluting solemnly and ludicrously in the Hitler Youth, killed all possible attractions of uniforms for me and made me permanently immune to the pull of any political charisma from any person, living or dead. I learned to use history as an argument. After all, the Nazis did so with their pseudo-history. But it soon became clear that my schoolfriends were quite impervious to rational and factual arguments. With a very few honourable exceptions they turned out not to be friends at all. As one outlet for my frustrations I flew a burgee of the *Paneuropa* movement on our little sailing boat on the river Dahme: a yellow circle (the rising sun?) with a red cross on a sky-blue background. I read avidly its inventor's books, one Count Coudenhove-Kalergi, an Austro-Hungarian-Belgian-Japanese aristocrat, I believe (the latest edition of the *Encyclopaedia Britannica* knows nothing of him), who argued, after the First World War, that Europe had to unite politically if it was not to commit suicide and if it wanted to survive between the great power blocs of America and the Soviet Union. He probably had some experience of English insularity, for he left the British Empire out of his proposed *Paneuropa*.

I don't know how far the French and German founders of the European Economic Community in the 1950s were influenced by Coudenhove-Kalergi's ideas. The Nazis, of course, disliked him intensely. But there were very few who knew about him, let alone about his flag. My flying it during the Nazi period – and I went on doing it during my summer visits to my mother right up to 1938 – was therefore neither a particularly hazardous nor brave act of defiance. I mention the whole insignificant episode only because it was part of my growing conviction that the approach to European history in the traditional way, through the history of national states, was fundamentally misconceived.

In 1934 my mother sent me as a boarder to Adams Grammar School, Newport, Shropshire, a school about which she had had good reports from different sources and also which, as far as boarding schools went, was relatively cheap. The ambience at Newport was very English with, however, some quite noticeable Welsh influences among the boys. It was one of the first things I learnt, that not everyone in Britain was English, nor wanted to be English. I myself, while fully accepted on a personal level – a great and very reassuring contrast to the betrayals in my last year at the *Realschule* Adlershof – I was clearly not English, or at least not yet; and, having effectively been rejected, together with my family, in Germany, I was also not German any more. Nor was I particularly Jewish, having been brought up, though without very strong convictions, as a Lutheran. Nor was there anybody in Newport who would have pushed me in that direction, and in any case, changing one set of identification for another was quite enough to be getting on with. Later, I also realised that I did not want to exchange one set of exclusive nationalism for another. And yet, in Newport I also realised that England and English society were not fundamentally strange, in fact much less so than many at Adams Grammar School believed. The young geography master asked me, 'Do they keep dogs and cats in your country?'

I had an excellent history master, at least for straightforward political history, even though he used a quite appallingly bad, jingoistic textbook.[3] Perhaps the very narrowness of this textbook emphasised for me that English history could be understood only in comparison with and in the context of European history. Some German myths on which I had been brought up disappeared quite rapidly, such as the supposed role of Edward VII in a policy of 'encirclement' of Germany. To balance matters, I could shock the English boys by doubting the role of Britain as a disinterested and honest broker in international affairs until the German invasion of Belgium in 1914. History, I was certain, had to get beyond the traditions of patriotic incantation, whichever side one was born to.

Much more positive was the emphasis on the role of parliament. This was something really new. The German writers of textbooks and the author of the nineteenth-century volume of my *Weltgeschichte* had not thought highly of the *Reichstag* or its predecessors, that is, when they had bothered to write about them at all.[4] I asked my History master Mr Humphries why this was. I don't remember what he said, but his answer did not get me very far. Here was a topic I would want to think more about, and I was now convinced that this could only be done by treating Europe as a whole, and not like the writers of English textbooks who tended to take parliament for granted as an institution demonstrating the superiority of English political *savoir faire*. Later, as an undergraduate, I read Otto Hintze's two splendid essays on representative institutions.[5] Here was a German historian who was thinking historically the way I thought one ought to think. Much later still, I began to wonder how far Hintze's model, for all the brilliance of its conception, provided a satisfactory answer to my original question.[6]

All this played little part in my first English examination, Matric. (later to be called O-levels and, later still, GCSE). I got a 'distinction' in History (later called A) and a 'good' (later B) in Mathematics. I had never bothered to learn the tables of the English measurements. In any case, the slightly better results in History won me the still somewhat sceptical approval of my family, and the enthusiastic support of Mr Humphries, to study History. He persuaded the headmaster that I should be allowed to skip other classes and to get a desk in the under-used biology laboratory. There, among dissected frogs and worms in evil-smelling formaldehyde, I could happily concentrate on the books I had to read for the Cambridge entrance examinations. In December 1936 I got an Exhibition[7] at Caius College for the following October. By itself, this was not nearly

Julius Carlebach

Francis L. Carsten

Edgar J. Feuchtwanger

John Grenville

E. P. Hennock

Helmut G. Koenigsberger

Wolf Mendl

Werner E. Mosse

Hellmut Pappe

Arnold Paucker

Sidney Pollard

Peter Pulzer

Nicolai Rubinstein

Walter Ullmann

enough to live on; but as a result of Higher School Certificate (A-levels) in the summer of 1937, I gained a scholarship from the West Riding of Yorkshire. This was due to the generosity of the county education committee, which was prepared to regard my holiday visits to my sister, then living in the county, as a sufficient proof of residence. From then on I was financially independent of my family, who would have found it very difficult, if not impossible, to pay for me at Cambridge. That aspect of being a historian I had won.

Cambridge (1937-40) exceeded expectations. Not that everything was beyond criticism. Lectures varied, from the brilliant (Michael Postan on English economic history, Herbert Butterfield on early modern European history, with strong emphasis on the history of science, a subject which I encountered for the first time) to the bizarre (Wellbourn on what he regarded as economic history) or the plain dull (Kenneth Pickthorn on English constitutional history). More important than the lectures, however, were the one-to-one supervisions. They were given by the historians of one's own college. Here again I was lucky. Zachary Brooke was a fine medievalist who knew the German historiography almost as well as the English and who had great respect for Karl Hampe, Ulrich Stutz and others. What he was contemptuous of were those he thought of as doing little more than paraphrasing the German historians. ('Does Mr Barraclough think that Otto the Great was afraid of Hugh of Arles?').

My other supervisor was very different. Michael Oakeshott was not so much a historian as a political philosopher. He suggested I read Hegel's *Philosophie des Rechts*. I disliked it, well, as much as I understood of it. That was probably not very much, but I knew then that I never wanted to be a philosopher, especially a German philosopher. But on Plato and Aristotle, on St Augustine and the Scholastics, on Hobbes, Locke and Mill, Oakeshott was fascinating and crystal clear, as well as on the nature of law and justice – he made me read Sophocles' *Antigone* – or on the nature of property and Karl Marx. His teaching methods were Socratic. He would politely ask you questions about your weekly essay until you realised that you had got it all wrong or, more rarely, that you had hit the nail on the head and done rather better than you thought you had. Later, I tried to imitate Oakeshott's method with my own students, but I don't think I ever managed it as elegantly as he did.

Undergraduate life in Cambridge was enchanting. There was its visual beauty: the river and the 'backs', King's College Chapel, the Gate of Honour in Caius, the Wren Library in Trinity; above all, there was the social and cultural life of the undergraduates. One could indulge practically any taste. For me and at my age, the long discussions of politics, literature and art and the omnipresence of music seemed an ideal life-style. Even my very amateurish violin playing was welcomed in college orchestras and chamber music groups. It all seemed a continuation of a greatly idealised version of my former home life.

It was, of course, an élitist life-style and I knew that it could not last. In my last year 'up', war had already broken out and, by degrees, Cambridge was shutting down. I could still choose the Italian Renaissance as my third-year special subject. I was quite clear in my mind that I did not want either an English or a German history special subject. Naturally, I read Jacob Burckhardt and Heinrich Wölfflin in German, but the core of the course was political history and the sources which we studied were Italian: Machiavelli, Guicciardini, Nardi, in Italian, Condivi and Cellini in English translation.

The end came suddenly, shortly before Finals, or Part II of the examinations, were due to start. As we now know from the Cabinet documents, it was Churchill himself who ordered the internment of all German and Austrian males in the eastern counties, ostensibly because they might be a 'fifth column' in case of a German invasion. Some historians, perhaps misreading the memoirs of the internees, have claimed that we, or at least a large number of us, welcomed this internment. If so, I failed to meet any of them. The English internment camps were not, of course, remotely like German concentration camps. It is also true that, once we were shipped to Canada, that is, those of us who were lucky enough not to be taken to Australia or torpedoed on the high seas, managed to entertain ourselves by organising lecture classes and, for the professional musicians, if they had portable instruments, almost unlimited time for practice. For me the most memorable classes were in the history of art, given by Johannes Wilde, expert on Michelangelo, and Otto Demus, Byzantinist and general art historian. Demus insisted on seeing art within its social-historical context, precisely the approach I had been looking for when studying the Italian Renaissance. The Marxist version of such an approach I had come across in the person of Alfred Meusel, in one of the transit camps in England, who insisted that Machiavelli was a representative of the rising capitalist bourgeoisie. Much later I heard from GDR (East German) colleagues that Meusel had achieved a leading role among the historiographical sharks of that country, only to end up being eaten himself. What this unfortunate character achieved with me was a lasting aversion to at least the more rigid concepts and phraseology of Marxist history.

From the beginning of internment there appeared in England a very vocal movement, both in and out of parliament, criticising this policy, and this at the most critical moment of the war. Characteristically, the government never admitted to having been wrong but quietly released most of those who had been interned at great expense, on the basis of information which the Home Office had had all along. As far as I know, in no other country was there such a reversal of policy during wartime. I was back in England and with a 'wartime degree' by January 1941.

There is an ironic footnote to this whole episode. In May 1990 there was a commemoration of the fiftieth anniversary of internment. It took place in the Imperial War Museum, in London, and a great number of those who attended had clearly made good their careers in Britain: university professors and high civil servants, barristers and high court judges, scientists and musicians of world renown. Evidently, Great Britain can successfully absorb its immigrants, even if the process takes longer and is not taken so much as a matter of course as it is in America.

In 1941 those of my Cambridge teachers who were still there advised me against joining the Pioneer Corps, the only branch of the forces then admitting 'enemy aliens'. 'You can surely do something more useful for the war effort than digging latrines.' More easily said than done, but after a while I got jobs teaching at grammar schools, first in Brentwood, Essex, then in Bedford. I enjoyed teaching history, French and German, but did not feel that I had a vocation for school teaching. After three years, in 1944, the Royal Navy suddenly decided they could use me. I served for about 18 months, mostly in destroyers, one of some thirty of 'His Majesty's most loyal enemy aliens', as we ironically called ourselves. With the great Edward Gibbon I can claim that a term in the military has had its uses for the historian.

By October 1945, the Admiralty had enough of us and gave us honourable discharges. I went straight back to Caius College as a postgraduate research student, funded by a government scholarship for ex-service personnel.

There was a slightly unreal feeling of reliving a part of one's life, five years later. It was certainly very enjoyable; but both Cambridge and I had changed. The old pre-war magic, between youth and adulthood, had been lost. I found that I had some sympathy even for that old faker, Talleyrand, who remarked, in old age, that no one who had not lived before the French Revolution knew the real sweetness of living.

My research had already been mapped out, while I was still teaching at Bedford School, in a discussion with C.W. Previté Orton, the professor who had taught the special subject of the Italian Renaissance. I wanted to carry on from there, but the obvious subjects, the Papacy, Florence and Venice, had been exhausted, he thought. How naive we were in the 1940s about the questions the historian could ask of his sources and how ignorant about the extraordinary riches of the Florentine and Venetian archives! The professor tentatively mentioned Sardinia, Portugal and Sicily. Sicily immediately appealed to me. Soon it became clear that this choice involved Spain, and I started to learn Spanish. While in the navy and sometimes on deadly boring guard duty on shore, I surreptitiously concealed strips of paper with Spanish verbs in my sleeves. Back in Cambridge, and with the splendid Acton Library at my disposal, virtually as a private retreat because nobody else was using it at the time, I could engage in being a professional historian, a feeling confirmed by having my first article, on the revolt of Palermo in 1647, accepted by the *Cambridge Historical Journal* (now called *The Historical Journal*) of 1946. I sent an offprint to Virgilio Titone, the Professor of Modern History at the University of Palermo. Apparently he was so pleased that anyone in England was interested in early modern Sicily at all that he gave the article a full critical review. Thus started a close friendship with one of the most extraordinary minds in modern Italy, a friendship which he later extended to my wife, both as a person and as a historian, and which lasted until his death in 1989 and has since continued with his students.

At home, Previté Orton, frail of body but acute of mind, was very good at suggesting where I might find my sources; but, being primarily a medievalist himself, he could give me little help in developing the conceptual framework of my dissertation on the government of Sicily under Philip II of Spain. Herbert Butterfield, who took over as my thesis supervisor after Previté Orton's death in 1947, did not pretend that he knew anything about Sicily or very much about Spain; but he did suggest searching questions and he knew everything there was to be known about how to write a thesis. This was exactly the help I needed at that point, for I was now clear what my thesis was about: how did an early modern monarchy run an overseas empire? What were its guiding principles and how were they put into practice? For here was a polity between the feudal empires of the Middle Ages and the commercial-bureaucratic British and French overseas empires of the eighteenth and nineteenth centuries.

Some years later, partly in parallel and partly in conversations with John Elliott, I gave up the concept of European empires in the early modern period. Instead, we developed the concept of composite or multiple monarchies, while keeping the term empires for the Ottoman monarchy and for the European overseas empires in America, Asia and Africa. For what happened in Europe was only rarely the conquest of one state by another or the planting of colonies but rather the dynastic unions of previously independent or autonomous principalities or parts of principalities, mostly regardless of whether this happened through war or simple inheritance or by a combination of the two.[8] Coudenhove-Kalergi's concept of *Paneuropa* and the present European Union have, in fact, had very respectable ancestries, even if, no more than the European Union at the time of writing, these ancestors never included the whole of Europe.[9]

My study of the government of Sicily in the sixteenth century led me directly to my next primary interest, and the question which I had posed, somewhat naively, already at school. In the seventeenth and eighteenth centuries the Sicilians claimed that they possessed the only effective parliament outside England. This claim was quite wrong, even if it was understandable. For had not the parliament of the Kingdom of Naples and the Cortes of Castile and Aragon disappeared in the middle of the seventeenth century? And why should the learned jurists and antiquarians of Sicily know anything about the States General of the United Provinces of the Netherlands, the *Riksdag* of Sweden, the *Sejm* of Poland or the *Landtage* of Württemberg and Mecklenburg? Many English historians were not much better informed or clung to the comfortable but erroneous idea that the Westminster parliament is the 'mother of parliaments'. But the question remained: why did so many of the European parliaments of the later Middle Ages disappear or become virtually powerless? And why had there been no parliaments in Orthodox Europe, nor in the great Muslim empires, in India or in China? And where they did exist, that is practically everywhere in Catholic Europe outside the city states, what were their different structures and powers, why had they, sooner or later, all clashed with the monarchies and why had most, but not all, monarchies managed to abolish or tame them by about 1700? Hintze had raised all these questions but he had given only rather sketchy answers, and many of them rested on arguments which were not tenable if one looked at them more closely.

In the 1950s I believed I would be able to answer these questions. This belief turned out to be much too optimistic, not to say hubristic. At that time I underestimated the sheer scale and complexity of the problems involved. The programme, however, came to colour much of my work in political history.[10] In 1952 my Manchester colleague John Roskell and the distinguished Cambridge and Harvard medievalist, Helen Cam, invited me to join the International Commission for the History of Representative and Parliamentary Institutions (Commission Internationale pour l'Histoire des Assemblées d'États), of which Helen Cam was then the president. Mainly through this commission, as its secretary-general and later vice-president and president, I met a growing number of historians from nearly all European and several non-European countries, with similar interests, if not always with similar views. It was an ambience that I found very congenial, especially during its annual conferences in different European university cities. In their representative institutions all Europeans had enjoyed similar, or at least parallel, experiences. This phenomenon was accepted even by our Marxist colleagues from the Communist countries. When the politicians were not present, relations were usually excellent; but when I tried to get support from the British delegation to the (then) European Economic Community for a conference in Strasbourg, I had first to persuade a Foreign Office mandarin that our elderly Polish and Czech colleagues would be most unlikely to throw bombs in the European Parliament building or to break out into a pro-Soviet propaganda speech. In 1972 in Hungary I overheard one of our Romanian members earnestly assure a Hungarian, 'Moi, je suis vraiment marxiste'. Perhaps I should have seen this apologetic remark as a clue to the coming collapse of Marxism in Eastern Europe. Alas, I cannot claim that at the time I had so much foresight.

If the International Commission was a bridge between 'East' and 'West', it was also a bridge between the historians of the Federal Republic of Germany and their western colleagues, something which, in the 1950s, could not yet be taken for granted. Through the commission my contacts with German historians, sporadic up to then, became regular and frequent. There is no question but that I learnt a lot from these contacts, from Dietrich Gerhard the importance in parliamentary history of its regional aspects. It was also, I believe, largely due to Gerhard that I was invited for a semester to

Washington University, St Louis (1964), and it was probably also because of this visit that I then spent seven years at Cornell University (1966-73). From Karl Bosl, and later Peter Blickle, I learnt something of the complexity and wide range of representation in southern Germany; from Heinrich Lutz learnt an internationalist view of German history and received my first introduction to the *Historisches Kolleg* in Munich; and from Gerhard Oestreich learnt the importance of Neostoicism in the development of the early modern state.[11]

With these and with many other German historians my contacts were both scholarly and, with many of them, also personal. Nor did these contacts only relate to the subject matter of the International Commission. I have had generous invitations to a whole string of conferences, symposia and lectures in different German cities. These included Eberhard Schmitt's invitation to take part in the academic steering committee in Bamberg of his project of publishing *Dokumente zur Geschichte der europäischen Expansion,* a quintessentially international project carried out mainly by German scholars. During a lecture in connection with one of my visits to Bamberg I tried, for the only time, to suggest a research topic to German historians, a topic which at the time was fashionable from Princeton to Moscow: the crisis of the mid-seventeenth century.[12] As far as I am aware, my suggestion had no effect whatsoever. The topic, unlike the protean subject of representation, was on its way out. There was no reason why anyone should have taken any notice of my suggestion.[13]

By far my most important experience of German academic life was my fellowship at the *Historisches Kolleg* in the year after my retirement from King's College London, my last academic position in England. The wonderful conditions which this provided for uninterrupted research, with secretarial backup, and the stimulus of discussions with colleagues and visitors gave me the chance to rethink the parameters of my principal research subject and to start rewriting my projected book accordingly. This is on the States General of the Netherlands in the fifteenth and sixteenth centuries. From being just a case study, it has moved to the centre of my comparative view of early modern representative assemblies. Since the northern Netherlands became a republic, I organised my obligatory colloqium as an international symposium on republics and republicanism in early modern Europe.[14] Its results will be incorporated in the major book which I now hope to finish shortly.

I have made some preliminary sketches of my overall thinking. The first was in my inaugural lecture at King's College, University of London, in 1975.[15] Effectively, this was a critique of both Otto Hintze and Norbert Elias, the latter an old friend whose views have greatly impressed me. Elias's model had the great merit of being dynamic but, from my point of view, it left out too much of the context of the development of monarchy, especially the prevalence of composite monarchies and the effect of this fact on the internal balance of power in the rivalry between monarchies and their parliaments. It also left out the effects of the intervention of outside states in such rivalries, an intervention which was particularly likely to take place during the sixteenth and seventeenth centuries when religion became involved with politics. If both these considerations are accepted, then an element of contingency is introduced into the problem of monarchies and parliaments and its solution purely by the methods of the French *Annales* school becomes impossible.

At the same time, my insistence on the validity of the distinction made by the fifteenth-century Chief Justice, Sir John Fortescue, between *dominium regale*, as in France, and *dominium politicum et regale*, as in England and wherever parliaments retained their power, has been criticised by the neo-conservative school of British historians, and most notably by Geoffrey Elton, who regarded the English parliament and, *a fortiori*, most Continental parliaments of the early modern period, as little more than instruments of the monarchies. The debate continues, now sadly without Geoffrey Elton.

Parallel with my interest in political history has been my interest in cultural history. Again, the original stimulus came from my father. Further confirmation was my first visit to Spain and Sicily, in 1947, and long discussions with Virgilio Titone about his Crocean view of the supposed decadence of the baroque period. This view was quite prevalent also in the rest of Europe. A visit to 'Die Wies' church in Upper Bavaria, as part of an International Commission conference in Munich, in 1963, illustrated for me the comic dangers inherent in the concept of decadence. The shocked reactions of many of our members to this masterpiece of the Bavarian baroque were hilarious. To the Italians, rather like Mozart's music to an Italianate Habsburg princess, it was 'una porcheria tedesca'. To the Belgians and the Irish it was, whatever else, not really Catholic. To the Calvinist Dutch and the Lutheran Swedes it was simply not Christian. The encounter with an unfamiliar style had misled intelligent people not only in their artistic judgement but had unconsciously shifted their judgement onto a quite inappropriate moral plane.

As early as a lecture to the Royal Historical Society in 1959 I had developed the concept of a shift in creative activity, with especial reference to Italy and Germany at the end of the Renaissance.[16] Later I developed and, I hope, refined this concept, especially in a lecture for the *Spätzeit* series which Johannes Kunisch organised for the 600-year anniversary celebrations of the University of Cologne, in 1988.[17]

Closely related to this type of historical analysis were attempts to study the historical connections between music and religion and between science and religion. Both problems were first posed by Max Weber.[18] My discussion of the problem of the history of science originated in an invitation by Gerhard A. Ritter to the *Deutscher Historikertag* in Hamburg in 1978.[19]

Three hypotheses are basic to my approach to cultural history. First, that there is a biological equality in the creative potential of different ethnic groups. The second is the psychological connection between individuals and the societies they live in. These societies are not biologically given but are the result of historical development, and as such the legitimate object of historical inquiry. These two hypotheses have a respectable ancestry, from Castiglione to Bodin and Voltaire. My third hypothesis, confirmed by my study of European history and the little I know of extra-European history, is that the appearance of creative talent is always limited to certain fields and never universal or all-inclusive. This means that it is hazardous for the cultural historian to draw conclusions, and especially moral conclusions, for the whole of a society. His endeavour should be rather to explain the clustering of creative activities in certain fields at certain times and places and the end of such clusters. It is here that I think the concept of shift from one type of creative activity to another, for instance from the visual arts to music or science, may be useful. It is a wide field on which, when I have finished with the States General of the Netherlands, I propose to spend my remaining time and energy.

What then was the significance of my German origins for my career and work as a historian? As I see it, although others may see it differently, not very much. My upbringing in a liberal-minded professional family was certainly important; but it would not have been very different in a similar family in England. The Nazi experience confirmed a hatred of dictatorship or any kind of tyranny, of racism and of political nationalism. There have been many in Great Britain and in America, both among my teachers and my contemporaries, who have shared these feelings. What was not always shared was my growing belief in the essential unity of European civilisation and history. I have found it very difficult to introduce this belief into the formal structure of English and, more curiously, of

American university teaching. But the resistance came from colleagues, rather than from the students. My own views of early modern history certainly contain German elements; but, apart from the ease with which I can read German, not really more than the elements they contain from the historiography of other European countries.

## Notes

1   I have still got a number of these drawings.

2   O. von Corvin et al. (eds), *Illustrirte Weltgeschichte für das Volk*, 8 volumes (Leipzig and Berlin, 1880-84).

3   Warner and Marten. In 1964 I was asked to give away the annual prizes at my old school. As a kind of joke I gave some examples of the more fruity nationalistic remarks in that book. Afterwards the young History master said to me, 'You have pulled the rug from under my feet. I still use Warner and Marten.' I imagine he changed his textbook after this incident.

4   Francis Carsten was not, of course, the first historian to write about the *Landtage*. But the emphasis which he placed on their historical importance, and the debates which followed his *Princes and Parliaments in Germany* (Oxford, 1959) were undoubtedly 'bahnbrechend' (epoch making) for the treatment of this subject.

5   Otto Hintze, 'Typologie der ständischen Verfassungen des Abendlandes' (1930), and 'Weltgeschichtliche Bedingungen der Repräsentativverfassungen' (1931), English translation of the 1931 article in Felix Gilbert (ed.), *The Historical Essays of Otto Hintze* (New York and Oxford, 1975), pp 302-353.

6   H.G. Koenigsberger, 'Dominium Regale or Dominium Politicum et Regale', Inaugural Lecture in the Chair of History in King's College, University of London, 1975, reprinted in H.G. Koenigsberger, *Politicians and Virtuosi* (London, 1986), pp 1-26.

7   The lowest form of scholarship. Later it was raised to a 'minor scholarship'.

8   The name of my chapter in the *New Cambridge Modern History*, volume 2, 'The Empire of Charles V in Europe', pp 301-333, was chosen by the volume editor, Geoffrey Elton. At the time I was not yet sufficiently clear about the distinction between an empire and a composite monarchy to insist on

changing the title of my chapter. To have insisted on a change for the second edition (1990), when all I did was to slightly expand the old chapter, would have seemed pedantic.

9    There were many in the sixteenth century, such as Charles V's grand-chancellor, Mercurino di Gattinara, who would have liked to see precisely such an inclusive union. Others, especially in France and England, regarded such a *monarchia universale*, as they termed it, with fear and horror.

10   There is a parallel problem in the continuity or discontinuity of the parliaments of the *ancien régime* and those of the nineteenth and twentieth centuries. I have mostly stayed out of this debate. But at a conference in Berlin I became involved in it when I found myself at odds with most of the senior German historians present (although not all of the younger German historians), when I argued that the nineteenth-century parliaments derived some of their moral authority from the continuity of the concept of representation. See 'Formen und Tendenzen des europäischen Ständewesens im 16. und 17. Jahrhundert', in Peter Baumgart (ed.), *Ständetum und Staatsbildung in Brandenburg-Preussen* (Berlin, 1983), pp 19-31. See also Jürgen Schmädeke, *Diskussionsbericht*, pp 494-95. The report of the debate in this volume, however, makes me out to be more of a Whig historian than I would accept.

11   In 1976 John Elliott and I suggested to Gerhard Oestreich the publication of an English version of his *Geist und Gestalt des frühmodernen Staates* (Berlin, 1969) for the series 'Cambridge Studies in Early Modern History' which we were (and still are) editing for the Cambridge University Press. Oestreich rewrote a considerable part of his book and, after his untimely death in 1978, his widow Brigitta Oestreich completed the rewriting. She and I then supervised the translation by David McLintock and edited the book as *Neostoicism and the Early Modern State* (Cambridge, 1982). Neostoicism, especially as propounded by the Netherlander Justus Lipsius (1547-1606), was a practical philosophy based on reason, Christian morality and classical learning, which stressed the power of the state and the need for political and social discipline of its citizens of all classes, and this during an age driven by religious-political passions and civil wars. Neostoicism was not the only political philosophy in the growth of state power, but it was often welcomed by political authorities in both Catholic and Protestant monarchies and

republics. In contrast to what is often said in Germany, it should be stressed that Oestreich did not argue that Neostoicism was the only, or often even the most important, ideology in the process of 'Staatsbildung'. On the term 'Staatsbildung', which has latterly become fashionable also outside Germany, I have considerable reservations. It fits some of the larger German principalities, but surely not the smaller ones. Was Goethe's Sachsen-Weimar really a state, and would there have been any advantage for it, or for Germany, if it had been? The term does not fit Western Europe at all, at least before the end of the sixteenth century, and even in the seventeenth it did so mainly in the minds of some jurists. Even at best, the orientation of historiography on state formation ('Staatsbildung') runs the risk of a teleology directed towards an ideal view of the nineteenth-century state – Whig history turned upside down but remaining just as teleological. I believe that all historiographical teleology, including that of Hegel, Marx and the recently fashionable feuilleton theories of 'the end of history' are basically unhistorical. I have expanded on this point because this essay is meant to be about my views of history and they show, if one wants to express it in this way, my assimilation of the Anglo-American positivist view of history. For me, this does not mean the rejection of the search for generalisations, models or theories, but of any attempt to apply them holistically to the whole process of history.

12  Published as 'Die Krise des 17. Jahrhunderts', *Zeitschrift für Historische Forschung* 9 (1982), pp 143-165. I did not realise at the time that Wolfgang Reinhard had treated this subject in a wider framework in 'Theorie und Empirie bei der Erforschung frühneuzeitlicher Volksaufstände', in Hans Fenske et al. (eds), *Historia Integra: Festschrift für Erich Hassinger zum 70. Geburtstag* (Berlin, 1977), pp 173-200. I can only offer my belated apologies to Prof. Reinhard for this omission.

13  In my book *Politicians and Virtuosi* (1986) I published a somewhat different version of the *ZHF* article as 'The Crisis of the Seventeenth Century. A Farewell?', pp 149-168.

14  *Republiken und Republikanismus im Europa der Frühen Neuzeit* (Schriften des Historischen Kollegs 11, Munich, 1988).

15  See note 6.

16    Reprinted in my *Estates and Revolutions: Essays in Early Modern European History* (Ithaca/NY, 1971), pp 278-297.

17    'Republics and Courts in Italian and European Culture in the 16th and 17th Centuries', in *Politicians and Virtuosi*, pp 237-261; 'Sinn und Unsinn des Dekadenzproblems in der europäischen Kulturgeschichte der frühen Neuzeit', in Johannes Kunisch (ed.), *Spätzeit: Studien zu den Problemen eines historischen Epochenbegriffs* (Berlin, 1990), pp 137-157.

18    Both articles reprinted in my own *Politicians and Virtuosi*, pp 179-210 and pp 211-235.

19    'Wissenschaft und Religion in der frühmodernen europäischen Geschichte', in K.-G. Faber (ed.), *Wissenschaft als universalhistorisches Problem: Beiheft zu Geschichte in Wissenschaft und Unterricht* (1979), pp 54-77.

**Wolf Mendl**

# A Slow
# Awakening

We were hardly typical refugees. One morning in April 1936 we arrived at Liverpool Street Station on the boat-train from Harwich, to be met by my great-uncle's chauffeur and car. I have a vivid memory of seeing my great-uncle in his study, reading *The Times*, before we sat down to our first English breakfast, with butler and parlour-maid in attendance. Later that day my parents took my sister and me to Bexhill-on-Sea to be thoroughly Anglicised by two unmarried ladies, while they looked around for somewhere to live.

I was nine years old, just turning ten, and not in the least bothered why we should be moving from Berlin to England. My father was an engineer in the employ of a German firm and had gone to London in the previous year to open a branch office. Now he was bringing over the family to live in the country and that was reason enough for me. Later, I learnt that the firm had sent him abroad chiefly to enable him to get out of Germany in good time, an example of how some people, who might have been favourably disposed towards the new regime, helped those whom the Nazis had vilified.

I was glad to leave Germany in one respect. I had spent the last year in a state primary school and hated it, receiving low grades in every subject except religion. On the other hand, I have happy memories of early childhood: of holidays in Harzburg where my grandmother had a house, on the estate of friends in the Spreewald, and on sandy beaches in East Prussia. In summer the sun seemed always to be shining. Breakfast on Sundays was taken on the balcony, with boiled eggs and 'Berliner Schrippen'. In winter we skated on the tennis-courts opposite our flat, which were flooded for the purpose. I would have made a cheerful Nazi. I was fascinated and attracted by the flags, the parades, the uniforms, the bands and the many holidays, one of which fell on my birthday.

I attended the school with the son of close friends of the family. He came to England with us and was to have a distinguished academic career here and in the United States. He, too, was Jewish and on one occasion was taunted by some boys on that account. Somehow I escaped such attentions and, though puzzled, remained strangely unaffected. My parents had kept the real reason for our emigration from me.

Eventually we settled in Watford and I attended the Grammar School there from 1936 to 1944. Gradually I came to understand the reason why we had to leave Germany without, however, thinking about it. In fact, I identified wholly with Britain and regarded it more of an accident that I happened to be of German nationality because I was born in Berlin. In my late teens, like all foreigners of German origin, I had to be classified as either category A (committed and dangerous Nazi), B (of dubious allegiance) or C ('friendly enemy alien'). I duly appeared before the local tribunal in St Albans. When they gave me the expected C category without further ado, after the chairman had found out that I was distantly related to Sir Sigismund Mendl, a businessman and at one time a Liberal member of parliament, I took this as evidence that I was regarded as being essentially British. It was only when I reached adulthood that I had to come to terms, emotionally and intellectually, with my background and the fact that I would probably have ended up as one of the millions who perished in the Holocaust, had it not been for a set of fortuitous circumstances.

I was born into a wholly Jewish family. My mother was German, though for some reason she had travelled on a Swiss passport before her marriage. My father was Austrian, born in Romania but schooled in Vienna. Both grandmothers were English and we had many English relatives whose language I was taught to speak from earliest childhood. Cosmopolitanism was therefore part of my background. This was one of several reasons why I was so slow in recognising my identity as a German-Jewish refugee.

Another reason was the fact that I suffer from a congenital defect of the eyesight. Nystagmus is a fairly rare condition.[1] In my case it is combined with a high degree of astigmatism. I have difficulty in focusing, which in turn has had various consequences. I am poor at mental and manual co-ordination, and in childhood quickly gave up trying to do tasks which required effort and close attention, withdrawing instead into a dreamworld of my own. People were always doing things for me either out of kindness or out of impatience with my clumsy slowness. In Germany I had not been allowed to cross a road on my own. Being so protected and sheltered as a child encouraged the flight into fantasy and from the need to work out and master practical problems, which may help to explain why I never seriously questioned what was going on around me and the circumstances that had brought us to England. My eyesight also partly accounts for my modest academic achievements in school and at university.

A third and probably the most important reason was the powerful influence of my mother. She died in 1974 and only recently have I become aware how greatly she affected my outlook and the development of my personal philosophy. As the youngest and rather delicate child of a well-to-do family, she grew up to be an ardent Anglophile. All that changed in August 1914. She was shocked and deeply offended to find that her beloved England was on the wrong side at the outbreak of war. During the war she and her English, though naturalised, mother turned part of my grandfather's villa on the Wannsee outside Berlin (he had died in 1912) into a convalescent home for wounded German soldiers. She was devoted to these men, whose photographs and tributes to their hostesses, a mixture of gratitude and sentimental German patriotism, were lovingly collected in scrapbooks.

Privately educated with a group of other Jewish girls, who became lifelong friends, my mother was a highly intelligent but also very emotional person. She never forgave England for its perfidy and this attitude accompanied her to Britain, where she professed never to have been happy, in spite of the fact that it offered her refuge from a barbarous fate. My father, on the other hand, did not identify with Germany, was proud of his Austrian background, but thoroughly at home in England, his mother's country.

My mother's patriotism was strengthened because she was a Christian. I was baptised in the Lutheran church and later confirmed in the Church of England. She drew a very clear distinction between Germans, whom she loved, and the Nazi regime whose origins she blamed on the Treaty of Versailles and its consequences. I owe it to her that I continued to develop my command of German during the war, though one did not speak it in public.

She suffered greatly as the war intensified, because she not only loved the country but had many friends there with whom she re-established contact as soon as the war was over. Nor is it surprising that she came into contact with Quakers, through her work for refugee children in Watford, and began to attend their meetings for worship. The religious philosophy, and particularly the Peace Testimony, of the Society of Friends spoke to her condition and she became a Quaker in the later years of the war. I began to attend meetings in 1942 and joined the Society in 1946.

A romantic and visual imagination predisposed me to the study of history. As a small boy I had been attracted to geography through a curiosity about distant lands as well as the shapes and colours of maps, but having to memorise the names of the cotton and wool manufacturing towns of northern England at school, soon put me off the subject. The history essays of my later schooldays reveal a nascent analytical ability, but were written in a rather pompous, rhetorical and emotional style, which sometimes got the better of my logic and judgement.

I was fortunate to have had sympathetic as well as scholarly teachers. Watford Grammar School was rightly proud of its high academic standing, but it was also imbued with a tradition of pastoral care, which turned out to be very important in my case. Difficulties in coping with formal academic disciplines and an easy-going if not lazy disposition did not make for bright prospects. Once, shortly before examinations for the School Certificate (the equivalent of O-levels), my father found me in the garden reading J.G. Lockhart's *The Life of Sir Walter Scott* instead of revising. In his anger he threatened to have me apprenticed to a baker if I failed the examinations. That helped to concentrate the mind. But my real salvation came from extra-curricular activities, which were strongly encouraged by some of the teachers. I even founded a flourishing historical society.

In my last year at school, an experience of tolerance and fair-mindedness made a lasting impression on me and confirmed my attachment to Britain as the country in which I feel truly at home. As a result of my association with Quakers and my awareness that there were 'good' Germans in spite of an evil Nazi regime, I had become an outspoken pacifist and refused to join either the cadet corps or the War Service Scouts, although that was strongly encouraged by the authorities. In spite of this dissent, I was appointed prefect.

At Cambridge in the years immediately after the war, I read history and was a pupil of Michael Oakeshott who, in a subtle and non-judgemental way, instilled some order into my rather chaotic thought processes. By now I had acquired a strong left-wing, though non-Marxist, political bias. In retrospect, the encouragement I received and the faith in me shown by my teachers at school and university, who mostly inclined to the opposite end of the political spectrum, was another example of that tolerance and fair-mindedness which transcends political and philosophical differences. As a student I was happy to give practical expression to my views by showing German prisoners-of-war round the ancient university town and entertaining them to tea in my rooms. I was also inspired by the left-wing Jewish publisher, Victor Gollancz, who came to speak in Cambridge on several occasions. His compassion for the suffering civilian population in defeated Germany made a deep impression on me, and I found his pamphlets, notably *What Buchenwald Really Means* (1945), very persuasive.

My undistinguished record in examinations seemed to rule out an academic career, and during the twelve years from 1950 to 1962 I was first a schoolmaster and then a voluntary worker in Japan and France for the American and British Quaker service committees. Japan was the last place in my mind when I offered for Quaker service, but the American Friends Service Committee (AFSC) asked me to organise international student seminars there. As a young man without family responsibilities I thought 'why not?' Thus began my love affair with a country of which I had only the faintest notions before 1955.

Family circumstances (I had a Japanese wife and infant son) forced us to leave Paris and return to England at the end of 1961. During my Quaker work with students in Japan and diplomats in France, I had become aware that, while there was a genuine appreciation of our efforts to promote international understanding and reconciliation, the bright students and seasoned officials generally thought of us as people who created an unusually pleasant and informal atmosphere for their discussions, but whose approach to international relations was too idealistic to have a great deal of practical relevance in the real world. Thus, when an unexpected turn of events forced a break in overseas Quaker work, I seized the opportunity, with the help of a grant from the Joseph Rowntree Charitable Trust, to equip myself better for this work in the future, hoping that my Quaker outlook would be taken more seriously.

I began my academic apprenticeship reading for a doctorate under the guidance of Michael Howard in the Department of War Studies at King's College London. The subject of French nuclear armament was a natural one to choose as it fitted well with Quaker concerns about disarmament and drew on my experience of three-and-a-half years in Paris. Instead of returning to Quaker work, I ended up in 1965 as Michael Howard's first colleague in an expanding department, and that is where I stayed until retirement 26 years later. A Quaker in war studies seems to be a contradiction in terms. But those who think I should have been in peace studies overlook the fact that war and peace are two sides of the same coin. Furthermore, just as no one would accuse a medical scientist of wishing to promote the disease he is studying, a student of war is not necessarily in favour of it.

The first thing that strikes me on looking back over my career is that things seemed to happen without my making them happen. I see no carefully thought out and planned pattern in my life. My intellectual development was haphazard and rather slow. It owes much to some remarkable, wise, humane and perceptive people who opened my eyes as I went along. In addition to such personal encounters, there were a few books which had a seminal impact on my thinking. Among them were Alan Bullock's brilliant *Hitler – A Study in Tyranny* (London, third impression, 1955) and K.M. Panikkar's *Asia and Western Dominance* (London, 1953). The latter, in particular, taught me that there was a different view of the 'Indian Mutiny', which he called 'The Great Rebellion' (p 143), from the one I had imbibed as a schoolboy, along with an uncritical acceptance of the benign and civilising influence of British rule over vast areas of the world. However, there was no deliberate attempt on my part to gauge the significance of why we left Germany, nor any effort to work out a coherent perspective which was based on that experience.

If I had been a more successful student, I would probably have gone on immediately to postgraduate studies and become an academic historian. Whether I would have chosen to concentrate on German or Anglo-German studies is more doubtful. Of course, it might have been so because I obviously thought of my German background as an important asset when I offered to work for the AFSC in 1954, having in mind their international affairs programmes in Germany and Austria, for which I had the necessary linguistic qualifications. As it happened, I began my academic career in French studies and later turned to the affairs of Japan and East Asia. All but one of my books deal with Europe and East Asia, mainly in the field of foreign and security policy.[2] If I have to be labelled, then it should be as a political scientist, though in whatever I write, the historical dimension always plays a part.

The circumstances of my childhood and youth may not have had a direct bearing on my academic work, but I realise now that they did have a significant, if indirect, influence on my later career and outlook. In this respect I attach special importance to my experiences during visits to Germany in the early years after the war.

Here, at last, I began to understand the nature of the Nazi regime and the reality of the war. Apart from two cousins who had spent the war in Holland – one hidden by a Dutch pastor and his family, the other in the underground resistance – none of my close relations had suffered severely under Nazi persecution or been sent to concentration camps. I was therefore relatively untouched by events. I did not have any inhibitions in mixing with German people, a good number of whom had been supporters of the regime. Their testimony, and especially the intellectual honesty of some whose ideological world had collapsed in the last stages of the war, had the initial effect of making me feel more rather than less sympathy for them.

The first post-war visits to my native land took place in 1948, 1949 and 1951. On each occasion I kept a diary of my visit. On re-reading these documents in preparation for this essay, I am struck by the gradual shift in my attitude and outlook.

In 1948, while still an undergraduate at Cambridge, I attended a seminar in Hamburg for German, British and a few other European students, which was organised by the Military Government of the British Zone of Occupation. It was intended primarily to introduce young Germans to the philosophical and social foundations of Western democracy. Setting off with enthusiasm and excitement on my journey of discovery, laden with gifts of food and other necessities for mother's many friends, I was shocked by the sheer scale of physical destruction in and around the city and by the evidence of much human misery. This strengthened my pacifist convictions. From what I wrote it is clear that I went to Germany in a very sympathetic state of mind, but with hindsight I can detect the slow emergence of a more balanced perspective on the past.

There was no mention whatsoever that I was conscious of my Jewish background, and no suggestion that I raised its implications in conversation with German people. Indeed, there is a singular detachment from the impact of Nazism on my fate. However, it does not mean that I was wholly unaffected by my background. I saw my identity and orientation as entirely British, which sat rather strangely alongside my pro-German sentiments. I think now that this was to compensate for an unacknowledged feeling of insecurity which led to the attempt, quite common among naturalised citizens, to be more British than the British. It was also the beginning of a rebellion against my mother's harsh and emotional criticism of Britain, which did not correspond to my knowledge and experience. Nonetheless, on the surface I remained very much under the influence of her views, especially as I was so warmly received by her friends. In addition, the influence of my Quaker faith is very marked. This led me to seek a more truthful understanding of things than might otherwise have been the case. It also helped me to avoid an excessive sentimentality to which I was prone at that time.

The visit in the following year was part of a wider European tour, and took place in the summer between graduation and the start of a teacher training course in Birmingham. This time I attended an international student seminar under the auspices of the AFSC, which was held at Heppenheim in the Odenwald. It brought together Germans, young people from neighbouring countries, Americans and a few from other parts of the world. In striking contrast to my 1948 diary, this one reflects a much more critical view of Germany (it was the time of the first elections for the *Bundestag* in the Federal Republic) and in particular the tendency to self-pity that I found among people. The more critical approach was encouraged by some of the Germans I met: Quakers, left-wing students, trade unionists, and those who had been in the resistance and had suffered under the Nazi tyranny. They included my Jewish godmother and her sons, who had only survived because her non-Jewish husband, who died shortly before the end of the war, had been a prominent and highly regarded citizen of Heilbronn. Incidentally, there is still no clear evidence that my Jewish background influenced my thinking. The diary contains a hint that some of the characteristics which had marked my early approach to the German problem were being transferred to the issues of East-West relations, ie a refusal to stereotype and to accept that the Russians were wholly in the wrong or evil.

When I returned to Berlin for the first time since the war, the focus had shifted from the significance of the Nazi era and the war to the burning problems of East-West conflict. In 1951 I paid a private visit to friends of the family and then served as a discussion leader in a seminar for high school students from West and East Germany as well as a few from other countries, which was organised by the AFSC in Berlin. The tone of the diary is more measured, the approach more objective, and there is a marked inclination to try and see things from different perspectives. I noted the tendency of some Germans to draw a veil over the recent past and to excuse their country on the grounds of the injustices inflicted on it by foreign powers from the Napoleonic era to the present day. I was not fooled by my visits to East Berlin (the communist-orchestrated World

Youth Festival of Peace and Friendship was in progress at the time) and there is some striking anticipation of the events to come in Berlin.

The visit also cured me of my early simplistic pacifism. I came to appreciate the moral dilemmas of decision-makers as well as ordinary citizens in the face of an implacable and utterly ruthless enemy. Later, war studies were to open my eyes to the complexity of human behaviour and to the flaws of a purely ideological and dogmatic pacifism. There are no simple or easy solutions to the problems of war, which should not be confused with problems of aggressive and violent behaviour in individuals. It is misleading to look for the roots of war in a single cause or in conspiracy theories.[3]

I have dwelt at some length on these personal, intimate and not particularly well written diaries because they reveal better than anything else how much my family background, my German origins and the emigration to England had affected my outlook. They also foreshadow to some extent the basic philosophy which has informed my academic career since then.

There were, of course, other influences at work, some of which could be considered as more important. They include the fact that I received most of my education in England, something which even my mother recognised as the best thing that could have happened to me. Then there was the impact of my Quaker faith, which had been greatly strengthened by three years of teaching history in a co-educational boarding school, run by a remarkable Quaker couple, Kenneth and Frances Barnes. I left Wennington School in 1953 to go to Pendle Hill, a Quaker centre outside Philadelphia, where I studied pacifism, making use of the excellent collection of peace literature in the library of neighbouring Swarthmore College. Perhaps most important is the experience of living and working in Japan and Paris, which was to provide the basis of my applied academic studies.

All of these influences are more relevant to my intellectual development as an adult than the fact that I am of German-Jewish origin. Nevertheless, I believe that they would not have existed nor had their particular impact if it had not been for that fact. The causal relationships are fairly easy to disentangle. Their relative significance is extremely difficult to assess, and one is always in danger of misreading the past, especially in an autobiographical context with its selective memory, emotional dimension and a deliberate or subconscious self-censorship.

As indicated above, German studies as such have played a minor role in my academic work. Lecturing on military sociology with special reference to the political aspects of civil-military relations has meant that I could not ignore the immense importance of Prussian/German thought and practice in the development of modern armies and military policy. But here I have always relied upon the work of established scholars. In my own studies of contemporary foreign and security policy, I have been interested in the similarities and differences in the development of the Federal Republic and Japan since the war.

My personal connection with Germany and the experience of living and working in Japan, as well as my Japanese family ties have, I believe, stood me in good stead when trying to understand the rather nebulous but real element of atmosphere and mood in each country. Regarding Germany, I did not have to overcome some of the emotional hurdles which faced those who suffered so grievously at the hands of the Nazis. I am thoroughly at ease when collaborating with German scholars in the areas I have chosen to work in.[4] Some of them have since become close friends.

Japan did not, of course, present the same problem. It was *terra incognita* when I went there in 1955. Here, too, I was inclined to be very sympathetic because I had been terribly shocked by the atomic bombings; so much so that I wobbled dangerously and nearly fell off my bicycle on the way to the station from a Scout camp, when I first heard the news of the fate of Hiroshima in the morning of 6 August 1945. But after a period of falling in love with Japan, I came to a more detached view with the realisation that, in a hidden way, what happened to Hiroshima and Nagasaki was often used to obliterate the shame of the atrocities committed by the Japanese armies in Asia.

More generally, I believe that the influences and impressions of my formative years have taught me not to allow personal convictions and strong emotions to interfere with my intellectual integrity, though I have not always been successful in doing so in practice. I am reluctant to pass final judgements on people and events – something which may be regarded as a weakness and which does not make for exciting reading. Experience and reflection have led me to try always to distinguish between our common humanity, regardless of cultural differences and historical background, and the institutional structures which we create to bring some order into our social existence. Human beings behave very differently when they are in an institutional setting than they do in relations on a personal level. This distinction makes me want to look for the real person behind the label which is used to classify people who belong to a particular country, ethnic group, religion, political party or profession. I have, for example, acquired over time a more sympathetic understanding of General de Gaulle and his policies than might have been expected of a pacifist.[5] Finally, I have acquired a profound mistrust of dogmatic assertions of what is *the* truth as well as any attempt to turn theory into dogma.

## Notes

1    *The British Journal of Visual Impairment* 12,3 (1994), pp 105-107.

2    They include: *Deterrence and Persuasion: French Nuclear Armament in the Context of National Policy 1945-1969* (London, 1970); *Issues in Japan's China Policy* (London and Basingstoke, 1978); *Western Europe and Japan between the Superpowers* (London and New York, 1984); *Japan's Asia Policy: Regional Security and Global Interests* (London and New York, 1995).

3    'A Quaker in War Studies', *The Friend*, 17 February 1989, pp 199-201. The evolution of my thinking on this subject can be traced in several of my writings, especially: 'Footnotes to Pacifism', *Pendle Hill Bulletin*, No. 119, February 1954, pp 1-7; 'Prophets and Reconcilers: Reflections on the Quaker Peace Testimony' (Swarthmore Lecture 1974, London, Friends Home Service Committee, August 1974, pp 106ff); *The Study of War as a Contribution to Peace* (Pendle Hill Pamphlet 247, Wallingford, Pennsylvania, February 1983, pp 28ff); 'Our Peace Testimony and a World in Turmoil', *The Friend*, 2 July 1993, pp 839-842.

4    My contribution to German publications include: 'Perspektiven der heutigen französischen Verteidigungspolitik', *Europa-Archiv* 23 (1968), pp 65-73; 'Die japanische Verfassung und Japans Sicherheitspolitik', *Beiträge zur Konfliktforschung* 3 (1976), pp 69-90; 'Sowjetische Japanpolitik zwischen politischer Konfrontation und wirtschaftlicher Kooperation', in Joachim Glaubitz and Dieter Heinzig (eds), *Die Sowjetunion und Asien in den 80er Jahren: Ziele und Grenzen sowjetischer Politik zwischen Indischem Ozean und Pazifik* (Baden-Baden, 1988), pp 265-285; 'Japans Aussen- und Sicherheitspolitik in Ostasien', and 'Die Japan-Politik Grossbritanniens', in Hanns W. Maull (ed.), *Japan und Europa: Getrennte Welten?* (Frankfurt/New York, 1993), pp 188-213, 322-336.

5    Compare my view of the General in *Deterrence and Persuasion* (London, 1970) with the conclusions in my essay on the occasion of his centenary: 'De Gaulle et la Politique Nucléaire', in *De Gaulle en son Siècle*, volume 4, *La Sécurité et l'Indépendance de la France* (Paris, 1992), pp 186-196.

**Werner E. Mosse**

# Self-Discovery:
# A European Historian

Viewed in retrospect, it is possible to see in my career as a historian the interaction of four different strands: German-Jewish, German, English and Russian. In the present context, the German strand inevitably assumes a disproportionate prominence.

The story begins with a sound German all-round education up to the age of fifteen. History and geography, together with German, were my favourite subjects. My early role model was an uncle, meteorologist and explorer, concerned, among other things, with measuring the movements of the Greenland ice-cap. An abiding interest in foreign countries was developed also by enthusiastic stamp-collecting. English governesses laid the foundations of an interest in matters British. I recall an English school reader showing a picture of rowing at one of the ancient universities and my feeling of regret that I had no prospect of ever seeing the reality.

One day – I may have been thirteen or fourteen – my father asked me what I would like to be. Among the possibilities we considered, the one which most appealed to me was diplomacy. The attraction, besides seeing foreign countries, was the imagined glamour. Enquiries, however, revealed that prospects for a young Jew in the diplomatic service of the Weimar Republic were nil. The early preference may have foreshadowed the later occupation with history as an alternative.

In 1933, aged fifteen, after my father had fallen victim to the Nazi regime, I moved to England with my mother and siblings. On the advice of English relatives, I became a day pupil at St Paul's School with its well-deserved reputation for extending a warm welcome to victims of oppressive governments.

At St Paul's, I was placed in 'Transitus B', one of two orientation classes between the lower and eighth forms. The form master responsible for most of the teaching, apart from trying to stimulate wider cultural interests, sought by means of the Socratic method to develop rational thinking and dialectical skills. His teaching, which would have an abiding effect, formed a 'classical' corrective to Germanic sentimentalism and romanticism. Whilst some of the latter would persist, my dominant world view became one of Anglo-Saxon pragmatism.

After a year, I had to choose my field of eighth-form specialisation. I opted for History in preference to language and literature. Classics and science, the other options, did not attract me. Whilst the choice of History did point to the future, it may well be that I simply preferred it to the alternatives.

Two years of intensive historical studies followed. The teaching of Philip Whitting, form master of the History Eighth and himself mainly a Byzantinist, helped to enlarge my knowledge and widen my horizons. Among others, Whitting tried to interest his pupils in the history of Russia. He also covered Chinese history as part of a broad historical education. I owe a great deal to St Paul's School and to the two masters who mainly taught me there.

Having gained my Higher School Certificate in History and German, I was offered the choice of sitting a scholarship examination for either Oxford or Cambridge. I chose the latter under the impression that it was the more 'middle class' of the two, as against 'aristocratic' Oxford. Within the group of colleges for which I applied, I selected Corpus Christi on account of its traditional links with St Paul's and because it offered a Closed Exhibition for Paulines. In 1936, I won a major open scholarship and registered for the historical tripos.

❖

Cambridge teaching, though the faculty boasted some prestigious names, left little lasting impression. It was strongly oriented, as indeed had been some of the teaching at St Paul's, towards British constitutional history. My first tutor and early mentor, Kenneth Pickthorn, a Tudor historian, failed to recruit a lesser Geoffrey

Elton. For my special subject I chose, perhaps not accidentally, a paper taught by G.P. Gooch and Harold Temperley on the Diplomacy of Imperialism 1890-1904. The course of lectures which most appealed to me, however, was one offered by Herbert Butterfield. The somewhat surprising topic, if I remember rightly, was the cultural history of the Mediterranean area.

Before moving to Cambridge, I had decided to acquire a knowledge of some 'exotic' language. The choice lay between Russian, modern Hebrew, Arabic and, I believe, Turkish. The first preference might have been Hebrew. However, an enquiry about the possibility of joining at some future date the international department of the Jewish Agency did not elicit so much as an acknowledgment. No doubt a non-Zionist of German origin was of little interest. What finally decided the issue in favour of Russian was its combination of an attractive literature and promising career prospects. In loose association with the Russian Department I acquired during my years in Cambridge a rudimentary reading knowledge of the Russian language.

In 1939 I graduated with a Double First in History and was awarded a Studentship at Corpus Christi. Being then interested in the constitutional arrangements under which different ethnic groups could coexist, however inharmoniously, in a single state, I chose as my topic for research the constitutional history of Canada after 1867. My early researches, however, were rudely interrupted by the outbreak of war and, soon after, internment as an 'enemy alien'. I would see Canada sooner than I had bargained for.

During my 'stay' in Canada behind barbed wire I was able, if I remember rightly, to regale some of my fellow-sufferers with talks on Canadian history. Not long after release from internment at the end of 1940, I volunteered for military service. I served in the army for five years. Two of these were spent in Italy, incidentally helping me to broaden my cultural experience and, as Liaison Officer with a unit composed of Italians, to acquire a good knowledge of the Italian language. I was demobilised in 1946 at the rank of Captain. My last commanding officer failed to entice me into a military career with the prospect of promotion and a junior staff course. I did not feel that my future lay in that direction. In fact, in my absence, Corpus Christi had offered me a Research Fellowship.

On returning to Cambridge, I registered for a PhD degree with Herbert Butterfield as my chosen supervisor. I intended to work in the Russian field. As research in Soviet archives was then impossible, I was advised to pick a diplomatic topic with Russian connections. I chose to investigate the international complications arising from the execution of the Treaty of Paris in 1856.

In 1948, at the invitation of the Foreign Office, I joined an international vacation course at the University of Göttingen. As a contribution to German 're-education', I read a paper on the revolution of 1688 as a study in political method. Of greater moment, however, was another event. To mark the centenary of 1848, a then well-known professor of German history expounded to a gathering of academics the familiar thesis of the 'Bismarckians': the Germans, in 1848, had tried to achieve unification by peaceful means. The attempt had been frustrated by the 'malevolent' intervention of the European powers. All that remained, therefore, was Bismarck's 'solution' of 'iron and blood'. The thesis, I felt, challenged contradiction. After a prolonged period of archival research, I published my first major study, *The European Powers and the German Question 1848-1871: with Special Reference to England and Russia* (Cambridge, 1958; American edition: New York, 1969). The book, I understand, is still consulted by scholars today.

My Research Fellowship at Corpus Christi had run out in 1948. For a variety of reasons I had not settled down well in the senior common room. I became a lecturer on Russian history at the School of Slavonic and East European Studies at London University. There, in 1950, I received my PhD (Cantab.). My doctoral thesis, in a greatly altered and expanded form, would subsequently form the basis of *The Rise and Fall of the Crimean System 1855-1871* (London, 1963).

❖

In 1952, I was appointed to a newly created post (under the Hayter programme, designed by Sir William Hayter, former British Ambassador in Moscow, to foster understanding in Britain of the countries of Eastern Europe, their peoples and their cultures) at Glasgow University as Senior Lecturer in Eastern European History. The appointee, under the terms of the Hayter scheme, was obliged to visit at regular intervals one of the countries of Eastern Europe. In 1953, I accordingly explored Yugoslavia from Slovenia in the north to Macedonia in the south, meeting people and gaining an impression of the land, its culture and its politics. Reinforced by an understanding of the history of Serbs and Croats, the study tour created an interest which has persisted.

Not long afterwards, I was invited by A.L. Rowse to contribute a volume to his series on major historical figures in the 'Teach Yourself History' series. I chose Alexander II, the 'Tsar Liberator', possibly through recalling the notes on Russian history dictated by Philip Whitting at St Paul's. *Alexander II and the Modernization of Russia* first appeared in 1958. It became a successful paperback. Eventually, it went out of print. Recently, there has been a new edition, both hard- and paperback, with a new introduction drawing attention to the topicality of the subject. In 1961, I provided a substantial entry on Alexander II for the *Encyclopaedia Britannica*. The book has become the standard life in English of one of the most important tsars of the nineteenth century. A by-product of the book, thanks to Rowse's severe editing, was a lasting improvement of my English style. Sentences became shorter, with the disappearance of abundant 'and's, the elimination of adjectives and a reduction in subordinate clauses.

Then my German-Jewish background unexpectedly intruded on my Russian academic pursuits. Early in 1958, I was invited by Robert Weltsch, its editor, to contribute a paper to the *Year Book* of the Leo Baeck Institute. The article, 'Rudolf Mosse and the House of Mosse 1867-1920', on my great-uncle, the well-known publisher, appeared the following year. I was then invited to join the board of the Institute. Under the aegis of Weltsch and with assistance from Arnold Paucker, the Institute's Director, I edited three voluminous symposia: *Entscheidungsjahr 1932: Zur Judenfrage in der Endphase der Weimarer Republik* (Tübingen, 1965, second edition 1966); *Deutsches Judentum in Krieg und Revolution 1916-1923* (Tübingen, 1971) and *Juden im Wilhelminischen Deutschland 1890-1914* (Tübingen, 1976). The volumes, to which I contributed, appeared in the 'Schriftenreihe' of the Institute. They have become frequently quoted standard works.

As a board member, meanwhile, I was helping to overcome the residual reluctance of some older members to associate more closely with German academics. Among others, I took a leading part in

1968 in a meeting in Berlin to discuss possibilities of future co-operation. Eleven German colleagues contributed to the three symposia. Three participants, Ernst Schulin, Rudolf Vierhaus and the late Werner Jochmann, became long-term partners of the London Leo Baeck Institute (LBI), as did the *Forschungsstelle für die Geschichte des Nationalsozialismus* in Hamburg.

⊨⇒

Work for the LBI and heavy administrative duties at the newly established University of East Anglia, where in 1964 I had been appointed to a chair of European History, did not prevent me from pursuing work in the Russian field. In 1964 I published in *Soviet Studies* an article 'Interlude: The Russian Provisional Government of 1917'. It was followed by two contributions in the same journal 'The February Régime: Prerequisites of Success' (1967) and 'Russia 1917: The February Revolution' (1968). I read papers at the triennial Anglo-Soviet historical conferences. At the fourth conference in Moscow in September 1968, my contribution attracted attention. Soviet colleagues, figuratively speaking, were hanging from the chandeliers to hear it, whilst the establishment mobilised three of its 'heavyweights' to criticise. An expanded version was published in *The Slavonic and East European Review* under the title of 'Makers of the Soviet Union' (1968). It was a quantitative analysis of the membership of seven successive Central Committees of the Communist Party, employing among other criteria social extraction, educational background, ethnicity and regional origins. Interesting patterns and shifts emerged. My participation in the Anglo-Soviet conferences ended in 1968 when I decided to have no further dealings with 'official' Soviet institutions whilst Russian soldiers remained on Czech soil. This phase of my work on Russian history concluded with two articles, 'A.F. Kerensky and the Emancipation of Russian Jewry' and 'Revolution in Saratov (October-November 1917)'. The second was based on reports of local Saratov papers preserved in the Hoover Institute at Stanford.

During this time, the direction of my research interests was changing. Whereas previously I had been forced to rely on printed sources, mainly in Helsinki University Library (a deposit library under the later tsars), access to Soviet sources was slowly opening up. Under a cultural exchange programme, I was able to work during several weeks at the Lenin Library in Moscow. Moreover the Soviet authorities, on an exchange basis, were willing to provide photo-copies of selected non-sensitive documents.

Taking advantage of the new research opportunities, I was able to collect material for seven papers on the tsarist bureaucracy published in a variety of learned journals between 1979 and 1981. Two final articles followed in 1984. It is a matter of regret that these papers were never collected. Between them, they present a thoroughly researched picture of a major aspect of the Russian *ancien régime*.

◁═══▷

I had at some point become interested in the history of *anciens régimes*. Like others, I had been struck by the similarities between Charles I, Louis XVI and Nicholas II with their foreign and widely unpopular wives. The comparison led to reflections on pre-conditions of successful revolution. A number of factors appeared to be present in each case. This line of thought led, almost automatically, to questions about the comparability of historical phenomena. I came to the conclusion that all phenomena described by the same term (*ancien régime*, revolution, outbreak of wars, peace treaties etc.) showed both typical features shared with others and specific ones which were unique. Whilst typical features represented similarities, the specific ones showed up the differences. It appeared a rough framework for comparison.

Reflections on comparability pointed in two different directions. They led me at one time to consider the possibility of writing a general study on the comparability of historical phenomena with illustrations chosen mainly from instances of the outbreak of wars and the conclusion of peace. It is a matter of regret that the project was in the end superseded by others and abandoned. All that remained was a general interest in problems of historical compara-bility and the basic concept of typical and specific features of comparable occurrences. The approach, as will be seen, would later re-surface in a different context.

The second possibility emerging from these ideas related to the late tsarist regime. Whilst ideally I would have liked to work on both the Russian and French *anciens régimes*, my primary concern with Russian history led me to concentrate on Russia. The series of articles I have mentioned formed part of the project. The interruption during the eighties due to concentration on German-Jewish history meant that the mass of material I had accumulated would remain for a time unused. Its utilisation, as will be seen, belongs to the final phase of my work as a historian of Russia.

---

The 'German diversion', meanwhile, was assuming serious proportions. In 1978, Robert Weltsch had given up his journalistic work in London and retired to Jerusalem. Shortly before he left, Hans Liebeschütz, the senior historian on the LBI board, came to ask my opinion as to whether the Institute should continue. Its future had become problematical, with the gradual shrinking of the original aged, largely non-academic and 'Germanic' membership. After some thought, I replied that the attempt should be made to continue. The board, no doubt at the suggestion of Robert Weltsch, had then elected me its chairman.

My early task as chairman had been to 'professionalise' and, at the same time, 'rejuvenate' the Institute. Over a period of time, younger British-trained academics of German-Jewish origin came to replace the founder-generation. At the same time, a succession of joint conferences intensified co-operation with German scholars and institutions. One conference held in Oxford in 1979 resulted in a publication, edited by myself, Arnold Paucker and Reinhard Rürup, *Revolution and Evolution: 1848 in German-Jewish History* (Tübingen, 1981). Publications by members, besides contributing to scholarship, helped to make the Institute more widely known. So did the annual *Year Book*, now edited by Arnold Paucker in succession to Robert Weltsch. The London Institute, by degrees, was turning into the institution it is today.

My own research interests, meanwhile, were turning towards German-Jewish economic history. I had already contributed a chapter 'Die Juden in Wirtschaft und Gesellschaft' to the 1976 symposium. Three years later, I had published in the *Year Book* an article 'Judaism, Jews and Capitalism: Weber, Sombart and beyond'.

Jürgen Kocka, during a visit to Glasgow, encouraged me to embark on a planned study of German-Jewish entrepreneurship. With his support following an initial exploratory grant from the German Academic Exchange Service (*DAAD*), I received a research grant from the *Deutsche Forschungsgemeinschaft*. I spent a year at the *Zentrum für interdisziplinäre Forschung* in Bielefeld, during which I carried out intensive researches in both business archives and in state archives in Koblenz, Merseburg and Potsdam. I worked closely with Jürgen Kocka who, for a time, doubted the legitimacy of treating Jewish entrepreneurs (capitalists) as a separate entity. His criticisms were helpful and I believe that, at the same time, by the end he had come to modify his views. The eventual outcome of my researches was a two-volume study, *Jews in the German Economy: The German-Jewish Economic Elite 1820-1935* (Oxford, 1987) and *The German-Jewish Economic Elite 1820-1935: A Socio-Cultural Profile* (Oxford, 1989). Regrettably, neither volume has been translated into German. However, in 1989, together with Hans Pohl, I helped to organise, under the auspices of the *Friedrich Naumann Stiftung*, a symposium on German-Jewish entrepreneurship. In 1992 the proceedings, in an expanded form, were published as *Jüdische Unternehmer in Deutschland im 19. und 20. Jahrhundert* edited by myself and Hans Pohl.

My studies of Jewish entrepreneurship also yielded a number of research-based by-products, among them 'Zwei Präsidenten der Kölner Industrie- und Handelskammer: Louis Hagen und Paul Silverberg' in *Köln und das rheinische Judentum* edited by Jutta Bohnke-Kollwitz et al.; 'Wilhelm II and the Kaiserjuden: A Problematical Encounter' in *The Jewish Response to German Culture* edited by Jehuda Reinharz and Walter Schatzberg; 'Jewish Marriage Strategies: The German-Jewish Economic Elite' in *Studia Rosenthaliana*; 'Drei Juden in der Wirtschaft Hamburgs: Heine, Ballin, Warburg' in *Die Juden in Hamburg 1590-1990* edited by Arno Herzig (Hamburg, 1991).

Between 1988 and 1992, I published four articles in the LBI *Year Book* on different types of partial Jewish integration in Wilhelmine society. By examining the Tietz, Wallich, Salomonsohn and Hirsch (Halberstadt) families I tried to identify the different frameworks within which partly successfully social integration could occur. In 1990 (Bochum) and again in 1992 (Hanover) I read papers on allied topics in the Jewish history sections of the German *Historikertag*. Finally, I contributed an essay-entry 'Juden im Wirtschaftsleben in Deutschland' to *Neues Lexikon des Judentums* edited by Julius H. Schoeps (Gütersloh, 1992).

Some time in the eighties, I was invited to join Jürgen Kocka's study group on the bourgeoisie in nineteenth-century Europe. I took part in meetings and discussions at the *Zentrum für interdisziplinäre Forschung* and contributed a paper to the eventual publication. 'Adel und Bürgertum im Europa des 19. Jahrhunderts – eine vergleichende Betrachtung', covering England, Germany, France and

Russia, was published in *Bürgertum im 19. Jahrhundert* edited by Jürgen Kocka (Frankfurt-am-Main, 1988). It was selected for inclusion in the shorter Italian (1989) and English (1993) editions.

◆━━━━▶

My teaching at the University of East Anglia (UEA) meanwhile included seminars on other subjects besides Russian history. Among them was European liberalism. I examined with students literary presentations of the conflict between the individual (and his conscience) and ruler, church, state and the 'solid majority'. On the agenda were Antigone, Socrates, St Joan, Luther, Galileo, Tomas Stockmann and, I believe, Winston Smith.

The interest in liberalism contributed to an early publication *Liberal Europe: The Age of Bourgeois Realism 1848-1875* (London, 1974). It made a later appearance in a joint conference of the *Friedrich Naumann Stiftung* and the Leo Baeck Institute, the basis for a bi-lingual volume *Das deutsche Judentum und der Liberalismus/German Jewry and Liberalism* (Sankt Augustin, 1986).

Following a family tradition now in its fourth generation I have always been a liberal and a democrat. My great-grandfather, a medical practitioner in a small Posen town, in 1848, unusually, supported the Polish national movement. He paid with a year in a Prussian fortress. My father in turn looked back to the traditions of 1848 and implanted in me a sense of loyalty to the republican colours of black, red and gold.

From my earliest years I was an avid newspaper reader with a lively interest in domestic politics. I identified with the *Deutsche Demokratische Partei* and, needless to say, loathed Hitler and the Nazi Party. In England, I was revolted by appeasement in all its manifestations. My sympathies for the Left – I was a Cambridge undergraduate during the 'golden' age of the Apostles – never strayed beyond the bounds of the Labour Party.

Not long after the war, I joined the British Liberal Party. I was an active party worker successively in Hampstead, Dumbartonshire and Norwich, and ended up as a founding member of the SDP. Now, utterly disillusioned with the British political system, I have withdrawn from active involvement. Only the threat of a substantial fine 'persuades' me to remain on the electoral register.

My general 'philosophy' of history rested on Locke and Montesquieu, more concretely on Benedetto Croce's *History of*

*Europe in the Nineteenth Century* (1932). Eventually this approach would be replaced by a more sociologically-oriented one, based on Comte and the pre-1914 German school: Robert Michels, Otto Hintze, Max Weber. I arrived at the view which I still hold today that the basic social and political unit in society is – possibly the family apart – the informal network. It is the structural building material of which élites, ruling classes, parties, unions, indeed all social and political entities and organisations are composed. My studies of the German-Jewish entrepreneurial class and, to a lesser extent, the tsarist bureaucracy have confirmed me in this view.

The finest expression of the liberal credo is that of Friedrich Schiller, not accidentally the icon of the German-Jewish sub-culture. It is contained in the closing dialogue of *Wilhelm Tell.*

Berta      Wohlan!
           So reich' ich diesem Jüngling meine Rechte,
           Die freie Schweizerin dem freien Mann!

Rudenz     Und frei erklär' ich alle meine Knechte.

<hr>

A second seminar I conducted at UEA was concerned with European nationalism. It was a subject which, in one form or another, touched me during most phases of my life. The excellent German education of my youth was permeated with a nationalist spirit. It was directed (understandably) primarily against France and the French. The young were fed with indignation at the Treaty of Versailles, exorbitant reparations, the French occupation of the Ruhr, the misdeeds of French colonial occupation troops (Zouaves) in the Rhineland, the French Foreign Legion and the Germans said to have been recruited into it. There was indignation at the treatment of Germans in 'Deutsch-Südtirol' (Alto Adige), in the 'Polish Corridor' and at the Upper Silesian plebiscite. To a limited extent I came to share these (partly justified) resentments.

Any possible tendency to hyper-nationalism was, however, counteracted by the influence of my father. A front-line officer with the Iron Cross of both classes, he had become, following the war, a staunch advocate of Franco-German reconciliation. He belonged to a Franco-German society devoted to this object. He welcomed the Briand-Stresemann initiatives and supported the *Paneuropa* movement of Count Coudenhove-Kalergi. We read the *Vossische Zeitung*, edited by the Francophile Georg Bernhard, dubbed by nationalists 'Gazette de Foch', in preference to the more Anglophile family paper, the *Berliner Tageblatt*. It may have been the *'Voss'* which at one point ran a youth competition for the best essay on Franco-German friendship. My father encouraged me to enter; needless to say, I did not win the prize, a visit to Paris.

The outcome of conflicting influences was a harmless brand of German nationalism. It found expression mainly in partisanship over international sporting events. One arena was the annual competition for the Davis Cup. On one occasion, if I remember rightly, Germany actually reached the final. I followed the progress of the German team with passionate interest, incidentally then unaware that the German champion Daniel Prenn was Jewish, or of Jewish origin.

After 1933 I loathed the Germans and all their works. The fact that during the transition period I had encountered an (all too small) number of decent and even courageous Germans in no way modified my hatred. Neither did the 'neutrality' of some teachers and fellow-pupils. The old national identification was gone, never to return, without a new one in sight.

My attitude towards Britain remained for years ambivalent. The policy of appeasement indulged in notably by members of the British upper classes, internment and my treatment by some British officers as a private in the Pioneer Corps did little to develop friendly feelings. Unlike some others, I felt no particular gratitude towards Great Britain as distinct from St Paul's, the helpful part of my British relatives, individual teachers and fellow-students and some 'ordinary people' encountered in everday life. Feelings warmed somewhat with the advent of Churchill and the emergence of a common urge to free Europe and the world from the scourge of Hitlerism. They were reinforced by a sense of loyalty resulting from Army service, more particularly as a commissioned officer. Naturalisation after the war further increased identification, if in a more formal sense. I came to appreciate living in a relatively toler-ant society with (almost) equal rights. At the same time, whilst a loyal British subject, I have at no time considered or described myself as English. If anything, my natural affinities lie with Scotland and the Scots. When I meet people with whom a rapport is easily established, I find that, as often as not, they have some Scottish or occasionally other non-English ancestry or at the very least North-country connections.

Werner E. Mosse

Though never a Zionist, I felt a strong involvement in the fight of the Palestinian Jews for statehood. I rejoiced at the creation of the state of Israel and its successful defence. At the same time I have always felt and still feel sympathy for the Palestinian Arabs. Like a number of early German-Jewish intellectuals who emigrated to Palestine, I would have preferred a bi-national to a purely Jewish state. My attitude to Israel remains one of sympathy and sympathetic solidarity but without close emotional identification.

After the end of the war, my hatred of Germany and the Germans gradually abated. One early factor was sympathy for the German resistance, another the readiness, due largely to Konrad Adenauer, to compensate, at some sacrifice, surviving Jewish victims of Nazi persecution. It gradually became clear moreover that Germany had become again a well-organised democratic 'Rechtsstaat'. My attitude towards East Germans however remained negative. For several reasons, I would not welcome 'Wiedervereinigung'. A gradual approximation of the two halves would have been greatly preferable, as would a 'Western' capital in Bonn. Over the years, I paid repeated visits to the Federal Republic, worked with German colleagues and made some friends. Germany has become for me almost a 'normal' country of the West similar to the rest – if with a difference. My cultural background, after all, if internationalised, has remained to a great extent German.

At the same time, especially during the past decade, my attachment to England has weakened with a steady deterioration of English manners and attitudes, the almost complete disappearance of the gentleman (or lady), both as a concept and in everyday behaviour, and his (and her) replacement by the demoralised 'go-getting' yobbo. British foreign policy, particularly in the Balkans, and the degree of sympathy I have always felt for the victims of Lloyd George's Irish partition also contribute. There has been a slow process of 'dissimilation'. Speaking the languages, and familiar to some extent with the culture and history, I also feel perfectly at home abroad, particularly in France and Italy.

Ever since the sixties, I have taken a keen interest in European integration. I recall study visits to the early European institutions in Brussels, Luxembourg, Strasbourg and Paris, as well as a gathering of pro-Europeans in the House of Commons. I regularly visit France and have got to know French people at more than tourist level. As already mentioned, as liaison officer with a unit of Italians, I lived and shared a mess with Italian officers and for years afterwards maintained some contacts. A knowledge of four major European languages has helped, as has familiarity, in varying degrees, with various literatures. Among my favourites are works by Honoré de Balzac, Edmond Rostand, Charles de Coster, Giuseppe di Lampedusa, Theodor Fontane, Thomas Mann and Selma Lagerlöf, to whose number one might add Viktor Scheffel, Gottfried Keller and Conrad Ferdinand Meyer. The only British names to add to the list would be the translator Edward Fitzgerald, Patrick White and Malcolm Lowry and, to some extent, Jane Austen.

Over the years, I have become a committed European (and British) federalist. The more extreme forms of nationalism, at least for developed Western countries, have had their day. Though surviving psychologically, the centralised nation-state has for many practical purposes become obsolete. Major decisions are taken by a variety of international bodies and multi-national organisations. In an oft-quoted phrase, the great panjandrum described patriotism as 'the last refuge of a scoundrel'. Only the term 'patriotism' is slightly inappropriate.

Withal, I do not feel a European. The federal Europe I welcome hardly evokes deeper feelings. It cannot become the basis of a new European nationalism, nor even patriotism. Emotional attachment following the eclipse of the nation-state could and should develop only towards (sometimes historically based) regions. I do have warm feelings for the South-West, as I once did for Scotland and to a lesser extent East Anglia. Decentralisation, the famous 'subsidiarity', should be the order of the day, and not only in the European Union.

In my UEA seminar on nationalism, the occasion of this digression, I tried to compare various manifestations, particularly in Germany and France. I drew attention to similarities but also to nuances. '… mit Henkerblut, Franzosenblut, o süsser Tag der Rache!' may bear a resemblance to '… qu'un sang impur abbreuve nos sillons'. Yet there is a difference in tone, in spirit and in the nature of the intended victims. What French nationalist could equal the bad taste of the ending of Karl Gerok's *Des Deutschen Knaben Tischgebet*:

> Spricht: 'lieber Gott, magst ruhig sein,
> Fest steht und treu die Wacht am Rhein.
> Amen!'

Could there be a French (or any other) equivalent to 'Deutschland, Deutschland über alles, über alles in der Welt'? 'Send her victorious, happy and glorious', even 'confound their politics, frustrate their knavish tricks, on Thee our hope we fix...' or 'Rule Britannia, Britannia rule the waves' are less bombastic and arrogant. The seminar, I recall, was not a complete success. The subject was of little interest to students. There may also have been language problems.

⬖⬗

The third UEA seminar which invites a brief digression was one on anti-Semitism. A small part of my teaching, it formed the background to much of my work on German-Jewish history. It was also a pervasive influence, particularly during my youthful years.

During my school-days in Germany, I do not recall open manifestations of anti-Jewish feeling. Neither teachers nor classmates showed hostility on ethnic grounds even in the early months of the Nazi regime. Yet it may be that an element of latent anti-Semitism contributed to an isolation due predominantly to social and economic causes. In the village elementary school, an inevitable social and cultural gulf existed between the child of the local landowner and the peasant children. In the secondary school of the nearby small town this persisted with regard to classmates with, in the main, a petty bourgeois background. Though friendly relations might develop in individual cases, I remained overall a complete outsider. Nor was my personality designed to facilitate personal contacts. Though Jewishness was not itself a prime isolating factor, it may well have been a subsidiary one.

There was also a political element. Whilst my own family supported one or other of the democratic parties, the political 'culture' in both village and small town was 'Deutschnational'. In the village, social contacts with peasant families were non-existent. There were friendly if unequal relations with some employees and their children. There was never a question of contacts with other landowners. Instead, the social circle consisted almost entirely of relatives and friends, mainly professional people, from Berlin. It was something like a 'natural' apartheid situation, in part inherent in the position of a landowning family in a still semi-feudal (Prussian) structure. Jewishness was merely an additional ingredient.

With the rise of National Socialism after 1928, a state of 'peaceful co-existence' gave way to one of increasing tension. A bankrupt shopkeeper from a nearby town set up shop in the village. Himself a fanatical Nazi, he was the father also of a middle-ranking (and later notorious) *SA* officer. Instead of buying at their (rather modest) shop, my parents continued to patronise their previous suppliers in the nearby small town. Disappointed, the two Nazis then started an openly anti-Semitic agitation against my father. Occasionally, they imported lorryloads of Brownshirts on missions of intimidation. Following violent incidents, and in the face of minimal police protection, the family finally was forced to escape to Berlin. The loyalty of a few employees during the critical months had been above praise. Even some of the peasants had adopted at any rate a neutral stance.

Throughout this time, teachers and fellow-pupils in my secondary school had behaved with consistent correctness. Before we left the village, I had been registered in the *Gymnasium* of a larger not too distant textile town (the secondary school lacking the three highest forms). I commuted, somewhat inconveniently, from Berlin. My new form master, an ardent Nazi, who once did not scruple to appear in class in *SA* uniform, behaved nonetheless correctly. His subject was English, and my knowledge of the language was good. His colleagues, in the main non-Nazis, showed no sign of discrimination. With classmates, there were few opportunities for contacts. During breaks, two went out of their way to keep me company. One was the son of a municipal medical officer with a Danish name and, I believe, background, the other the son of a Social Democratic schoolteacher in a neighbouring village. I recall their gesture with gratitude.

Pupils at the *Gymnasium* contained a significant minority of Nazis. When in school assembly the Brandenburg hymn 'Märkische Heide...' was intoned, there was regular competition between non-Nazis and the others. Whilst the former sang '... dem Vaterland die Treue, getreu bis in den Tod ...' the Nazis shouted '... dem Hakenkreuz die Treue...' For the moment at any rate, the non-Nazis just 'had it'. Overall through these years and months the situation in the two schools, if often uncomfortable, was not intolerable.

In England, racial anti-Semitism hardly existed. Instead, without ethnic distinction, Jewish and other refugees were subsumed under the wider category of 'bloody foreigners'. I have quite recently had a pertinent experience. A speeding 'fellow-citizen', having just failed to run me over, stopped and became abusive. During the exchange which followed, he asked, 'Why don't you go back to where you came from?' This is a sentiment perhaps quite widely shared if not openly avowed, but could it be called anti-Semitism?

My Norwich seminar involved a comparative study of German and French anti-Semitism. It was, at his suggestion, conducted jointly with a Gentile colleague, an expert on late nineteenth-century French anti-Semitism. As part of my own contribution, I analysed a large number of anti-Semitic propaganda leaflets. Students, however, showed little interest and, having been offered once, the seminar was then discontinued.

In fact, in my work on Jewish history I have, on the whole, fought shy of the subject of anti-Semitism. Not only has it never attracted me, but I seriously doubt how far it should be treated by a Jewish historian. Unavoidably, the necessary detachment would (some would say should) be lacking. Anti-Semitism is primarily a Gentile – in this case more specifically a German – problem. It should be left in the main to Gentile historians.

The same is true, and to an even greater extent, of the shoah, misnamed the Holocaust. This is in my view only marginally a proper subject for a historical approach. It is an emotive subject, much of it para-historical, best left to theologians or pathologists. I moreover suspect the motives of not a few of its practitioners. The depiction of Jewish victims of Nazi atrocities can all too easily be used for a form of moral blackmail. Again whilst many focus on the shoah for entirely honourable reasons it will in others reflect a morbid curiosity and satisfy pathological cravings. Last and not least, there is in 'Holocaust studies' an almost unavoidable element of sensationalism. In fact, historical study of the Holocaust is best left to Gentiles, the moral evaluation to theologians and philosophers. As an eschatological phenomenon, it lies essentially outside the purview of the historian.

In fact the founding fathers of the Leo Baeck Institute wisely limited the scope of its activities to the period before 1933. They may well have felt misgivings about extending it beyond this date. It is a matter of some regret that over the last few years the Institute has partially departed from this policy.

⬤━━━⬤

In the course of my involvement with German-Jewish history, I have become increasingly concerned at some of the terms and concepts employed. Too many are ill-defined, loaded or plainly inappropriate. At the same time, important phenomena remain unrecognised. There are difficulties even in matters of translation. 'Gentile' and 'Nichtjude' are not synonymous, nor is the latter term a particularly felicitous description. Some dictionaries actually translate 'Gentile' as 'Heide'.

Among others, the term 'anti-Semite' is both woolly and incapable of definition. 'Wer Antisemit ist, bestimme ich', in adaptation of a classical formulation. Who can rightly be called an anti-Semite? Gustav Freytag? Theodor Fontane? Thomas Mann? On a different plane Schacht, Hugenberg, Papen? Again, in another context, Walther Rathenau or Otto Weininger? Does it make sense to speak of 'Jewish anti-Semites'? Is anyone with a (mild) dislike of Jews to be lumped together with Hitler, Streicher or Goebbels?

In general, students of anti-Semitism frequently overlook the existence of the 'non-anti-Semite', for whom there is not even a learned term. Too often, the Gentile world is divided into anti-Semites and 'philosemites', an infinitesimal minority. What about the rest, all those either indifferent to or unaware of a 'Jewish question'? What about those, possibly a majority, with a slight, if not openly expressed, anti-Jewish sentiment? What about people with mild Jewish sympathies? Why, in any case, should a sympathetic attitude be assumed as the 'normal' Gentile stance? When and where have the majority feelings towards members of a minority been other than ambivalent? Even the question of possible Jewish 'anti-Gentilism' could be raised.

In short, there is a variety of feelings both for and against. Whilst theoretically these could perhaps be ranged in a continuum, this in practice is impossible. The intensity of feelings can be neither measured nor quantified. Even could it be done, at what point does the 'anti-Semite' start? And are there not conspicuous examples of people changing their attitudes in the light of reflection or personal experiences? Mankind (and womankind) in short does not divide neatly into anti- and philosemites. And 'anti-Semite' is not the only term or concept calling for careful evaluation by the historian.

━━◆━━

I now turn to the final phase of my activities as a historian. In 1989, in close co-operation with Reinhard Rürup, I was responsible for setting up the *Wissenschaftliche Arbeitsgemeinschaft des Leo Baeck Institutes in der Bundesrepublik Deutschland*. At a meeting of the international executive in New York, I moved the resolution under which the LBI achieved its long-standing objective of creating a German partner-institution. Reinhard Rürup then came to London. In long hot sessions during a heat wave we sketched out, with assistance from Arnold Paucker, the outlines of the new organisation and of its relations with the LBI. 'Die zu gründende Arbeitsgemein-schaft,' ran the minutes, 'ist eine Einrichtung des LBI, für die Herr Mosse zu einer Gründungsversammlung einladen wird.'

On 8 December 1989, in Frankfurt, I accordingly opened the proceedings in the presence of 18 German colleagues and represen-tatives of the LBI centres in New York and Jerusalem. After I had handed over the chair to Reinhard Rürup, the meeting elected a five-member executive. Rürup became its chairman, Monika Richarz his deputy. On the nomination of the LBI representatives from Jerusalem and New York, I was appointed an additional member.

The *Arbeitsgemeinschaft* under Reinhard Rürup's chairmanship has since flourished in close co-operation with the LBI institutes. It has gained wide scholarly recognition. I have been involved in its deliberations whether in person or by correspondence. In concluding this section I might add that, following my retirement in 1983 as professor emeritus, I held for one year a guest-professorship for Jewish history at the University of Munich.

❦

In the course of the eighties it was becoming clear that the scope for original work on German-Jewish history was rapidly shrinking. Three decades of research, much of it under the auspices of the LBI, had come close to exhausting the possibilities. At the same time, German historians had increasingly indicated a desire for German-Jewish history to be 'Germanised', absorbed into general German history, in one extreme formulation 'repatriated'. I had reached the conclusion that remaining work should be left largely to German colleagues. The LBI, instead, must diversify its approach. One possibility lay in the direction of comparative Jewish studies.

In 1988, I had been invited to join a research planning group to work on a project comparing Jewish emancipation in various countries. Meetings at the European University Institute in Fiesole (1989) and in Paris (1990) became the basis for a subsequent pub-lication, *Paths of Emancipation: Jews, States and Citizenships* edited by Pierre Birnbaum and Ira Kaznelson (Princeton/NJ, 1995). It included my chapter 'From „Schutzjuden" to „Deutsche Staatsbürger jüdischen Glaubens": the Long and Bumpy Road of Jewish Emancipation in Germany'.

Concurrently, I had pioneered a study of the cultural role in Britain of German-Jewish immigrants. A conference at the Steinheim

Institute in Duisburg had raised in my mind the question as to the fate of the German-Jewish sub-culture after 1933. It was clear that it had in the main migrated to the Anglo-Saxon countries. After a major project to include also the USA had proved unfeasible, it was decided to limit the study to the UK. A conference in Cambridge in 1988 paved the way for a monumental study, *Second Chance: Two Centuries of German-Speaking Jews in the United Kingdom* (Tübingen, 1991), on which I was co-ordinating editor. The theme of the pioneering work is now being taken up by others.

The next step was a project to compare the Jewish experience in Germany and Italy from the Enlightenment to fascism. Based on a programme designed by Reinhard Rürup, Mario Toscano of Rome University and myself, a major conference was organised at the *Centro Culturale Tedesco* (Goethe Institute) in Rome. My own contribution, predictably, dealt with the role of Jews in German economic life. Among the joint sponsors, besides the LBI London and the *Centro Culturale*, the *Arbeitsgemeinschaft* also figured prominently.

The success of the venture only partly justified expectations. In many cases, two papers from different contributors did not match, making comparison difficult if not impossible. One reason was the relative paucity of Italian research. The conference was nonetheless valuable in drawing attention to general problems of comparative Jewish history. It also helped to stimulate the interest of Italian colleagues in the history of their own Jewish communities. An Italian volume edited by Mario Toscano is in preparation.

The Rome experience contributed to the planning for the next venture I initiated, a detailed comparison of aspects of Jewish history in Germany and Britain. The 'Two Nations' project, extending over three years, is now entering its second year. Some twenty scholars of distinction – German-Jewish, Anglo-Jewish, German and British – are participating. Rainer Liedtke, the project secretary, apart from scholarly work in the field of comparative Jewish history (German and British), is familiar also with the general problems of comparative history. It is largely at his suggestion that both the German and British aspects will, in the great majority of cases, be dealt with in a single paper by one author. We are lucky to have found a sufficient number of both linguistically and academically qualified participants, who met for a preliminary conference in Oxford in 1996. The main conference took place in Cambridge in September 1997. If successful, the pioneering project may become a model for other similar ventures.

Towards the end of one's active career, as is well-known, one tends to return to one's earlier interests. In my case, these are Russian and, to a lesser extent, family history. In 1992, I published *Perestroika under the Tsars*, a study of successive attempts between 1856 and 1914 to introduce far-reaching economic and political reforms – with mixed success – in the Russian empire. Parallels with present-day developments are readily apparent. The book is now being published also in a paperback edition as *An Economic History of Russia, 1856-1914* (London, 1996). Simultaneously with *Perestroika*, my earlier book on Alexander II was re-printed with a new introduction drawing attention to its topical interest. It also appeared as a paperback. A further large study, *Dormant Volcano: Russian Society on the Eve of the Revolutionary Crisis*, is currently in the hands of a publisher. Intended for a wider public, it has in flattering terms been described as 'a wonderful text written as history should be written – wide-ranging, vivid and illustrated with contemporary materials, the literature of the period, full of striking and memorable quotations, based on the most extensive research and documentation...', an unexpected though gratifying testimonial.

I am involved also in local lecturing on the historical background to contemporary events: Russia, Eastern Europe, Yugoslavia, Germany, most recently Britain and the world. There are members of an insular British public who take at least some serious interest in world affairs.

A returning interest in family history, meanwhile, was signalled by an article 'Albert Mosse: a Jewish Judge in Imperial Germany'. My great-uncle was notable, among others, as adviser (1886-1890) to the imperial government of Japan on secondment from the German judicial service. In that capacity, he had the major share in designing the new institutions of local and regional government (largely on the Prusso-German model).

In 1990 I was approached by Elisabeth Kraus, research fellow at the *Institut für Neuere Geschichte*, at Munich University, about making the Mosse family the subject of her *Habilitationsschrift*. I was able to encourage and to help her, particularly at the early stages. In 1994 she presented to a colloquium at the University of Bielefeld an outline of her thesis 'Geschichte der jüdischen Bürgerfamilie Mosse (1800-1970)'. More recently, I have seen a paper on my great-grandfather, the GP who backed the Poles in 1848, a version of Kraus's first chapter. The thesis will be interesting, showing as it does the evolution of an extended Jewish family through four generations from acculturation in the early nineteenth century to almost the present day.

———◆———

Some broader reflections should conclude the present sketch. The German background which made me presently virtually bi-lingual was, at the same time, an advantage and a handicap. I have retained a German accent or, more accurately, intonation. This has, on more than one occasion, made me self-conscious and undermined confidence. On the other hand, familiarity with both languages has enabled me to do work I could not otherwise have done. Again, I have retained from my German youth a characteristic German (or is it German-Jewish?) work ethic and a thoroughness occasionally bordering on the pedantic. Again my sense of humour, though not lacking, is not of the English variety. As already indicated, though underneath a thick layer of Anglo-Saxon pragmatism, a residue of German sentimentality, idealism and tendency to abstraction remained.

A more direct influence on my career as a historian has been the German-Jewish connection. It was this above all which diverted me from a 'normal' academic career as a Russian historian into the marginal field of German-Jewish history. It did not further integration into the British academic establishment. Furthermore, intensive occupation with German-Jewish history was to some extent dysfunctional in creating split interests and a permanent dichotomy between teaching and research. It almost certainly meant fewer research students than I might otherwise have attracted. Single-minded concentration on one or other of the two subjects might well have produced greater results.

German background and intonation as well as my German names marked me out as an easily identifiable member of a minority group. In the army, with encouragement from the authorities, I had Anglicised my name. After the war, I was given the option of keeping the Anglicised form. I decided to return to my original name, partly from pride, partly because almost as soon as I opened my mouth I would still have been identified as a 'foreigner'. At the same time, I have more than once felt embarrassed by my un-English and never correctly pronounced first name. On occasion, I have compromised by using an Anglicised form.

Whilst in tolerant British academe and relatively tolerant society 'Jewishness' was never a problem, 'Germanness' was, more particularly during and after the war. Someone with a German-Jewish background, unlike the native-born British Jew (though even he might be 'given away' by his name), was and remained a 'foreigner'. Though this might act as a spur to achievement, it was not always an asset in the private sphere.

---

My contacts with German historians and institutions, as seen from the foregoing, were close from the moment of my involvement with German-Jewish history. Relations, on occasion cordial and some-times fruitful, were rarely problematical. So far as I personally was concerned, though it was never forgotten, the past rarely cast a shadow. My attitude came fairly early to relate to individuals, not a collectivity.

---

What as a British historian, or, indeed, a historian *tout court* has been my 'contribution' (a term used with some reluctance)? First and more briefly in the organisational field. As has been seen, the continuance of the London LBI in 1978 was the result of my deci-sion. As chairman, I have largely directed its activities with unstint-ing support from senior colleagues. Later, as has also been seen, I became the originator of the *Arbeitsgemeinschaft*, in whose work I have since participated. I also played a part in organising the suc-cessful (if modest) appeal of the London Institute. Overall, I played a significant role in developing Anglo-German co-operation in the field of German-Jewish history. My role as a founder-member of the School of European Studies in the University of East Anglia, as its second Dean during the 'student troubles' and as the long-time head of its historical sector, lies outside the scope of the present profile.

My scholarly contribution is perhaps the more significant. Publications dealing with the German-Jewish *haute bourgeoisie* and particularly its entrepreneurial activities have drawn attention to an important section of German Jewry until then largely neglected. I have helped to make its study 'salonfähig' following prolonged disdain from socialist and Zionist quarters. In the process, I have dented the crude Scholem thesis of the (alleged) German-Jewish 'symbiosis' and its (alleged) failure. ('Symbiosis' for several reasons is, of course, one of the numerous terms best avoided.) I have instead presented a truer and more differentiated view of the 'Jewishness' of members of the group and of their partial integration in German society. In opposition to the theory about the identity of Jewish and Gentile capitalist decision-making, I have drawn attention to distinctive social and cultural influences contributing to the emergence of a Jewish economic sub-culture. I have established, quantitatively, the part of people of Jewish origin in the development of the German economy. Similarly, I have helped to identify the 'contribution' made by German-Jewish immigrants to the social, economic and cultural life of Britain.

I have, to the best of my ability, tried to counteract the widespread tendency to view all earlier German-Jewish history under the aspect of the Holocaust – the Jewish variant of the 'Whig interpretation' of history. In the same spirit, I have rejected the still surviving view of German-Jewish history in Germany as a progression from emancipation and acculturation through 'failed symbiosis' and Zionism to the creation of the state of Israel, another variant of the Whig approach. In a similar spirit, I have tried to resist the pervasive temptation for the Russian historian to see late tsarist history through the distorting mirror of the Bolshevik revolution. Those who went before did not know what was to follow.

What may be a final contribution is the attempt to develop new methods of comparative Jewish history. The focus of attention has been shifted from German Jewry to international comparison identifying both the sub-stratum of common 'Jewishness' and specific variations introduced through contact with surrounding Gentile societies. It may be a way of integrating German-Jewish into wider Jewish history. Here a perspective for new work also on German-Jewish history may be opening up.

<hr />

To look back over the years and perhaps try to assess one's own part may be, as the ancients knew, a cathartic exercise. I am grateful to the editor of this volume and the German Historical Institute London for having furnished the occasion for such self-examination. It has helped me to discover myself: a European historian.

## Selected Writings of Werner E. Mosse

Books

*The European Powers and the German Question 1848-1871: with Special Reference to England and Russia* (Cambridge, 1958; American edition: New York, 1969)

*The Rise and Fall of the Crimean System 1855-1871* (London, 1963)

*Alexander II and the Modernization of Russia* (London, 1958; new edition: London and New York, 1992)

*Entscheidungsjahr 1932: Zur Judenfrage in der Endphase der Weimarer Republik* (Tübingen, 1965, second edition 1966)

*Deutsches Judentum in Krieg und Revolution 1916-1923* (Tübingen, 1971)

*Juden im Wilhelminischen Deutschland 1890-1914* (Tübingen, 1976)

*Jews in the German Economy: The German-Jewish Economic Elite 1820-1935* (Oxford, 1987; Italian edition 1990)

*The German-Jewish Economic Elite 1820-1935: A Socio-Cultural Profile* (Oxford, 1989

*Perestroika under the Tsars: An Economic History of Russia, 1856-1914* (London, 1996)

*Albert Mosse: a Jewish Judge in Imperial Germany* (London, 1983)

*Liberal Europe: The Age of Bourgeois Realism 1848-1875* (London, 1974)

*Das deutsche Judentum und der Liberalismus/German Jewry and Liberalism* (Sankt Augustin, 1986)

Articles and Editorships

(co-ordinating ed.), *Second Chance: Two Centuries of German-speaking Jews in the United Kingdom* (Tübingen, 1991)

with Hans Pohl (eds.), *Jüdische Unternehmer in Deutschland im 19. und 20. Jahrhundert* (Stuttgart, 1992)

'Zwei Präsidenten der Kölner Industrie- und Handelskammer: Louis Hagen und Paul Silverberg', in Jutta Bohnke-Kollwitz et al. (eds), *Köln und das rheinische Judentum* (Cologne, 1984), pp 308-341

'Wilhelm II and the Kaiserjuden: A Problematical Encounter', in Jehuda Reinharz and Walter Schatzberg (eds), *The Jewish Response to*

*German Culture* (Hanover and London, 1985), pp 164-195

'Jewish Marriage Strategies: The German-Jewish Economic Elite', in *Studia Rosenthaliana* (1985), pp 188-202

'Drei Juden in der Wirtschaft Hamburgs: Heine, Ballin, Warburg', in Arno Herzig (ed.), *Die Juden in Hamburg 1590-1990* (Hamburg, 1991), pp 431-447

'Juden im Wirtschaftsleben in Deutschland', in Julius H. Schoeps (ed.), *Neues Lexikon des Judentums* (Gütersloh, 1992), pp 485-487

**Hellmut Pappe**

# The Scholar
# as Businessman[1]

I was born on 29 January 1907 in Liegnitz, the capital of the former Prussian province of Lower Silesia. Liegnitz had been German for some 700 years. It was there that the Mongol invasion came to an end in 1241, and it has been known as one of the main centres of the Silesian poets school.

On my paternal side I come from an industrialists' family. I grew up in a pleasant villa on the outskirts of the town. My mother was a North German who came from Stadtoldendorf in the Solling. Her father, Carl Ullmann, was a professional farmer and had gypsum deposits on his land. My family's historical background goes back well over the whole of the previous century, that is for about two hundred years; my parents were thus upper middle class. Speaking in stratification terms they were the leading Jewish family in the town, but not actively involved in Jewish religious life. My grandfather had been an atheist and my father an agnostic. However, they had both continued to keep, though not to occupy, seats in the synagogue. They were totally emancipated and secularised.

I went to school in Liegnitz. It was the oldest school in town, founded in 1309, the Municipal Protestant *Gymnasium*. It had a humanist and a realist division: I was in the humanist division. Most of our teachers were dedicated and kind people. I passed my *Abitur* after twelve years at school in 1925. I started university in Freiburg im Breisgau, then moved the next winter to Breslau and the following summer to Geneva. I was a law student, and the subjects of particular interest to me were legal history and the sociology of law.

In the beginning there were no teachers who really influenced me particularly, but when I was in Freiburg I attended lectures by Otto

163

Lenel, who was one of the leading Romanists in the country, a lively and interesting man. I heard the philosopher Edmund Husserl and that means, thank goodness, not Martin Heidegger. I still regard the latter's philosophy as capricious in its subject-matter and pretentious in form. Heidegger stands and falls with his new ontology, which is a farrago of peculiar assumptions concerning the meaning of being and the essence of man. As he puts it, 'the idea of logic gets dissolved in the maelstrom of basic questioning'.[2] However, I found Husserl a dry old man and soon stopped attending his lectures. Another remarkable professor was Hermann Kantorowicz who taught sociology of law. He had just written a book on Germany and the spectre of encirclement,[3] and that led to a great deal of unrest at the university. In Geneva there was nobody of real importance for me. Jean Piaget, the psychologist, I heard not as a student, but only on later visits. But it was in Geneva that I discovered Ernst Cassirer and C.G. Jung. More recently I have greatly valued the friendship and intellectual support which I have received from two Geneva scholars, Antony Babel and Jean Starobinski.

I was influenced most strongly during my university days by Eugen Rosenstock-Huessy who taught at the University of Breslau, and whose book *Die europäischen Revolutionen* was later rewritten for publication in America under the title *Out of Revolution*.[4] He was extremely stimulating. I attended some of his lectures and actually was his last assistant (*Fakultätsassistent*) from 1931 until 1933.

Rosenstock-Huessy was in the law faculty; in fact he held, since 1923, the chair which Otto Gierke had filled in the 1880s. He had been first *Privatdozent* (lecturer) in legal history at Leipzig, but he was a man of many interests such as history, theology, philosophy of language, psychology, social reform, labour conditions and labour law. He founded the *Akademie der Arbeit* in Frankfurt. One of his students in Leipzig before the First World War was Franz Rosenzweig, the theologian and translator of the Bible. Rosenstock-Huessy thought that it was then that Rosenzweig had imbibed the philosophy of 'Ich und Du', and that Rosenzweig had passed it on to Martin Buber.

Rosenstock-Huessy was a very innovative historian. He wrote on the Royal household and the Germanic tribes,[5] and defined the meaning of German as part of the *lingua franca* in the Frankish realm. That had a bearing later on his political views when, like many people today, he felt that the end of the war was also the end of the nation-state in Germany. In order to escape from itself, Germany would have to be recreated as part of a Greater Europe. I was unable to share Rosenstock-Huessy's notion of history, stimulating though it was in its details. He stood close to the Anglican concept of history as depicted by Duncan Forbes.[6] The desire to reconcile religion and philosophy put its advocates under constant restraint, resulting in mysticism as well as rancorous misrepresentation of the thought of lucid and humanitarian sages such as Descartes, Condillac, Condorcet and John Stuart Mill. My own credo has been the dialectic of necessity and freedom, the pursuit of the facts of truth and the values of happiness, the critique of historical unreason and the *Friedensstiftung* (pacifism) of Hume and Kant, the true history of the past in combination with the history of a better future,[7] that is, a free choice of responsibility within the confines of the traditions of time and place.

In 1929 I passed my legal examination, the 'Referendarexamen', in Breslau. I was a 'Referendar' (candidate for the higher civil service) first at a small *Amtsgericht* (district court) in the Silesian town Haynau and after that in Breslau. From the spring of 1930 I combined the *Referendariat* with teaching at the university (*Fakultätsassistent*). In 1933 Rosenstock-Huessy went to Berlin for a year on loan to the Ministry of Justice to work on law reform, but he could not come back because he would have been arrested. I was not dismissed after Hitler's seizure of power in 1933, but the post expired and was not renewed. That had more to do with Rosenstock-Huessy than with me. I was not dismissed from state service until August 1933. With Rosenstock-Huessy's help I saw the cultural attaché of the French embassy in Berlin, who offered to take me and a few others to the Sorbonne. He had the idea at the time, and stuck to it for about a year or two, that it might be useful for the French to have young Germans in Paris with authentic knowledge of German attitudes.

However, I could not go because, returning from Berlin, I went on a walk with a friend who smoked and I suffered a lung haemorrhage. I should have mentioned before that in *Obertertia* in school I had suffered a pernicious pneumonia and I had a relapse in the year of my *Abitur*. So for the next few years, from 1933 to 1936, I was a patient. I spent this time partly in Germany and partly in the Slovak High Tatra, including half of 1934 in Matliary, the sanatorium in which Franz Kafka had been a patient. I did not really recover from my illness, although we thought I had.

I got married in December 1936. My wife and I had been friends for a long time. She came from an old Jewish family. On her father's side the family's firm Hirsch S. Krieg had constantly been in the hands of the family since 1812. Her maternal grandfather, Louis Waldenburg, was a professor at the University of Berlin and a chief consultant at the Berlin hospital, the Charité. After our wedding we moved to Berlin. By that time I had decided that there was no point in joining the German opposition; this meant people I had been friends with from the *Boberhaus* which was the creation of Eugen Rosenstock-Huessy. It had been built by the architect Hans Poelzig in Löwenberg in Silesia. There, Rosenstock-Huessy had arranged three of his voluntary *Arbeitslager* (work camps). Out of them arose the Kreisau Circle (*Kreisauer Kreis*), the resistance movement, whose leading members were Helmuth James von Moltke and Horst von Einsiedel. At the *Boberhaus* we also had an interdisciplinary seminar on liberty in which I took part. That was in August or early September 1930. On that occasion I made friends with the historian Peter Rassow, who later became professor in Cologne and President of the Academy of Mainz. In 1954 we spent several wonderful days together again. We remained close friends until his death in 1961.

In January 1933 I became an active member of the Zionist Organisation. Apart from that I was a columnist with Jewish newspapers. At that time I had completed my doctoral dissertation on marital law, *Methodische Strömungen in der eherechtsgeschichtlichen Forschung* which was published in 1934. My supervisor was originally Eugen Rosenstock-Huessy, but when he had to leave Breslau, Walter Schmidt-Rimpler, who was later in Bonn took over.

At Easter 1937 we went to Berlin, and I became the secretary-general of the German Friends of the University of Jerusalem. I relished the friendship of my predecessors Joachim Prinz and Konrad Kaiser as well as of David Schlossberg, Walter Gross, Ernst Hoffmann and Eleazar Sukenik. It was during my time in office that we were closed down by the *Gestapo* during a meeting in the house of Otto Warburg, who was a professor at the University of Berlin and a member of the Prussian Academy. He had been the world president of the Zionist Organisation. At the beginning of 1938 I started work with the Jewish support group *Jüdischer Hilfsverein* in Berlin. I wrote for them part of a book on the United States of America and how to become an immigrant there. While working with the *Hilfsverein* I had another haemorrhage and had to go to Davos where my wife's uncle Adolf Loewy was head of the Swiss High Altitude Research Institute. I stayed at a Jewish sanatorium until July 1939. My wife came out of Germany and joined me. She had obtained a three-week permit for Switzerland because the chief of police in Davos had been a friend of my wife's uncle. After the three weeks had expired she had to leave and went to England. She had been there before; she had friends in Cambridge and was staying with them until I followed in August 1939. Through the work on my dissertation I had learnt to read English without difficulty.

My wife, who had a doctorate in French Romantic literature and had been teaching English at the *Landschulheim* Caputh near Potsdam,[8] was allowed to come to England because she had a permit to go to New Zealand as a tutor on a sheep station in the Southern Alps, as had I as her companion. After a fortnight together in Cambridge we boarded a ship to New Zealand. The sea journey took the best part of three months because war broke out after we had just passed the Suez Canal. We were on a Dutch ship and supposed to change in Ceylon onto an English boat which was, however, recalled for war service. We were thus taken to Java where we had a fortnight in the mountains. We then continued our journey, with all the men sleeping on deck and the women in the cargo hold, on a freighter to Sydney, and after another fortnight on to New Zealand. We arrived there in October 1939. My wife's employer was a New Zealand farmer with a liberal English wife.

The couple had a son of fourteen and a daughter of thirteen who had been at school at Bedales in England. However, the parents brought them home because of the clouds of war on the horizon. They had tried to find an English tutor unsuccessfully, and so this position was offered to my wife. She had told these kind people that she had a husband who suffered from tuberculosis. They wrote back saying that they had the best climate in the world, and welcomed us both. This proved to be my unique opportunity at the time before antibiotics. The farm was a sheep-run of 24,000 acres at a height of between 1,400 and 3,000 feet above sea level, with 7,000 Merino sheep. The owners had a hut built for us, at some distance from the house, and we lived there for the next ten years. We then moved to Christchurch, the main city of the South Island, because it so happened that the farmer, William Hamilton (later Sir), was not only an outstanding sportsman and mountaineer but also an engineer of genius. He came from a family of Scottish origin, his wife from a distinguished English liberal family. She had come to New Zealand after her favourite brother, one of the early flying men, had been killed in the First World War. After our first three months at the farm, our boss asked me whether I would like to help him as a secretary to build up an engineering firm. He had designed some earth-moving equipment such as bulldozers and related machinery.

He offered me £1 a week as a salary, so I was earning something myself. The firm took on a number of munitions contracts which established manufacturers did not want because they were difficult to handle. But these presented no problems for our engineers.

We started manufacturing in Christchurch with a view to the post-war period. We wanted to be ready for peace. I resumed at this time some scholarly work. The problem was, of course, that in New Zealand one is at a great distance from the rest of the world. This is the reason why there is some sort of brotherhood amongst the intellectuals and the artists of the country. After a short time we knew many of them, not only the people in the south, but also in the North Island, including a short correspondence with Karl Wolfskehl, who was then living in Auckland. Friends came at times to visit us in our solitude, including the historians Leicester Webb (later Canberra) and Peter Munz, the philosophers Arthur and Mary Prior (later Manchester and Oxford), the painter Eve Page, the poet and editor of *Landfall* Charles Brasch, and the musicians Frederick Page, Douglas Lilburn and Lily Krausz. On the whole, it was not a difficult time for us in New Zealand. There was temporarily the danger of a Japanese invasion but one more or less disregarded it. Actually, we were not unhappy at all because amongst books I had read in earlier times, particularly in my last school years, there were some of a somewhat romantic nature such as books by Friedrich Nietzsche and Fyodor Dostoevsky. My wife and I had often said we should experience mountain life for a period of time, like Nietzsche.

We had simply started a new life in New Zealand. As it happened, all our books, manuscripts, pictures and everything that we were allowed to take with us from Germany were on a German freighter which got as far as Curaçao in the Caribbean. Then the phoney war broke out. When, in 1940, the real war started, the ship tried to break the British blockade and, when it did not succeed, it was scuttled by its crew. We lost everything, in some respects we lost our whole past. Otherwise it was a happy time in New Zealand, with skating and skiing in the winter and with all sorts of other sports. I gradually grew stronger, and my wife took part in the sheep work on horseback and similar things whilst preparing the children for their matriculation. When war came to an end the firm had a brand new factory in Christchurch and developed into an important engineering firm.

Against this background, my first scholarly paper was accordingly entitled 'Manufacturing in New Zealand'. I was now joint chief executive of a pretty considerable firm, dealing, on behalf of the company, with the Government as well as with the administration. I was never interned as an alien because Bill Hamilton vouched for us. We made friends within the community and fitted in extremely well. I had the confidence both of the boss and the staff. In the best times we had a staff of about 450 engineers, which in heavy engineering is not negligible.

In 1948, on invitation, I applied for a lectureship in politics. The University of Christchurch appointed me, with a view to creating a new department, senior lecturer in charge of politics. But it took two years before the funds came through. By that time I needed more money because we wanted my mother to come to live with us in New Zealand. As I earned more in the firm than at a university I stayed on in business for a while. We spent the year 1954 overseas, partly on business and partly as some sort of sabbatical. On our way back we stayed a month at the Australian National University in Canberra where I took a number of seminars. The National University is a research university.

Things having become easier for us in the 1950s, I resigned from the firm at the end of 1957. As we had no children there was no point in getting rich. Early in 1958 I joined the Australian National University as a research fellow in social philosophy and stayed there for three years. It was a time when I could publish a great deal. We were quite happy in Canberra. The climate is wonderful. The place is about 700 metres above sea level in the mountains. It is a very popular venue among academics, very much like Princeton in the United States. One has a lot of time for research and few teaching obligations. My book on John Stuart Mill, which I wrote in Canberra, was published in 1960. The National University was loved by many people who came there as guests for half a year or so. There we made friends with visitors such as Harry Court, the author of the *Concise Cambridge Economic History*, Sir Alec Carr-Saunders of the London School of Economics, the anthropologist Max Gluckman and the editor Norman MacKenzie. They encouraged us to come to England.

The most eminent visitor we met in Australia was Asa Briggs (later Lord Briggs of Lewes). He arranged a lectureship for me at the new University of Sussex near Brighton. I had once sent him an article from the farm for a periodical which he published, together with Italians, called *Oriente*. It was an article about German disciples of Edmund Burke, and I had enclosed an article on John Stuart Mill. The lectureship in sociology was the only vacant position at the time.

Two years later, in 1960, the vice-chancellor invited me to apply for the foundation chair in sociology at Sussex. However, I refused to do this because I did not want to enter into any administrative commitments. In the end, I was ten years at the University of Sussex, five years full-time. Thereafter, I got a part-time readership in the history of social thought. We were thus able to spend most of the springs and early summers in Tuscany, and worked there in the archives of Pescia. The offer to come to Sussex was made in 1961 but we did not arrive in England before October 1962, having spent a year in Geneva in between. I retired from the university in June 1972.

I enjoyed the first few years in Sussex because at that time you knew everybody, the scientists as well as the colleagues in the arts faculty. In the second year of the university we had fifteen members of staff and about 300 students. There were Asa Briggs, David Daiches, the Dean of English, and Martin Wight of International Relations. We had animated lunches and so on, and all got on extremely well. The new University of Sussex was supposed to be strictly inter-disciplinary. However, it became less and less so because very few people could or wanted to co-operate. They, instead, favoured their own disciplines. I was prejudiced in favour of interdisciplinary work because, already when at school, I had read Friedrich Schiller's inaugural lecture in the chair of history at Jena, with its differentiation between 'Brotgelehrter', a materialist academic, and a 'wahrer Gelehrter', a true scholar.

When asked to sum up my life, I may safely say that I felt at home both as a scholar and a businessman. During my time in New Zealand, Australia, Geneva and England I had kept contact with German academics. I had stayed in correspondence with Peter Rassow and the classicist Kurt von Fritz. Moreover, I had a school friend, Dr Christoph Andritzky, who had left East Germany and became *Stadtdirektor* in Mannheim and Senator at the city's university. My wife and I visited Germany frequently, at least once a year, mainly on our way to Geneva or Tuscany. We used to stay with friends in either Mannheim or Heidelberg. In 1969 I read a paper at the German *Werkbund*'s annual meeting in Stuttgart.

As I have already said, the years in Canberra and then at Sussex gave me time to think and write. One of my research subjects was John Stuart Mill, on whom I published various papers and a booklet. When we came to England I wrote a number of articles for the *Encyclopedia of Philosophy*, including ones on Arnold Gehlen, Ernst Jünger, Werner Sombart and philosophical anthropology.

While at Canberra I discovered Jean Charles Léonard Simonde de Sismondi. He was a highly innovative and fertile mind. With Madame de Staël, his intimate friend, he created the discipline of literary criticism in French.[9] He inaugurated modern French historiography with his *History of the French People*. He was the first, after the annalists, to lay the foundations of modern Italian history with his *History of the Italian Republics in the Middle Ages*. As an economist, he originated the neo-liberal welfare economics of the social market; and, following Adam Smith, he introduced the concepts of time and place into economic analysis, half a century before the historical school of Wilhelm Roscher. He carried on the tradition of Niccolò Machiavelli, James Harrington and the great Scots of the eighteenth century. So, rather than John Stuart Mill, my main subject has been Sismondi. My field of research was the history of ideas, or *Geistesgeschichte*.

I believe my German upbringing has had a substantial influence on my academic life and work. First, when I got up to university, even at school in the last two years, I read a great deal because of my illness. There were, *inter alia*, two works which influenced me. My mother owned the favourite work of her father's, who as I mentioned was a farmer. That was Wilhelm Heinrich Riehl's *Naturgeschichte des deutschen Volkes*, published between 1851 and 1869. The other thing was that my father had a good library on political economy. There were, apart from a book by Alfred Weber on the origins of the state,[10] the *Erinnerungsgabe für Max Weber* which had come out in 1923 and contained an article by Werner Sombart on 'Die Anfänge der Soziologie'.[11] Although I did not understand all the ideas and controversies, I found them highly thought-provoking. As far as the English academic tradition is concerned, I was strongly influenced by the eighteenth century, especially by the Scots, that is the Scottish Enlightenment, including the non-Scots Immanuel Kant and Edward Gibbon. I have completed the first volume of a biography of Sismondi, as well as most of a book on Sismondi's impact on his own time. But so far I have not approached any publishers, a matter of old-age indolence. I should have liked to do a study dealing with the continuities I have observed in John Stuart Mill, Friedrich Albert Lange and Wilhelm Dilthey, but there is no time left for it. Since the late 1970s, we have been handicapped by illness and major operations. On the positive side, however, we have been able to turn our bungalow and its secluded garden into some kind of earthly paradise.

Considering my international background, and looking back on my life, my true compatriots live in England, Germany, Israel, New

Zealand, Australia, France, Geneva and Italy. I am a cosmopolitan, or a European. So it would be too narrow to describe me either as German or British.

A good deal of my life has been happy despite the terrible experiences of the Nazi period. That I can end on an optimistic note is partly possible thanks to a very happy marriage, partly due to the loyalty of good friends and partly to the satisfaction derived from stimulating work. Having had to emigrate is a matter of mixed feelings. As a consequence, I have been deprived of twenty-five years of scholarly work. To that extent Hitler has beaten me. But then, I had the New Zealand episode, and I found a congenial environment in England, neither of which I would like to have missed.

## Notes

1       This essay is based on an interview with the editor which took place in Brighton on 2 June 1996.

2       I have treated this in my paper 'On Philosophical Anthropology', *Australasian Journal of Philosophy* 39 (1961), pp 59-64.

3       Hermann Kantorowicz, *Der Geist der englischen Politik und das Gespenst der Einkreisung Deutschlands* (Berlin, 1929).

4       Eugen Rosenstock-Huessy, *Die europäischen Revolutionen: Volkscharaktere und Staatenbildung* (Jena, 1923); Idem., *Out of Revolution: Autobiography of Western Man* (New York, 1938).

5       Eugen Rosenstock-Huessy, *Königshaus und Stämme in Deutschland von 911 bis 1250* (Leipzig, 1914).

6       Duncan Forbes, *The Liberal Anglican Idea of History* (Cambridge, 1952).

7       Compare Wilhelm Dilthey's distinction between *sichere* and *wahre* history.

8       See Hildegard Feidel-Mertz (ed.), *Ein verlorenes Paradies: Das jüdische Kinder- und Landschulheim Caputh 1932-1938* (Frankfurt-am-Main, 1994).

9       J.C.L. Simonde de Sismondi, *De la littérature du Midi de l'Europe*, 2 volumes (Paris, 1813; English translation second edition: London, 1846).

10      Alfred Weber, *Die Krise des modernen Staatsgedankens in Europa* (Stuttgart, 1925).

11      Melchior Palyi, in collaboration with Gerhart von Schulze Gaevernitz, Werner Sombart, Franz Eulenburg et al. (eds),

*Hauptprobleme der Soziologie: Erinnerungsgabe für Max Weber* (Munich and Leipzig, 1923).

## Selected Writings of Hellmut Pappe

### Books

*Methodische Strömungen in der eherechtsgeschichtlichen Forschung* (Würzburg, 1934)

*John Stuart Mill and the Harriet Taylor Myth* (Melbourne and Cambridge, 1960)

*Sismondis Weggenossen* (Geneva, 1963)

(ed.), *La Statistique du Département du Léman de Sismondi* (Geneva, 1971)

### Articles

'Manufacturing in New Zealand', *New Zealand Geographer* 1946, pp 329-344

'Some Notes on T.S. Eliot's concept of culture', *Landfall* 1950, pp 230-243

'Wakefield and Marx', *The Economic History Review* 4 (1951), pp 88-97

'On the Validity of Judicial Decisions in the Nazi Era', *The Modern Law Review* 1960, pp 260-274

'Rocking the Cradle of Erewhon: Samuel Butler and Darwin', *Historical Studies* (Australia) 1961, pp 106-111

'On Philosophical Anthropology', *Australasian Journal of Philosophy* 39 (1961), pp 47-64

'The Early Draft of John Stuart Mill's Autobiography', *The Journal of English and Germanic Philology* 1962, pp 655-661

'Mill and Tocqueville', *Journal of the History of Ideas* 25 (1964), pp 217-234

'The Early Letters of John Stuart Mill', *Mind* 1967, pp 442-449

'Enlightenment', in *Dictionary of the History of Ideas*, volume 2 (Oxford, 1973), pp 89-100

'La formation de la pensée socio-économique de Sismondi: Sismondi et Adam Smith', in S. Stelling-Michaud (ed.), *Sismondi*

*Européen* (Geneva and Paris, 1976), pp 13-34, 107-110

'Sismondi et John Stuart Mill', *Economies et Sociétés* 1976, pp 1150-1160

'The English Utilitarians and the Athenian Democracy', in R.R. Bolgar (ed.), *Classical Influences on European Culture 1700 to 1870* (Cambridge, 1978), pp 295-307

'Sismondi's System of Liberty', *Journal of the History of Ideas* 40 (1979), pp 251-266

**Arnold Paucker**

# Mommsenstrasse to
# Devonshire Street

If I am to assess my own modest contribution to historiography – which in my case is that of a minor historian, editor and *Wissenschaft*-organiser – I am confronted with a curious dichotomy. My triple role was determined by my appointment some 37 years ago as director of an institute for the study of German-Jewish history in the United Kingdom. Given my subject, it is obvious that both my research and my organisational activities are rooted in my German-Jewish past, however distant it may now seem. Yet, on the one hand my preoccupation with historical processes reflects beliefs I have firmly adhered to since my youth, and on the other it constitutes a conscious revolt against prejudices with which I was inculcated at the very same time.

I was born in 1921 into a fairly affluent Berlin Jewish family which was then living in a commodious flat in Charlottenburg's Mommsenstrasse, where I grew up. My parents were assimilated, emancipated and as much integrated into German society as a Jewish family could then be. My father was a manufacturer of leather goods which were sold in a number of shops he owned in Berlin. He was a kindly man and a benevolent employer, so much so that his former employees continued to visit him after 1933 and even after 'Kristallnacht', and up to my parents' almost last-minute emigration (to Shanghai), a touching sign of the human values which persisted even under relentless pressure. My parents' Gentile friends stood by them as well. In religious and political matters, my parents were nominally liberal in their outlook – and no more than that. A dash of German patriotism was *de rigueur*. My parents were not intellectuals, but they were cultured in a way then expected of the Jewish middle class. By 1932 they were already impoverished on account of the depression years, and also politically confused. It was left to their precocious twelve-year-old elder son to advise them to vote Social Democrat after the collapse of the liberal centre which, like so many of their co-religionists, they duly did.

It was only too easy for the very young to become politicised in the early thirties. I remember insisting that I and my younger brother should have the three-arrows symbol of the anti-Nazi republican *Eiserne Front* stitched onto our bathing trunks, and our being beaten up at the Halensee swimming baths by some Nazi oafs as a result. That was in 1932. I remember seeing the marching columns of the *SA* and the counter-demonstration of the *Reichsbanner* and the *Rotfrontkämpferbund* in our neighbourhood in the centre of Berlin. I can conjure up the scene of the frenzied crowds cheering the torchlight parades down the Kurfürstendamm on the way to Unter den Linden on the night of 30 January 1933, when the Nazis took power. And I know that I, like other Jewish boys and girls during the early years of the Nazi regime when I was still in Germany, was not only aware of the absolute wickedness of this so-called National Resurrection, but also saw the grotesque, even ludicrous, aspects which are clear to many young Germans today.[1]

I had been earmarked for the usual *Gymnasium*/university run in conformity with my Jewish social group, though nothing was to come of it. The brief spell at a *Gymnasium* revealed a bent for German and history before I was expelled with the other Jewish pupils from my school, the *Kaiser Friedrich Realschule*. Here my formal education was abruptly terminated, only to be resumed in the United Kingdom in the early 1950s.

It was very much the custom in my circles to join a youth movement. My choice in this was by no means guided by my parents, either in Weimar Germany or under Nazi persecution. Given my background, it seemed almost natural that I should become a 'Pimpf' in a German youth movement in the two years before 1933; the idea of joining a Jewish youth movement would not have occurred to me. The *Deutsch-Republikanischer Pfadfinderbund* (*DRPB*), into which I was recruited, was less nationalistic than other youth movements, and staunchly republican. Probably about one third of its members came from the Jewish middle class. Relations between Jews and Gentiles were untroubled. When the *DRPB* was dissolved by the new rulers in the summer of 1933, the non-Jews were absorbed by the Hitler Youth; those young Jews who remained attached to the youth movement ideal either joined 'assimilationist'

Jewish *Bünde,* such as the *Schwarzes Fähnlein,* or what I would call the moderate Zionist, actually culturally still very German *Werkleute,* which I myself joined. Some historians of the *Werkleute* would differ with my assessment, which discerns many trends: a Martin Buber-inspired Judaism, a continuing deep involvement with German culture, a socialist Zionism, even an anti-fascist indoctrination, all depending on whatever *Führer* one had in charge.

Anyone who was involved in the German youth movement is tempted to write volumes on the élitist, manipulated, *Führer*-orientated, culture-imbued German and Jewish *Bünde* in Germany. They mark their disciples even in old age. As an editor I was later to allot almost excessive space, between the years 1965 and 1990, to the evaluation of the various Jewish youth movements by historians of German Jewry. And while the Jewish youth movements kept clear of any illegal activities against the Nazi regime, on the strict advice of the official leadership of the Jewish community and the *Führer* of the youth organisations, some one per cent of its members paid no heed to this admonition. I myself was very marginally and fleetingly enrolled in such 'resistance' activities before leaving Germany.

At the end of 1936 I left for Palestine. Significantly, I was given two good-bye parties, one by my Gentile friends of the *DRPB,* now wearing Hitler Youth outfits and one by my more recent *Werkleute* friends. I emigrated with a *Werkleute* group. Almost by chance we were not sent for the customary two-year Kibbutz training, but by a decision from above, my group was channelled to Ben Shemen, an out-of-the-common school which exercised a marked influence on its pupils.

Official accounts of the school tend to skate over the surface, in the bland manner of such productions.[2] Ben Shemen went through various phases: founded by its Director, Dr Siegfried Lehmann, as a school for orphans from Lithuania and problem children from Tel Aviv, it began life almost as a corrective establishment for social re-training, somewhat in the style of A.S. Neill's Summerhill, though Lehmann himself was influenced by Kurt Hahn's Salem School. With the coming of the Nazi regime and the influx of German-Jewish youth groups and, later on, socialist youth groups from Poland, it became better known for its cultural and élitist qualities, producing many remarkable personalities (the former Prime Minister of Israel, Shimon Peres, was a pupil two years below me). After the war, giving a new life to young concentration camp survivors, it was to change character again.

During my time there it was distinguished by many interesting features. First of all, it was co-educational and 'free' discipline was firmly advocated, very much in the wake of modern school movements in other countries. Functioning, however, primarily as an agricultural high school, training the future cultivators of the soil of Israel, it was for me and my kind educationally unsuitable. After attending a few lessons I abandoned any form of school attendance, though doing my stint of agricultural work, and evolved a course of reading to suit myself. The establishment preached a 'Dorfkultur', attempting to create a sort of enlightened peasantry, at once musical and literary, a cultural aim which also produced an undercurrent of discontent in those for whom a preparation for a future village culture was not enough. There was the reading and re-reading of the Bible *à la* Buber/Rosenzweig, which resulted in a Bible-weariness and the ironic disapproval of part of the school population. Yet Ben Shemen had many more positive aspects too. The predominant political tendency was a moderate socialist Zionism with the emphasis on Arab-Jewish understanding – Lehmann was a close friend of Martin Buber – which had a lasting effect on many of its pupils. For a time some turned away from Zionism altogether, seeking Jewish salvation in the delusive notion of the universal brotherhood of the proletariat, which was certainly not the founder's intention. Looking back, though as a wilful pupil I received no formal education there at all, the atmosphere of Ben Shemen remains vivid. I feel its impact even today.

One formative experience of the years 1936-1939 which I spent in Ben Shemen was the civil war in Spain. It is not easy to explain some sixty years later how the fight of the Spanish people against fascism stirred us. Too young to join the International Brigades, the battle absorbed us totally; victories of the Republic were announced by the staff and celebrated by the school. The Brigaders were our heroes. The defeat of the Republican forces dismayed us, its significance for Europe and the Jews was to us all too clear. That so many Jews – so many German-Jews – had fought in Spain deeply impressed us. Again, this was reflected later in editorial projects of mine.

At the end of 1941, I volunteered for the British Army. For my generation this needs no explanation; it was our duty to fight Nazi Germany. German Jewry was strongly represented in all the Allied armies. (Adding here a footnote to my own more humdrum military service: all those younger members of my extended family who were lucky enough to escape Nazi extermination were either involved with the German resistance, fought with the partisans, or served with the British commandos.) Chronicling the contribution of the German Jews to the Allied war effort and the victory over Nazi Germany was to become in recent years one of my editorial concerns.

I saw service first in the Middle East and then, from the autumn of 1943 to the end of 1946, in Italy. In May 1945 I was reunited with my brother at the Italian/Swiss frontier post in Chiasso. He had escaped from the deportation of his entire Jewish school in France, and with the help of the Maquis had reached the safety of Switzerland. I had witnessed the liberation of Northern Italy; it is difficult to convey, more than half a century later, the almost revolutionary atmosphere of this short period: the national uprising, encounters with the partisan brigades, the jubilation over the fall of fascism. One views the events more coolly today: they were less clear-cut than they seemed at the time, when one was more easily swayed. Fascism was not dead: the images of liberation from half a century ago are now marred by recent political happenings in Italy. Even with these reservations, I am left with a lasting affection for Italy and its culture. My time in Italy also opened the way to connections later on with Italian friends and colleagues, which led eventually to lectures and publications in Italy on the themes of Jewish self-defence and Jewish resistance. I lived in Florence for quite some time after my demobilisation, and there met my future English wife during a summer course at Florence University. I came to live in England early in 1950.

It must have been my service in the British Army which made integration into English provincial life so easy. I felt at home at once. When some thirty-five years later I found myself for a spell in an open ward of a London hospital, surrounded by British ex-servicemen of my own age, I had a sense of complete belonging. This was my group. England had now been my country for a long time.

In 1951, the total lack of formal educational qualifications forced me, if ever I was even to have the hope of attending a university, to turn myself back into an adolescent schoolboy, apart from working for a living, as an export clerk at the James Motorcycle Co. in Greet, Birmingham. For some two years, from the age of thirty to thirty-two, I had to pass, at every level, all the examinations needed for university entrance. It might seem rather a harsh fate, but it had its compensations. Most of my studies were meant to fulfil only the basic requirements, but my work in A-level history left me with an abiding interest in and an enthusiasm for Puritanism, Whig politics, radicalism and the British socialist movement. Reading for A-level English generated a deep affection for English literature, and I became an avid book collector. The collecting and reading of a wide range of authors and browsing in second-hand bookshops occupies my leisure, and also, in some ways, affects my approach to my subject and my style of writing.

Except for purposes of study and later on for professional needs, I began to read less and less German literature and to identify more and more with the English historical past and with English customs. The importance of the niceties of tea-making and serving impressed themselves on me very early. As my English friends often remark, British naturalisation should have been awarded me for my skills in this particular art alone.

I entered the German Department at Birmingham University in 1953, which then ranked, after Cambridge, as the best in England. That was entirely due to Roy Pascal and his well-chosen staff: William B. Lockwood, Siegbert Prawer and Richard Hinton Thomas. Pascal was undoubtedly the leading British Germanist of his generation. What singled his department out was a new attitude to German studies which would appear less revolutionary today but was quite novel in the late forties, when he first came to Birmingham as a young professor. Not content with the dissection of texts, the analysis of poetry, and the learning of Middle High German grammar by rote, his three-year course attempted at the same time to encompass the study of German social and political life, and to generate in his students a real understanding of Germany's complex history and those elements leading to the ultimate evil of National Socialist dictatorship. Pascal was the first of four outstanding figures in the United Kingdom who had a strong effect on my work. It is not surprising that I am not the only Pascal Germanist who became a historian.

Oddly enough my first return to Germany was the result of British university stipulations: the compulsory term one had to spend at a German university in order to become more proficient in the German language, rather superfluous in my case. In 1955 I chose the then still sleepy Bonn, and the Rhineland seemed strange, almost alien to me, except that the natives spoke my mother tongue. It could have been Switzerland as far as I was concerned (an alternative offered to me by Pascal, who thought I might not wish to go to Germany). Berlin, to which I came back some eight years later when I was invited to lecture there, was different. The return to the scenes of my childhood was an emotional experience.

Having obtained a First in my Finals meant that I was able to apply for a grant for further study. For my research – 1956 to 1959 – I turned to a then out-of-the-way subject, Western Yiddish, which, considering my background, was rather unusual. Yiddish was disdained by the assimilated German Jew as 'Mauscheldeutsch' and 'Jargon', while in fact Western Yiddish, originating in Germany some thousand years ago, was a true German 'Nebensprache'. It was the influence of Pascal's teaching on Reformation literature and the early German prose novel which made me select as the topic of my thesis a comparative study of the transfer of German 'Volksbücher' to the Yiddish of the German ghettos; but soon Solomon Birnbaum, the great Hebrew palaeographer and the founder of modern Yiddish studies, became my mentor. Without his guidance I could hardly have pursued my research. This was the time when Germanists such as Frederick Norman, Leonard Forster and Peter Ganz also stimulated me; they had begun to pay some attention to Old Yiddish within the curriculum of German studies at British universities. Yiddish studies now flourish everywhere, and much of what I did then has been superseded. Yet I would claim that I made here my first contribution to Jewish history, establishing that the Jewish public was far more familiar with German popular literature than had been hitherto assumed, that a wholly literate Jewish readership was at times supplied with more editions than their largely illiterate German neighbours, that versions for Jewish readers departed substantially from the German texts and were not merely 'women's' literature and so on. For me it pointed a way to a wider study of Jewish history.

In 1959, when I completed my studies, the London Leo Baeck Institute, which had been founded whilst I was still an undergraduate, was looking for a Director with a German-Jewish background and a British university education. A professional historian would have been preferred, but the Board settled for me although I was then a Germanist. One should add that an émigré organisation – and at the time the Leo Baeck Institute was exactly that, though certainly not so today – would always find it difficult to appoint a candidate from the older generation, whom those in the Institute all knew, and thus would not be able to come to a unanimous decision on anyone. They needed an unknown, and here was I, a neutral element, a non-Londoner from a provincial university. So they found it easy to appoint me, and were, I was amused to see, very much intrigued by my preoccupation with Western Yiddish. I had originally thought of a career as a university teacher, but quickly realised that an institute of this type might give me more scope. I have never regretted this choice.

My first mundane task in 1959 was to supervise the Institute's move from rather ramshackle accommodation in the Finchley area to more generous quarters in the West End in the house of the Wiener Library in Devonshire Street. That was quite in keeping with our expanding activities and our links with the Wiener Library, and we have been there ever since.

The Leo Baeck Institute, founded by the generations of my fathers and grandfathers for research in modern German-Jewish history, is well known today. I have written elsewhere on the London Institute in great detail.[3] It was then in its infancy and is now in its fifth decade. As most of its founders died many years ago, it is now run by another generation more rooted in English life.

And here I come to the third great influence on my work, Robert Weltsch. It was Solomon Birnbaum to whom I owe my enthusiasm for Jewish learning; but it was Weltsch who taught me my trade as editor and initiated me into recent German-Jewish history. There is as yet no biography of this intriguing Prague Jew. Robert Weltsch was Chairman of the London Leo Baeck Institute from 1955 to 1978 and the founder editor of its *Year Book*. When the idea of a year book on German-Jewish history was first mooted, the choice automatically fell on him. Weltsch, who had edited the famous *Jüdische Rundschau* in Berlin, has undoubtedly been the greatest editor of a Jewish journal in this century. A man of deep Jewish knowledge, steeped in European culture, a humanist Zionist, he was also a sceptic in his view of human nature. As an editor he was impatient of certain exaggerated reputations, and, as he saw it, of pompous and conceited scholars. Indeed, he looked at all potential authors with a cool eye. Having to work mainly with non-professionals in the fifteen years of his editorship, he often welded diffuse material into unified volumes, prefacing them with well-crafted introductions which are generally recognised as shrewd and wide-ranging essays on German-Jewish history.

When, in 1970, I inherited the *Leo Baeck Institute Year Book* from such a masterly editor, I decided it was the right time for a change of direction, using the work of a new generation of professional scholars fresh to the subject. In my farewell introduction to *Year Book* 37 in 1992, I tried to outline some of my editorial aims.[4] I can only make a few brief comments here. Moreover, the *Year Book* has been analysed by others, complete with charts and tables setting out the composition of its authorship. The *Leo Baeck Institute Year*

*Book* had, in its early years, of necessity relied largely on eye-witnesses, participant observers, politicians and functionaries, in addition to reputed scholars such as Hans Liebeschütz. It is now generally agreed that we succeeded in transforming it into a professional journal largely written by historians. Had we not achieved this, the *Year Book* would not have lasted as it has. I also felt that we had manoeuvred ourselves into a somewhat parochial Prussian-Jewish rut, something which had to be overcome by extending the scope of the *Year Book* to cover all the German-speaking Jewries. We also had to redefine who exactly we were to consider as 'Jewish' for the purpose of historical research. No limitation such as professing the Jewish religion or belonging to a Jewish community could render justice to, say, the function of the Jew in German political life (to take only the November Revolution and the Bavarian Soviet Republic or, later, the anti-Nazi resistance). I introduced the topic of Jewish resistance in my first (1970) *Year Book*, with Western Yiddish as the second main theme. We began to lay more emphasis on the period of Nazi rule, which had previously been neglected, including also an assessment of the reluctance of the older generation to tackle a phase in which many of them had taken an active part. We now shifted our attention to the comparative study of German-speaking Jewries with other Jewish groups, and with other European minorities, which considerably broadened our range of authors. The *Year Book* was now increasingly written by historians who had no personal experience of life prior to the Second World War, by Jews and Gentiles, by those of German-Jewish descent, and by a new generation of German scholars. I can here single out only some salient points of editorial policy, and must refer the interested reader to the above-mentioned Introduction to *Year Book* 37, and to an excellent survey by Christhard Hoffmann of the development of the Leo Baeck Institute and its *Year Book*.[5] In conclusion, I have always tried to maintain the *Year Book* as the forum of German-Jewish historiography, with often provocative points of view and a healthy clash of controversial opinions. And I have consistently maintained that the 'ideological' aims of some of the founders, such as the transmission of Jewish 'values' to future generations, are not the function of a historiographical publication. After a tenure of twenty-two years, I handed over the editorship of the *Year Book* to Professor John Grenville of Birmingham University (see pp 55-72).

In more than four decades the London Leo Baeck Institute has launched many projects, held many conferences, published many monographs. But apart from the *Year Book*, the most important

contribution I feel we made to historical knowledge is our series of
'Sammelbände', in all of which I had my share. For the first three
symposium volumes I collaborated with Professor Werner Mosse,
whom the Institute had appointed as Editor-in-Chief, and who was
then already an established historian while I had only recently come
to the trade. I served as Editor or Co-editor for the five succeeding
volumes. In the beginning, we had only one volume on the last
phase of the Weimar Republic in mind, and *Entscheidungsjahr 1932*
has indeed been our greatest publishing success. But we were to
embark on a series spanning the period 1800 to 1943, from the
entry of the Jews into German society to the final deportation of the
remnant. Admittedly, there remain some gaps to be filled, yet the
existing volumes have come to be regarded as standard texts for the
student of German-Jewish history. They chart the chequered and
disrupted course of Jewish emancipation in Germany up to its
revocation by the Nazi regime, the position of the Jews in the
German polity, their place in German politics, the development of
modern anti-Semitism and the various Jewish responses to its
growth. I would call its central theme the 'Spannungsverhältnis'
between Germans and Jews. And we quickly realised that among its
many authors a sizeable contribution from the new generation of
German historians would be vital. It is here that intensive collaboration with our German colleagues began. This was mainly initiated
by Werner Mosse and myself. Mosse succeeded Robert Weltsch as
Chairman of the London Leo Baeck Institute in 1978.

Thus both the editorial policy of the *Year Book* and the concept
of our symposium volumes has led to close links with German historians over thirty years. In many instances these also developed into
personal friendships. Here I must mention first of all Hermann
Greive, who was assassinated by a deranged student over ten years
ago, and Werner Jochmann, my oldest post-war German friend,
who died in 1994. It was not only Hermann's profound knowledge
of Judaism and Werner's searching analysis of the structure and
nature of German anti-Semitism which impressed me so very much
and enriched my work; their learning and competence was coupled
with very strong moral support and a warm humanity. At this point
I must say that I never had the problem of the much-disputed
notion of German-Jewish reconciliation. I have always regarded the
reconciliation industry with a great deal of suspicion, as something
concocted by fulsome politicians. I can never be reconciled to those
who brought disaster to the Jewish people, to Europe, to Germany
itself. But I can be friends with those of the succeeding generations

who carry no personal guilt or responsibility for the past, and those who share my outlook and concerns. As it is the historical profession – so much transformed from former times – which occupies us here, I must say that I have often pondered on the phenomenon that those present-day German historians who have made German-Jewish history their subject reflect so strongly the progressive leanings and political orientations which once characterised the Jewish group in Germany. While individual motives and impulses lead the scholar in certain directions, the object of research is bound to exert an influence on the researcher as well. If I name here as friends and colleagues Stefi Jersch-Wenzel, Konrad Kwiet, Monika Richarz, Reinhard Rürup, Wolfgang Scheffler, Ernst Schulin and Rudolf Vierhaus, with whom I have been connected since the sixties and, more recently, Peter Alter, Ingrid Belke, Wolfgang Benz, Helmut Berding, Ursula Büttner, Ludger Heid, Arno Herzig, Gerhard Hirschfeld, Christhard Hoffmann and Barbara Suchy, they stand as representatives of a much larger group which has become indispensable for our joint writing and understanding of German-Jewish history. For the last thirty years or so I have been regularly invited to lecture at German universities and to conferences.

In 1994 I was a Visiting Professor at the new University of Potsdam, at the *Moses Mendelssohn Zentrum* directed by Julius H. Schoeps, who had initiated German-Jewish studies in the former German Democratic Republic. As a child, Potsdam, where my mother's sister and her family lived, had been a second home, so I knew it well. My aunt and her younger daughter were deported to their death in the East. The older daughter survived in Berlin, hidden by socialist and communist friends. I had first returned to Potsdam in the early sixties to work in the archives there. In 1996, for my seventy-fifth birthday, the University of Potsdam awarded me an honorary doctorate.

My long-term interests have been Jewish self-defence in Wilhelminian Germany and the Weimar Republic, and Jewish resistance in Nazi Germany. As to *Jüdischer Abwehrkampf*, I myself wrote the first studies; in the case of Jewish resistance, I was in a position to direct the research and work of others. By self-defence, I mean primarily the activities of the *Centralverein deutscher Staatsbürger jüdischen Glaubens (CV)* from 1890 to 1933 (and a little beyond), for which I was to conceive the phrase 'The Jewish Defence'. In opting for this as my major subject, I really did turn against the preconceived ideas I had held for so long. Members of my group and generation who became historians of German Jewry often took the

Jewish nationalist line. They treated the 'assimilationist' defence endeavours of their fathers, who had proudly defined themselves as Germans, with undisguised contempt, or from a Socialist point of view they scorned the 'bourgeois' limitations of the *Centralverein*. Those who came from the Zionist socialist youth movements dismissed the views of the parental generation altogether. After 1945, for some twenty years, the 'obsolete' *Centralverein* disappeared as a subject of serious historical concern.

Painstaking analysis of this chapter of the German-Jewish past was soon to redress what was a one-sided picture. Since I myself set in motion what was to become an avalanche of 'defence' studies – some 250 publications to date at the very least – I have achieved the somewhat uncomfortable status of a sort of patriarch of defence scholarship. The topic has preoccupied me now for a good thirty years, from my book, *Der jüdische Abwehrkampf* (1968/9),[6] which was presented as a thesis for my doctorate from the University of Heidelberg, to my last study on the liberal Jewish middle class in the Berlin *CV*, published in 1995. But one must acknowledge the many historians who followed on and who added immeasurably to our knowledge and, notwithstanding their critical judgements, have completely changed the former image of the leaders of the *Centralverein* as misguided Jewish functionaries deluded into believing there was a German-Jewish co-existence, or symbiosis, or whatever one likes to call it. The *Centralverein* has again become respectable.

As to my own contribution, I must now measure it against the work of many others. I therefore restrict myself to the claim that I initiated the historical rehabilitation of the *CV*'s reputation, and that I was the first to establish that in the last years of the Weimar Republic the *Centralverein* mounted a considerable anti-fascist propaganda campaign – largely camouflaged – against National Socialism in defence of the Republic and the Jewish community. This all-out attack on fascism, instead of merely the warding-off of anti-Semitism and the safeguarding of Jewish rights – for which the *Centralverein* had ostensibly been founded – constituted a remarkable feat for a liberal middle-class organisation, and this has found general recognition today. And as I also attempted an analysis of the problems of Jewish defence strategies both before and after the First World War, I must acknowledge here the debt to the fourth figure who exercised a very strong influence on my work, Eva G. Reichmann, now a centenarian, and the sole survivor of the founder generation of the Leo Baeck Institute. This fine sociologist and historian is one of the most remarkable women German Jewry has produced in this century.

As to the subject of Jewish resistance, I have always been distressed by the constant harping on Jewish passivity in the face of Nazi persecution. The fact is that there was another form of response on the part of many Jews. Some of the people involved were personally known to me. Therefore I felt it right to take on the task of integrating resistance studies into German-Jewish historiography. I have described elsewhere how I did this despite the objections of an older, more conservatively inclined historians' élite. The crux of the matter was, of course, that many of those who engaged in militant illegal activity against the Nazi regime were peripheral to the organised Jewish community, often only nominally Jewish. Here again a broader definition of what was a Jew conflicted with a narrower view of German-Jewish historiography. This has been overcome. Jewish resistance studies, which were first introduced in the *Year Book* in 1970, have spread widely, and the considerable contribution German Jews have made to resistance, first in Germany, in Spain, and then in European partisan warfare, has now been fully documented. Helmut Eschwege, Konrad Kwiet and many other Jewish and German scholars deserve much recognition for this, while I myself have attempted to summarise their findings, to highlight the problems inherent in resistance, and to draw certain conclusions whilst adding some research of my own.

Finally, another contradiction: I stress how completely I feel at home in England (despite my speaking the language with a strong German accent, as do many others of my kind).[7] Yet my niche in academic life here is both a German and a Jewish one, brought about by a chance encounter one morning in the corridors of an English university.

After a lifetime in German-Jewish studies, I must admit that I have derived immense satisfaction from a fascinating subject, though of course it is darkened by the sense of tragedy, the ever-present thought of what German Jewry might still have been, for itself and for Germany, had catastrophe not overtaken it in 1933. I have added my share to the elucidation of its history, but beyond my personal contribution I see myself very much as the representative of an organisation formed for the study of German Jewry and as part of a circle of British scholars of German-Jewish origin engaged in this task.

## Notes

1   Arnold Paucker, 'Zum Selbstverständnis jüdischer Jugend in der Weimarer Republik und unter der Nationalsozialistischen Diktatur', in Hans Otto Horch and Charlotte Wardi (eds), *Jüdische Selbstwahrnehmung in Mitteleuropa, 1870-1939* (Tübingen, 1997).

2   Norman Bentwich, *Ben-Shemen: A Children's Home in Israel* (Jerusalem, 1959).
     Sender Freies Berlin, Feature-Abteilung, Ben-Shemen. Zuflucht und Heimstätte. Die Geschichte eines Judendorfs in Palästina. Ein Feature von Kurt Kreiler.

3   On the London founder generation see Arnold Paucker, 'History in Exile: Writing the Story of German Jewry', in Siglinde Bolbecher, Konstantin Kaiser, Donal McLaughlin, J. M. Ritchie (eds), *Zwischenwelt 4: Literatur und Kultur des Exils in Großbritannien* (Vienna, 1995), pp 241-266.

4   Arnold Paucker, 'Preface/Introduction', *Leo Baeck Institute Year Book* 37 (1992), pp ix-xxix.

5   Christhard Hoffmann, 'Deutsch-Jüdische Geschichtswissenschaft in der Emigration: Das Leo Baeck Institut', in Herbert A. Strauss, Klaus Fischer, Christhard Hoffmann, Alfons Söllner (eds), *Die Emigration der Wissenschaften nach 1933: Disziplingeschichtliche Studien* (Munich–London–New York–Paris, 1991), pp 257-259, esp. pp 267-273.

6   An earlier, shorter version, with only a brief documentary appendix, had already appeared in Werner E. Mosse (ed.), *Entscheidungsjahr 1932: Zur Judenfrage in der Endphase der Weimarer Republik* (Tübingen, 1965, 1966), pp 405-499.

7   Arnold Paucker, 'Speaking English with an Accent', in Charmian Brinson, Richard Dove, Marian Malet, Jennifer Taylor (eds), *'England? Aber wo liegt es?' Deutsche und österreichische Emigranten in Großbritannien 1933-1945* (Munich, 1996), pp 21-31.

## Selected Writings of Arnold Paucker

### Books

*Der jüdische Abwehrkampf gegen Antisemitismus und Nationalsozialismus in den letzten Jahren der Weimarer Republik* (Hamburg, 1968, 1969)

*Jüdischer Widerstand in Deutschland: Tatsachen und Problematik* (Gedenkstätte Deutscher Widerstand Berlin, Beiträge, No. 37, Berlin, 1989, 1995)

*Jewish Resistance in Germany: The Facts and the Problems* (Berlin, 1991)

*Standhalten und Widerstehen: Der Widerstand deutscher und österreichischer Juden gegen die nationalsozialistische Diktatur* (Essen, 1995)

(ed.) *Leo Baeck Institute Year Book* 15-37 (1970-1992)

(ed. with Cécile Lowenthal-Hensel, *Ernst Feder: Heute sprach ich mit...: Tagebücher eines Berliner Publizisten 1926-1932* (Stuttgart, 1971)

(ed. with Hans Liebeschütz), *Das Judentum in der deutschen Umwelt 1800-1850: Studien zur Frühgeschichte der Emanzipation* (Tübingen, 1977)

(ed. with Werner E. Mosse and Reinhard Rürup), *Revolution and Evolution: 1848 in German-Jewish History* (Tübingen, 1981)

(ed. with Sylvia Gilchrist and Barbara Suchy), *Die Juden im Nationalsozialistischen Deutschland/The Jews in Nazi Germany 1933-1943* (Tübingen, 1986)

(ed. with Ludger Heid), *Juden und deutsche Arbeiterbewegung bis 1933: Soziale Utopien und religiös-kulturelle Traditionen* (Tübingen, 1992)


Articles

'Yiddish Versions of Early German Prose Novels', *The Journal of Jewish Studies*, volume X, Nos 3 and 4 (London, 1959), pp 151-167

'Das deutsche Volksbuch bei den Juden', *Zeitschrift für deutsche Philologie* 80 (1961), pp 302-317

'Das Volksbuch von den Sieben Weisen Meistern in der jiddischen Literatur', *Zeitschrift für Volkskunde* 57 (1961), pp 177-194

'"Gerechtigkeit!": The Fate of a Pamphlet on the Jewish Question', *Leo Baeck Institute Year Book* 8 (1963), pp 238-251

'The Letters of Moritz Steinschneider to the Reverend Bandinel: From the Workshop of the Catalogus Librorum Hebraeorum', *Leo Baeck Institute Year Book* 11 (1966), pp 242-261

'Searchlight on the Decline of the Weimar Republic: The Diaries of

Ernst Feder', *Leo Baeck Institute Year Book* 13 (1968), pp 161-234

'Jewish Defence against Nazism in the Weimar Republic', *The Wiener Library Bulletin* 26 (1972), pp 21-31

'The Yiddish Versions of the Schildbürger Buch' (in Yiddish), *YIVO Bleter* 44 (New York, 1973), pp 59-77

'Documents on the Fight of Jewish Organisations against Right-wing Extremism', in *Michael* 2 (Tel Aviv, 1973), pp 216-246

'La posizione degli Ebrei e loro autodifesa in Germania dal 1890 all' avvento del Nazismo', *Atti della Società Leonardo da Vinci*, volume 73 (Florence, 1975), pp 65-81

'Zur Problematik einer jüdischen Abwehrstrategie in der deutschen Gesellschaft', in Werner E. Mosse (ed.), *Juden im Wilhelminischen Deutschland 1890-1914* (Tübingen, 1976), pp 479-548

'Die Haltung Englands und der USA zur Vernichtung der europäischen Juden im Zweiten Weltkrieg', in Ursula Büttner (ed.), *Das Unrechtsregime*, volume 2 (Hamburg, 1986), pp 149-162

'Die Abwehr des Antisemitismus in den Jahren 1893-1933', in Herbert A. Strauss, Norbert Kampe (eds), *Antisemitismus: Von der Judenfeindschaft zum Holocaust* (Schriftenreihe der Bundeszentrale für politische Bildung, volume 213, Bonn, 1984-1986), pp 143-171

'Jewish Self-Defence', in *The Jews in Nazi Germany* (Tübingen, 1986), pp 55-65

'Jewish Defense against Antisemitism in Germany, 1893-1933', in Jehuda Reinharz (ed.), *Living with Antisemitism: Modern Jewish Responses* (Hanover–London, 1987), pp 104-132

'La reazione dell' Inghilterra e degli Stati Uniti alla deportazione degli ebrei', in Enzo Collotti (ed.), *Spostamenti di popolazione e deportazioni in Europa 1939-1945* (Bologna, 1987), pp 224-235

'Self-Defence against Fascism in a Middle-Class Community: The Jews in Weimar Germany and Beyond', in Francis R. Nicosia and Lawrence Stokes (eds), *Germans against Nazism: Non-conformity, Opposition and Resistance in the Third Reich* (New York/Oxford, 1990), pp 59-76

'Das Berliner liberale jüdische Bürgertum im "Centralverein deutscher Staatsbürger jüdischen Glaubens"', in Reinhard Rürup (ed.), *Jüdische Geschichte in Berlin: Essays und Studien* (Berlin, 1995), pp 215-228

'History in Exile: Writing the Story of German Jewry', in Siglinde Bolbecher, Konstantin Kaiser, Donal McLaughlin, J.M. Ritchie (eds), *Zwischenwelt 4: Literatur und Kultur des Exils in Grossbritannien* (Vienna, 1995), pp 241-266

'Resistance of German and Austrian Jews to the Nazi Régime 1933-1945', *Leo Baeck Institute Year Book* 40 (1995), pp 3-20

'Speaking English with an Accent', in Charmian Brinson, Richard Dove, Marian Malet, Jennifer Taylor (eds), *'England? Aber wo liegt es?' Deutsche und österreichische Emigranten in Großbritannien 1933-1945* (Munich, 1996), pp 21-31

'Zum Selbstverständnis jüdischer Jugend in der Weimarer Republik und unter der Nationalsozialistischen Diktatur', in Hans Otto Horch and Charlotte Wardi (eds), *Jüdische Selbstwahrnehmung in Mitteleuropa* (Tübingen, 1997)

'Responses of German Jewry to Nazi Persecution, 1933-1943', in Edward Timms, Margarete Kohlenbach, Ritchie Robertson (eds), *The German-Jewish Dilemma: From the Enlightenment to the Holocaust* (Lampeter, 1997)

'"Non solo vittime": Riflessioni sulla resistenza degli ebrei tedeschi e austriaci contro la dittatura nazista', in Giuseppe Lissa (ed.), *Olocausto: La Sho'ah tra interpretazione e memoria* (Naples, 1997)

with Konrad Kwiet, 'Jewish Leadership and Jewish Resistance', in David Bankier (ed.), *German Society's Responses to Anti-Jewish Policy* (Jerusalem, 1977)

'Eva Gabriele Reichmann (1897)', in Hans Erler, Ernst Ludwig Ehrlich, Ludger Heid (eds), *'Meinetwegen ist die Welt erschaffen': Das intellektuelle Vermächtnis des deutschsprachigen Judentums* (Frankfurt/New York, 1997), pp 279-284

**Sidney Pollard**

# In Search of a
# Social Purpose

It was shortly before my thirteenth birthday that Hitler's troops invaded Austria. They were greeted with jubilation by large crowds, recorded at length in radio and newspaper reports. But there were some who were quietly fearful. They included such leading socialists as had retained their freedom from the existing repressive regime; but above all they included the Jews.

Without fully understanding the cause, I sensed the deep anxiety of family and friends that began immediately to pervade our lives. Before long I felt the effects directly: we were driven out of our council flat and had to move, the three of us, to a one-room flat in the ghetto of the Leopoldstadt; my father lost his income; and on the way to school I saw the horror of the notorious 'scrubbing', as well-dressed, middle-aged people were on their knees in the street, forced to clear the pavements, with toothbrushes and other unsuitable gear, of the painted election slogans, surrounded by jeering crowds. We children were told to creep about quietly and not draw attention to ourselves: the fear of crowds driven by vicious and irrational hatred has remained with me to this day.

Some time later, when living in a community consisting of about one half Austrians, and one half 'Reichsdeutsche', we Viennese were astonished by the comparatively gentle and restrained anti-Semitism in Germany, at least before 'Kristallnacht'. Austrian anti-Semitism – Hitler's anti-Semitism – it seems, was of a different order. It was not merely that six years of growing persecution across the border were telescoped into a few months in 1938 in Austria, and were therefore felt more harshly; there was a unique populist bite to it. While one heard of truckloads of *SA* men in Germany driving round to attack

Jewish shops and those trading in them, in Vienna there was no need of organised terror: the populace attacked, looted and humiliated without command from above.

In December 1938 my parents managed to get me onto one of the 'Kindertransporte' to Britain. There were some 500 of us on board the special train, seen off by our families. I was never to see my parents again: they ended up in an extermination camp, I am not sure which. On their fiftieth anniversary in 1988, much was written in Britain about those transports. I remember the subdued fear as we reached the Dutch border in the early hours of the morning, and the unbelieving relief when we had really crossed it. I still feel my tears swelling up when I think of the ladies – bless them – on the platform in the first Dutch town we reached in the cold morning hours, distributing bags containing fruit and rolls spread with butter – by then unknown at home – and grated chocolate. I remember the friendliness of the crew on board the ferry to Harwich, and the slow recognition that the British bobbies we saw had no wish to harm us, but might even smile at us refugee children.

Some months in unsuitable holiday camps on the East coast followed, interrupted by a stay in the comfortably heated dormitories of a girls' boarding school standing empty over the Christmas holidays: a succession of self-perpetuating measles cases had kept us in quarantine. Eventually I ended up, together with some 180 children, at Whittingehame, the Balfour family home in Scotland, to lead a communal life and prepare for a future in a Kibbutz in Palestine. As many of us were still of school age, technically it was called a 'farm school', but there was no education in the accepted sense. We had English and Hebrew lessons, and classes on any other odd subject the 'teachers' in charge were capable of delivering. I remember scraps of astronomy and chemistry, unorganised and unexamined. A proportion of us worked 'in house', cleaning, cooking, washing up etc, turn and turn about; the rest worked in the fields of the proprietor, Lord Treprain, presumably to help pay the rent. 'Outside work' was full-time and allowed no education.

We were highly politicised – not perhaps surprisingly since politics had wrenched our lives out of their courses - and tended to be contemptuous of the philistines who did not think politics the most important thing in their lives. In principle, our political attitude was Zionist, but there was also a strong streak of socialism, and an equally strong belief, derived from the early Kibbutz movement, that there was something highly moral and good for the soul in doing manual work, a curious echo of the Benedictine and

Cistercian ideal. There was also the Fourierist notion that conditions should be created for everyone to be able to engage in both physical and intellectual labour. Working on the land in Scotland would be a good preparation for such a life.

After two years the funds, subscribed by Jewish families in Scotland, ran out. A small group of the older ones among us had left for Palestine, but when our turn came all the sea routes were closed, and we had to stay in Britain. I ended up working as a market gardener in Cambridge, food production then being classed as a reserved occupation which one could not leave. Agricultural wages were at the bottom of the pay league, and the pay of a sixteen-year-old was meant as a supplement to a family income, not a living wage. As a result, sharing a bed-sitter with another Whittingehame boy in a working-class suburb, I had left, after paying for board and lodgings, 2s 6d per week (twelve-and-a-half pence). It was a distant cousin resident in Britain, John Katz, who helped me out by paying for my correspondence courses and examinations, first for the London Matriculation exam and then for the External BSc (Economics) Intermediate (ie first year) examination of London University.

I prepared for these in the evenings and at weekends, and usually managed to send off my fortnightly essays to the correspondence college tutors on time. To my surprise I found that the education provided in the Viennese *Realgymnasium* was so far ahead of that available in English schools that with less than seven-and-a-half years of schooling in Vienna I had little to add to my knowledge in school subjects to pass the London Matric. (*Abitur*), which was meant to be taken after some twelve years' schooling. I had difficulty with English, however, and with Geography, which was mostly on the British Isles, and for which I lacked both academic knowledge and the kind of knowledge of one's own country which eighteen-year-olds could be expected to have. On the basis of the Intermediate Exam. results, the London School of Economics (LSE) promised me a student's place when I returned from war service.

Why did I choose academic study in these somewhat difficult circumstances? In part, as an avid reader in my free time, I wanted some guidance to a structured acquisition of knowledge, which I had sorely missed since leaving school at the age of thirteen. In part, in the longer term I wanted to escape from my agricultural labourer's work, which I hated. But at the time I had no specific profession in mind, and did not really see myself in a white-collar job, though by then I had given up the notion of joining a Kibbutz.

Why did I choose economics? There were two main reasons. For one thing, it reflected my passionate interest in politics and my desire to understand its mechanisms. But secondly, my natural bent was for generalising, abstract thought, and I was always impatient of exceptions and details which did not fit: thus mathematics was easily my best subject at school (and history my worst), while my innate tendency towards reductionism would have pleased mathematicians, but is much frowned upon by historians. However, to read mathematics I would, in the earlier stages, also have to take some other natural sciences, and there was no way I could get near a laboratory or specimen collection: so it had to be a subject to be mastered from books only. In those circumstances, economics seemed the arts subject nearest to a scientific approach.

As soon as the law allowed, I volunteered for army service. It was an obvious thing to do. Unlike my British fellow soldiers who were conscripted to fight a conventional war against an enemy state, at least in the early stages, for me it was to fight pure brutal barbarous evil which had wrecked my life and threatened to destroy civilisation as we know it. But I was also very conscious of the fact that while the normal soldier had family and friends who would grieve if he did not return, no one would shed a tear if I were to die: a girl I was very close to had been killed in an air raid on London, and while in fact a number of uncles, aunts and cousins had managed to escape to Palestine, I did not know that at the time. I was therefore morally more suited than most to risk my life for a good cause. Furthermore, I had the strong feeling, which I have since learnt is common among people with my experience, of guilt at having survived when my family had perished, and that in some way, dying would make things right again.

I was posted to the Reconnaissance Corps and saw active service in Belgium and Germany, staying on in the army of occupation in Germany after the fighting ended. Since, technically, my studies had been interrupted by joining the forces, I became eligible to early ('class B') release from the army, timed to coincide with the beginning of term in October 1946. However, the army mislaid my papers for three months, so that I had to wait until January 1947 before entering the LSE as a student. Having gained an external Intermediate before joining the army, I was excused the first year's internal study. Now, losing another term, I had in fact only five terms' full-time study before the finals instead of the usual nine. It did not seem to make much difference academically, but I missed out on the usual induction information, and never having attended a British school either, I had for a time great difficulty in finding my way about in practical matters.

Looking back, I seemed to have taken all this for granted. The LSE had accepted me, the army had taken care of me and released me earlier to take up my studies: I was a passive recipient of decisions by others with very little effort on my part. Nevertheless, full-time study for a degree turned out to be the decisive turning point in my life, pointing in a completely new direction. Looking back, all my earlier experiences, home in Vienna, Zionist preparation, agricultural labour and army service in the ranks were not the background of which university was the recognised culmination. Going up to university sometimes has a tendency to destroy relationships with family, friends or home town, but I had no relevant previous history. In some ways, I was starting with a clean sheet, and was floating freely in my new life without obligations or ties, though I have since come to realise that my then conception that, therefore, I was also free of prejudices, was quite mistaken.

I was lucky to find digs with an elderly, childless couple, the Ransomes, who took me to their heart as I did them. They lived in a council house and were lifelong Labour supporters, of the kind who do the eternal grind of addressing envelopes and knocking at doors without ever expecting a return. My respect for the British working man has its roots with that couple. They told me about the Holiday Fellowship, for which I ran some centres as 'secretary' in the following summers, and where I also met my first wife.

Meanwhile I explored London on my bicycle, went to concerts and theatres (in the gods for 6d) and became convinced there was no other city in the world to compare with it. But much of what makes up the usual student life was missing. Most of the men (less so the women) had lost four, five or six years in the forces and were too old and earnest to engage in the usual student larks, being keen to make up for lost time; of course, like all war generations, we could never make up for the lost carefree years of our youth. At the same time, as might be expected in an institution devoted to the social sciences, and with several members of the academic staff highly prominent in the political life of the country, politics in the wider sense were a burning and live issue for most of us.

Those were the days of the post-war Labour Government, of the formation of international peace organisations and the beginnings of the rehabilitation of the devastated continent. The world was full of hope, and Wordsworth's 'bliss was it in that dawn to be alive' would not have been an inappropriate description. The 'right' side had won the war. Full employment, in contrast to the pre-war scourge of unemployment, brought hope even to the problem areas of the country, though we did not then know just how successful Keynesian counter-cyclical policies would turn out to be. National-isation of some key industries, the remarkable construction of a complete welfare system and, as a result, a softening of employers' attitudes and more humane treatment in the workplace brought to an end the worst aspects of the traditional capitalist social order. For many of us, what had been vague ideals inspiring hope in the war years became reality, and the LSE, where student societies could easily call on politicians and top administrators to address us, and where recruiting parties from the new welfare ministries were almost regular attenders, seemed to be in the midst of it. In the face of the temporary reversion of much of the continent to a more primitive form of life and the discrediting of its traditional leaders (as well as the very different and inappropriate conditions in the USA) Britain seemed once again to be leading the world, a model and pioneer for others to follow.

My own sympathies were with Marxism and the Communist Party. Marxism, reducing all social observations, at any rate of the more recent centuries, to one single explanatory system, obviously suited my scientific temperament. It also had its heart in the right place, being on the side of the poor, of the underprivileged and the oppressed in all countries. With my past as a reluctant and badly-paid wage worker, the notion of an exploited and oppressed working class found a ready echo. In the Soviet Union, the new social system appeared to work: while the rest of the advanced world had stumbled into depression, waste and war in the 1930s, her economy had been expanding at an unparalleled rate. Much of what information I had on the USSR was derived from the literature of the Left Book Club, of which I had become a member. In the war, the Soviet people had suffered the heaviest losses in the fighting, and had done more than any of the other Allies to win it. But above all – and that for me was the deciding factor – when it came to the crunch, it was the Communists who had stood up most bravely and consistently to the fascist terror everywhere in Europe, while the adherents of other parties had all too frequently been ready to compromise. The Hitler-Stalin pact was to be explained by the need of the Soviet Union to gain time, and as a reaction to the appeasement policies of an unreliable West.

In my youthful enthusiasm I, like many others, drifted into the LSE branch of the Communist Party. But being a full-blown

Communist implies a great deal of activism and personal devotion to politics. I found that I was not a political animal in that sense; moreover, I had the nagging feeling that as a foreigner – though I had acquired British nationality by then – I ought not to engage directly in political action in my host country. I left the party again after some six months: that period of membership was, however, to have considerable consequences later in life.

The economics degree of London University at the time had a large compulsory economics component, but, in addition to some subsidiary papers, candidates could choose from a number of other social sciences to make up a considerable part of their examination. I was attracted to statistics, which I thought would be easiest for me, but found that I lacked some of the necessary mathematical base. Moreover, it did little to illuminate my quest for an understanding of the mechanism of politics. Instead, I chose modern economic history: it seemed to be the best gateway to an explanation of the rise of the modern world, while being closest to the Marxist approach. The choice was purely driven by academic interest: I was so full of the excitement of finding myself in an academic community, with companions with whom, unlike agricultural labourers or young fellow soldiers, I could relate, that I had no thought for the morrow, and for the likely utility of my chosen option in finding a job afterwards. There was a vague background notion that in some way I should 'do good' to society within the British context, though it was not at all clear how a history degree would help in that endeavour.

I found my courses, both those of economic theory, and economic history, fascinating and satisfying. The lone study out of books in the days of my correspondence college course, while leading a totally separate personal life, had led to a kind of detachment from reality which made the subjects themselves unreal and academic in the negative sense. Now, in the collective interest of fellow students and teachers, the subjects came alive. While the LSE had few tutorials, and those with large groups only, so that there was little personal contact with the tutors, at any rate for undergraduates, it had some excellent lecturers on its staff. Many of their lectures became occasions, much debated afterwards, especially as fleshed out by the lecturers' writings and the daily political events.

The economic history we were taught was centred on the British industrial revolution, its antecedents and consequences. The topic was significant in at least two respects. Forming one of the major turning points in the development of modern society, it allowed a wide-ranging quest for the moving forces in history. But at the same time it raised the question of the miseries of the working families who had to live through it, as described in much of the literature and thus, at a higher level, on the moral basis of capitalism itself. The issue was in due course to lead to a lengthy debate between 'optimists' and 'pessimists' in the profession, a debate not unrelated to the political approach of the historians concerned, and which has remained unresolved to the present day.

The focus on economic history, set in a framework of economic theory, rather than of political history, broadly tended to confirm the Marxist view. Though not necessarily placing much emphasis on the class struggle which was one of the motivating drives in Marx's view of history, what might be called orthodox economic history saw the major trends and development, at least of the western world in recent times, in terms of the logic and the requirements of the economic sector, of man's need to make a living as a social being. 'Capitalism' and 'feudalism' were terms disliked by some of our teachers, but much of the thinking behind these concepts and the apparently irresistible way in which one had changed into the other everywhere was necessarily to be found in one form or another in every school of economic historians. It led to the thought that capitalism, too, was passing through what could well turn out to be its fatal difficulties, which would make way for a higher stage of social development.

Having done well in the finals, I was offered a scholarship to work for a PhD degree at the LSE. I had in any case to put in an additional year's residence in order to make up the three years required for an internal degree, and accepted with alacrity. As a topic I wanted something down-to-earth, possibly the history of an industry. On the suggestion of F.J. Fisher, I chose the British shipbuilding industry in its heyday, 1870-1914. I was given two supervisors, T.S. Ashton and H.L. Beales, and since each of them falsely thought the other was looking after me, I was left very much to my own devices. This caused no problems, though I had some difficulty within the LSE establishment to convince authorities that I ought to visit some shipyards to see with my own eyes how ships were built and launched, rather than work from archives only: my interest in Barrow-in-Furness derived from one such visit.

Seen in perspective, the success of the late Victorian and Edwardian shipbuilding industry was truly astonishing. In spite of subsidies and hidden support by other nations, British yards launched, even at the end of the period, some 60 per cent of the world's tonnage, or in other words 50 per cent more than the rest of the world combined. Yet by then some foreign yards had more modern equipment installed than their British counterparts, and Britain also tended to be conservative in some aspects of ship and engine design. How, then, was the continuing success to be explained? Apart from cheap steel and a favourable coastline, the critical British advantage lay in the skill of the shipyard workman; but that, although not at the time recognised, was a wasting asset as machinery and design teams were about to replace manual skills. It formed a useful lesson for me on how easy it is for something that was once an advantage to turn into a fetter on progress as the old, successful ways are clung to, and also how industrial methods reach their apogee just before being replaced by new ones. But at the same time it strengthened my view, derived both from the history of the industrial revolution and from the condition of Europe in the late 1940s, that Britain was destined to be among the leaders in the economic sphere. After completion I was told that the university library typescript copy of the thesis was much consulted, but the text was not published until much later by Harvard, after conflation with a thesis by Paul Robertson.

By the autumn of 1950 the thesis was about to be completed and I was looking for a job. I applied and was interviewed for assistant lectureships, then the entry grade for university teachers, at four universities, and was turned down by all of them in favour of candidates who looked less well qualified on paper. This caused me to panic. I was married by then, and with a background of deep insecurity I was more conscious of the difficulty of finding a non-academic job with a doctorate in history, should my hope for a lectureship be disappointed, than of the chances which a good first economics degree might still give me. In any case: what had gone wrong? The London University appointments officer assured me that I interviewed well: was it then anti-Jewish prejudice? But at least one of the successful men was also a refugee. Finally someone whispered the answer in my ear: the head of department, T.S. Ashton, was in his references warning prospective employers against me because of my dangerous communist beliefs. At the time, being only too familiar with political prejudice, it caused me little surprise, though it did nothing to lessen my all-pervading anxieties. Since then, having been in a position to supply references myself, I have come to consider the action of my head of department quite unacceptable within the British tradition, though it might be said in Ashton's defence that he was then engaged, together with Friedrich von Hayek, in a polemic against Marxism in history.

I was saved by the newly established Knoop Fellowship in economic history in Sheffield. As a limited three-year appointment with no teaching duties, Ashton saw no reason to block my appointment to it; once there, I could be promoted to a permanent teaching post without his intervention. And at Sheffield I remained, gradually running up the promotion ladder to a professorship, for thirty years until 1980.

The name of Sheffield, then as now, has a grim ring to it, and I went there, as did so many others, with the intention of leaving again as soon as I could. But, like others, I came to love the city, and soon considered that there was nowhere else that could offer more, though at one time I did consider very seriously an invitation from Cambridge. Sheffield is large enough to have all the cultural facilities of a city, including concerts, theatres and libraries, and it was then engaged in a vigorous, though not perhaps aesthetically very satisfying, programme of rebuilding and expansion. Yet at the same time it has open country close enough to reach it on foot if one is fortunate enough to live in one of the western suburbs. I have since seen many countries and visited numerous famous beauty spots; but for me there is nothing to beat the range of gentle hills of the Peak District on Sheffield's doorstep, with its ploughed fields and trees giving way to rough grazing and, past the dry-stone walls, the blue heather as the eye travels upwards. In my eyes it has a rightness about it − as if I had been born there.

Coming from the riches of the LSE library, Sheffield University's library facilities seemed very limited as a base for research, though it stood then on the threshold of an extraordinary phase of expansion. Nor were there many archive collections in the city apart from those relating to local and regional history. I therefore chose a local theme for my research programme: a history of labour in Sheffield since 1850.

It was a theme, needless to stress, which was not unconnected with my left-wing political views. Perhaps it should be inserted here that though that commitment has remained unchanged to the present day, I found myself drifting away from the active politics of the Communist Party or even the Labour Party, not only because of the moral compromises which all party activism entails, but because my leftness seemed to differ from that of others. Their loyalty, when it came to the crunch, was to their left-wing organisations, while mine was to the underdog, and not to his would-be leaders, whenever these diverged. Thus, to anticipate, the Left would support the governments of the ex-colonial countries in Africa and parts of Asia because they had fought imperialism in their day and mouthed suitable anti-capitalist and anti-colonial slogans. As far as I was concerned, however, looking rather to the fate of those they governed, many of these governing élites were made up of corrupt and incompetent oppressors, a disaster for their unfortunate subjects.

Possibly the most searing conflict of conscience which derived from that attitude arose in the face of the great miners' strike of 1984-5. Miners are the quintessential ideal proletarians: hard-working, well-organised, living in closely-knit communities in which humanity has room to flourish. Their strike became a focus of left-wing support, their leader, Arthur Scargill, the darling of the Left. Yet I found myself totally opposed to that strike from the start. It was, to begin with, really the result of a one-man decision, Scargill having tried several times before, as he was to try several times after, to bring the men out. He had always lost the vote for it until on this occasion he managed to get the strike launched by by-passing the voting procedures laid down. His demand, that no pit be closed, no matter how uneconomic, until the coal gave out, was obviously preposterous if taken literally. Moreover, there was from the beginning a nasty streak, in the attempt to use the steelworkers, whose jobs were much more precarious, as cats' paws, and of using large numbers of strong men for violent action on the streets and against the men still at work: I had seen enough of that tactic to abhor it. Above all, a long drawn-out strike would inflict endless misery on the mining communities such that, even if the miners had 'won', whatever that had meant in the context, they would never recover the incomes they had lost, or get over the effects of prolonged idleness and the hatreds engendered within families and communities. More than this, coal was everywhere in the western world under threat from cheaper fuels, and a sensible leader would seek to secure its markets, among other means by making sure of its regular delivery, whereas a big strike was certain to wreck permanently many of the remaining outlets for coal, and thus the miners' future. As for the miners themselves, my heart went out to them, as I saw them not as fighters in a good case but as victims, the victims of political ambition. My hope was that they would end the strike quickly, to limit the damage done by the ruthless abuse of the tradition of loyalty of a fine body of men and prevent the emasculation of a powerful union which would give great comfort to the Conservative Government.

To return to Sheffield in 1950: Labour history up to that time had been largely the history of organisations, such as the trade unions, and of Labour politics. It was natural for me to determine to write the history of the workers themselves, to sketch their lives from their own point of view. Since then, this field has expanded enormously, much sophisticated history has been written, and history from below, or of everyday life, or based on live interviews, has expanded beyond recognition. Compared with that efflorescence, my history now looks colourless and limited. Yet the attempt to see how working people really lived in an industrial city, including their economic, social and cultural experiences, was novel then and stood at the beginning of a new trend. Liverpool University Press, my publishers, were amiable but somewhat unbusinesslike: they allowed the book to become out of print almost at once, and it was not reprinted until 1993, by Gregg Revivals.

Arising from that preoccupation, I became a founder member of the Society for the Study of Labour History, and a co-editor of its *Bulletin*. I was also drawn to co-operation, which in Britain is largely a working-class movement concerned with retail shops. Here was an organisation built up by humble people putting in many unpaid hours to help their own class and beat capitalist proprietors and managers at their own game – at least until they had to compete with monster supermarket chains. What I found attractive additionally is that co-operation, unlike trade unionism, is non-confrontational and combines practical achievement with an inspiring ideal.

The ideal derives, in some respects, from one of the most fascinating figures of the industrial revolution, Robert Owen. The lasting attractiveness of Owen, which has survived to the present day, is based on the fact that he looked on workers as full human beings, not merely, as did his contemporaries and as most economists have done since, as passive recipients of orders. His deepest insight was to realise that economic welfare is not to be measured merely by the wage packet at the end of the week, but also, and possibly even more, by how that week is spent, by satisfaction, fellow-feeling, 'happiness' in the place of work. It is thus the very antithesis of Thatcherism which, starting with the not unreasonable notion that the rate of profit is the best indicator for making choices in a market economy, then goes on to make the maximisation of profits the main objective of Government. Having in the process deliberately created insecurity, speed-ups, a low wage economy and achieved the longest hours of work in Europe, the then Conservative government was left wondering why the 'feel-good factor' failed to materialise despite a rising overall national income. Robert Owen could have told them.

In view of my well-known commitment to labour, it caused some surprise that my next study put the capitalist at its centre, by concerning itself with management in the industrial revolution. Much of it, it is true, still dealt with the treatment and control of labour in the early factories, but the main theme was indeed a different one. It arose, in one sense, out of the intellectual's curse of seeing that there are two sides to each question, including the question of the exploitation of the working classes in the industrial revolution. But there was also the feeling that moral concepts were commonly wrongly applied in that context. In some sense, workers did indeed lead more moral lives than many of the mill owners and shopkeepers of their day; but that was not due to an innate moral superiority, but to their position in society. Had the roles been reversed, the starving and exploited handloom weavers would no doubt have acted just as their employers did, and vice versa. It was interesting, then, to see what drove the mill and mine owners, and that led to the question of what problems they faced: the book has been widely used in following up that topic.

However, for me the heart of the study, as it developed, lay on a different plane: it had to do with the freedom of choice of the individual. Given their background, the need to survive within their society and its accepted framework of behaviour, how much choice did the typical factory owner, not endowed with Owen's unshakeable self-assurance, have to act differently, and is there much point in 'blaming' him for his heartlessness? It is a problem which in principle has exercised most historians, and it is essentially insoluble, for it depends on what we begin by taking for granted. In the extreme case, if we take a man's background, his character, motivation and experience all as established, there is only one way in which he will act in any given circumstances. Take away any of these qualifying preconditions, and his choice becomes more open. My own prejudice, coloured by my innate quest for scientific certainty, has come to be towards the constraint end of the spectrum of possibilities, and to be impressed by the limited freedom of action possible for any but the most exceptional individuals.

Meanwhile I had been persuaded by the publisher Edward Arnold to write a textbook on modern British economic history. I chose the period since 1914 and, thinking to fill a gap in the existing literature and offer some advice to students and tutors on further reading, I supplied it with a generous choice of sources. Somewhat to my surprise, *The Development of the British Economy* turned out to be a great success, even helping to put Sheffield on the map as a place in which graduates wished to undertake their research. As it brought the story practically up to date, it fell in due course behind current reality and required extension. Fitting both the material for the later years as well as the new literature on the earlier years into the same number of words turned out to be an increasingly painful exercise as time went on. The fourth edition now runs to 1990. Significantly, I found myself introducing a subtle change with the passage of the years, from the optimism on the economic future of Britain in the first edition to the pessimism of the last.

From the late 1960s onward, the issue of the relative decline of the British economy since the war became one of my main preoccupations. The other was the economic development of modern Europe, seen as a single process. For me, possibly surprisingly at first sight, these two were related, for it was because, for obvious reasons, I never ceased to look at the continent that I first began to discern a fateful failure in Britain to keep up with the rate of growth and of innovation across the Channel. No doubt British growth was quite satisfactory on its own terms, but lacking the traditional self-confidence of British economists, I remember my frustration to be told, in discussion with a large sample of them over many years, that the continent was merely catching up, and there was no chance, given the industrial lead which Britain had at the time and her comparative political and social strengths, that continental countries would ever overtake her. It was years before public opinion in this country caught up with my early fears.

Now that Britain's failure to make the most of her opportunities has become only too obvious, numerous explanations of that failure have been put forward. My own view was that any set of explanations would have to be general, at least as far as manufacturing was concerned, since it was unlikely that all industries together would simultaneously fall victim to poor management; it would have to be something of which the other Western European countries were free; and it would have to be steeped in history or, as it is nowadays fashionable to express it, to be at least partially 'path-determined'. It would also have to accord with the facts.

My starting point was the strikingly low rate of productive capital investment in Britain: it immediately hit the eye in any statistical comparison, while it accorded with common sense that any rapid economic progress must depend, among other things, on new or improved capital, including human capital. That emphasis was strengthened in my own mind by my work on capital formation and its significance in the industrial revolution. It was also based, in part, on personal observation, as visits to steel works and car factories in Britain, Germany and Japan had made it only too obvious how far the equipment with which British workers were supplied had fallen behind.

Why was investment so low? There was a possible short-term cause at the end of the war, in the expectation, by citizens of a victorious nation, of a rapid rise in their standard of living, and thus the demand for too much in immediate incomes. Their counterparts on the devastated continent, by contrast, knew that there was much reconstruction ahead before gains in incomes could be hoped for. But there was also a more pervasive, long-term cause, which was linked to Britain's economic past: that was the dominance in economic policy-making of the finance and commercial interest, widely known as 'the City', over the (mainly provincial) industrial interest. The Treasury, meaning the economic policy-making apparatus as a whole, never wearied of this preference, in the apparent belief that unless the nominal relationships which interested the City, such as the internal or external value of the pound or the balance of payments, were right, no prosperity could have a lasting existence in the real economy. Thus, whenever any of these showed any weakness, as in a full-employment economy they were bound to do from time to time, a severe bout of deflation was ordered, and deflation, in the context of the time, meant a cutback in investment. Thus a series of 'stop-go' phases ensued, the real economy being weakened still further in every stop phase against its rivals abroad by cut-backs on modernising investment, which made the next cycle inevitable and still more damaging.

I set out this theory in *The Wasting of the British Economy* and in numerous minor writings. There were, no doubt, other contributory causes of Britain's failures, such as the over-extension of her military activities and the technical and often also managerial incompetence of her industrialists, but so far as an initiating and main mechanism was at work, I saw no reason to change my emphasis in the passing of the years. The destructive impact of Treasury policies was unaffected by political change, since Labour and Conservative cabinets alike were in the hands of the 'experts' in this matter, supported as these were by financial journalists and most economists, who also made 'the City' their starting point. These policies survived into the Thatcher years, with their high unemployment and other novel facets, with only minor role switches. Thus the balance of payments gap which so exercised the economics establishment in the 1970s has today come to be totally neglected, though the gap has widened to an order of ten times as large; instead we have inflation as the bugbear, to be held in check once again by the same investment-inhibiting policies.

It comes as no surprise that those responsible for the failures sought to shuffle off responsibility onto alternative scapegoats. A favourite explanation centred on the long-term trend of British relative decline, dated by many to well before the First World War, of which the post-war failure was alleged to be but a natural contin-uation. It is indeed true that Britain lost ground in the decades after 1870, but that was inevitable, given the quite extraordinarily domi-nant position of the mid-Victorian age, and implied a catching up, rather than overtaking: even in 1914, Britain was still far ahead in income or output per head, in trade, finance, foreign investment or any other relevant measure of all European countries including Germany; only the USA, with her immeasurably more favourable resource base, had overtaken her. To counter the facile diversion from current failures by shifting blame onto earlier generations, I wrote *Britain's Prime and Britain's Decline*, though in the writing a number of other topics also came to be covered.

Meanwhile I had begun to explore the theme of a common economic development and a common history which bound Europe together, though it has always remained unclear to me how far to the east Europe extended. One root of this specific interest was the real-isation that the European Economic Community (EEC) represented but the last stage in a long process of European economic integration. A more powerful urge still derived both from my own origins and from numerous travels in post-war Europe. It was based on the conviction that many of the borders which divided Europe and had set one set of citizens against another in the past were artificial, and that, despite the great regional and cultural diversity to be found on the continent, there was far more that was similar, the outcome of a common heritage and a common fate over the centuries.

Following some minor writings on the subject, I set out these ideas in *Peaceful Conquest*, published in 1981. Its main point is often taken to be the emphasis on regionalism, and in particular the notion that industrialisation in Europe was a regional phenomenon. That, to me, has always seemed obvious. In so far as I wanted to say something new, my basic intention had gone in quite a different direction: it had been to show that the industrialisation which grad-ually covered the greater part of Europe in the two centuries after 1760 was a single process, involving the adoption of similar tech-nologies and the similar social and organisational changes made necessary by them in one country after another. The origins of that process lay in Britain but, having caught her up, other societies were quite capable of originating innovations in their turn. At every stage, industrial regions tended to have more in common with similar regions abroad than with their non-industrial hinterlands, and every 'economy', meaning the totality of economic life within one country, turned out to be an assembly of separate components each of which, *mutatis mutandis*, could be duplicated abroad.

That book was written in one go in a year spent at the *Zentrum für interdisziplinäre Forschung* in Bielefeld. Conditions there, in a life shared with other scholars but freed from administrative or teaching duties, were ideal in many ways, and the months spent there were among the happiest in my life. They followed a term as visiting professor in the History Faculty of the then new University of Bielefeld which I had found equally congenial, and when an invitation came to take up a permanent chair, I accepted, to spend the last ten years of my teaching life, 1980-90, as professor at that university.

It had not been the first visiting professorship or the first invitation from abroad. The most portentous of these was an invitation to move to Berkeley, again following a year as visiting professor. The attractions were obvious: an ideal climate, a fine city, one of the world's greatest libraries, a brilliant group of colleagues in the Departments of History and Economics, and some outstanding students. I had accepted, and actually resigned from Sheffield, but pulled out at the last moment. That decision has been widely misunderstood. It has been put down to the refusal of the American authorities to grant me a visa because of my brief membership of the Communist Party in my student days. In fact, I did obtain a visa, but it was of a temporary nature only because of my Communist association, and in spite of the assurance of the American colleagues that there would be no problem in prolonging it, I felt too insecure to entrust my family and myself to an uncertain future abroad. There were other problems too: problems concerned with the move itself, with the student rebellion in California and the reactions of the Governor, Ronald Reagan, to it (the period was 1969-70) and, more than anything else, the drug culture then rampant in the San Francisco area, to which my teenage children, who were only too impressed by all that they saw there, would be exposed.

My move to Bielefeld has caused some raised eyebrows: people usually migrate westwards, I was told, never to the east. Though not entirely correct, there was some truth in that observation, but there were good reasons for my decision. On the positive side there was, by common consent, the most brilliant faculty in the field of what in Germany was called social history, but would perhaps more correctly be called universal history. Moreover, unlike other close associations of outstanding scholars, it was a faculty which worked in an excellent spirit of friendliness and collaboration. There was also the challenge of something new at a time when it had become clear that little more could be accomplished in Sheffield, with its well-running curriculum, in a department that was unlikely to expand any further.

Among the negative factors was the threat of Thatcherite attacks on British universities, which in the event turned out to be even more devastating than I had expected. There were also personal problems. My marriage was breaking up and I had to get away: divorce and re-marriage did, in fact, follow in 1982.

I presume that from Bielefeld's point of view, the intention was that I should widen the educational base of students by introducing something of the Anglo-Saxon tradition of economic history. But the move also necessarily served to jerk my own outlook out of its wonted ruts. Though I carefully avoided teaching any aspect of German history, I could not avoid being struck by the differences in approach, and unconsciously absorbing at least some of the German one. Thus, as far as earlier centuries were concerned, there was the contrast between the British historians' view of seeing their country within the context of a wider overseas world, whereas for Germans, Germany was a world in itself, battles, intrigues, trade and economic warfare taking place *within* the German orbit. For more recent periods, I found that the discontinuity and the collapse of civilisation in 1933 dominated the thinking of German historians in a way quite strange to those brought up on British history; this prompted puzzlement *inter alia* as to what indefinable quality there was in British, Australian or American society that ensured that, no matter how devastating the economic crisis of the 1930s, democratic government was never remotely in danger, or its survival a serious topic for historians.

I have never regretted the move to Bielefeld, though on my retirement in 1990 my wife and I did decide, with something of a heavy heart, to leave and return to Sheffield. Family and friends were there and other happy associations, including an honorary post at my old university.

At the time of writing I am in the process of putting the finishing touches to a book which I had begun to write in Bielefeld. To be called *Marginal Europe*, its original inspiration was the paradox that the British industrial revolution had its main locations in regions far from the centre of things and from the wealthier cities and counties, and were on the contrary among the poorest, least favoured by nature and political influence: the uplands of Lancashire and Yorkshire, the heathlands of the West Midlands or the valley of the Clyde. Areas like these, often seen as marginal lands in literature, which usually included mountains, forests and marshes, are generally described as poor, backward and discriminated against in history. Yet a brief review of European history showed that the eighteenth century in Britain was not the only time and place when it was precisely these sorts of area which took the lead in innovative action. The book discusses the features usually ascribed to European societies living on the 'margins', and the reasons why, in spite of their bad press, they were so frequently the location of the springs of progress, at least on a temporary basis. The theme combines much which has moved me in the past: the unity of European developments, the significance of regions, the sources of economic development and the fate of the underdog.

This may be a good note on which to end an autobiographical narrative. Having been obliged to put down, for the first time in this form, the events of my life with the emphasis on my development as a historian, they seem to show neither unity nor purpose, either in their personal or their academic aspects; yet, living through my time, the way ahead always appeared quite clear and logically marked out. Though fully at home in Britain, I never lost the feeling that I was not quite like those born here: any feeling of Jewishness has long since dropped away – except when Jews are persecuted for their race – but it is the consciousness of the continental heritage which obtrudes itself, possibly more with advancing age than before. In one way, I feel the call to interpret the rich cultural world of the continent to my British hosts, and at the same time to make clear to continentals the values, the vigour, both intellectual and commercial, the adventurousness and, not least, the innate and unshakeable attachment to the freedom of the individual as against any social organisation to be found in the Anglo-Saxon culture. It is, possibly, an acquired prejudice which sees all continentals as having much in common, with a break in that pattern as one crosses the Channel: the way in which towns and houses are built are an obvious example of this. Yet I also see the commonness, clearly evidenced when matched against extra-European cultures. The conflict over the divisive power of the Channel is, at the time of writing, expressed most clearly in the political field, in the hesitancy and genuine puzzlement over how far Britain should give up her individuality to an integrating Europe.

In one sense, I am able to feel above that battle: both the fears and the expectations are needlessly magnified by the protagonists in Britain. In another sense, it is one which has gone on inside myself ever since I arrived, one winter morning, on the Harwich ferry, to come to terms with a society which insists on being different, for example driving on the left and, until recently, dividing its currency not into 100, but into 240 pieces. The feeling of not wholly belonging anywhere remains.

## Selected Writings of Sidney Pollard

*Three Centuries of Sheffield Steel* (Sheffield, 1954)

*Sheffield Trades Council 1858-1958* (Sheffield, 1958)

*A History of Labour in Sheffield, 1850-1939* (Sheffield, 1959)

*The Development of the British Economy 1914-1950* (London, 1962)

*The Genesis of Modern Management: A Study of the Industrial Revolution in Great Britain* (London, 1965)

*The Co-operatives at the Crossroads* (London, 1965)

with D.W. Crossley, *The Wealth of Britain, 1085-1966* (London, 1968)

*The Idea of Progress: History and Society* (London, 1968)

(ed. with C. Holmes), *Documents of European Economic History*, 3 volumes (London, 1968-73)

(ed.), *The Gold Standard and Employment Policies Between the Wars* (London, 1970)

with J. Salt (eds), *Robert Owen, Prophet of the Poor: Essays in Honour of the Two Hundredth Anniversary of His Birth* (London, 1971)

*European Economic Integration, 1815-1970* (London, 1974)

with P. Robertson, *The British Shipbuilding Industry, 1870-1914* (Cambridge/Mass., and London, 1979)

(ed.), *Region and Industrialisierung: Studien zur Rolle der Region in der Wirtschaftsgeschichte der letzten zwei Jahrhunderte* (Göttingen, 1980)

*Peaceful Conquest: The Industrialisation of Europe 1760-1970* (Oxford, 1981)

*The Integration of the European Economy Since 1815* (London, 1981)

*The Wasting of the British Economy: British Economic Policy 1945 to the Present* (London, 1982)

*The Neglect of Industry: A Critique of British Economic Policy Since 1870* (Rotterdam, 1984)

with P. Mathias (eds), *The Cambridge Economic History of Europe*, volume 8: *The Industrial Economies and Social Policies* (Cambridge, 1989)

*Britain's Prime and Britain's Decline: The British Economy 1870-1914* (London, 1989)

*Typology of Industrialisation Processes in the Nineteenth Century* (London, 1990)

*Wealth and Poverty: An Economic History of the 20th Century* (London, 1990)

(ed. with K. Ditt), *Von der Heimarbeit in die Fabrik: Industrialisierung und Arbeiterschaft in Leinen- und Baumwollregionen Westeuropas während des 18. und 19. Jahrhunderts* (Paderborn, 1992)

(ed. with D. Ziegler), *Markt. Staat, Planung: Historische Erfahrungen mit Regulierungs- und Deregulierungsversuchen der Wirtschaft* (St Katharinen, 1992)

*The Metal Fabrication and Engineering Industries* (Oxford, 1994)

*Marginal Europe: The Contribution of Marginal Lands Since the Middle Ages* (Oxford, 1997)

**Peter Pulzer**

# From Danube to Isis:
# A Career in Two Cultures

Most historical writing – at any rate writing on modern history – is also autobiography. Often this works indirectly. The writing may be entirely impersonal and drily objective, with no visible connection to the author's life story. The details may be derived from archives, newspapers or interviews, and therefore not part of the author's own experience. But what about the choice of subject itself? The agenda? The questions to be addressed and the conclusions to be formulated? Are they chosen at random? Do they derive from some purely external stimulus? Or do they come from inside the scholar, because something that once happened to him goes on growing inside, because the world as he has experienced it has features that cry out for an explanation?

No doubt no two historians are alike. The ambition to write the definitive work on medieval China or Renaissance Mantua may have no connection with the author's own life. But more often than not, when the subject is the nineteenth or twentieth century, there is a link between person and subject, though here, too, it is safe to say that no two links are alike. In my own case there are certainly links, though not all of them are the obvious ones. Indeed, the request to write this essay has encouraged me to explore them a little more thoroughly than I have so far bothered to do in the course of a rather busy professional career.

I was born in Vienna in 1929 at the beginning of the world economic crisis. My parents were secularised, non-practising Jews of the professional middle class, not particularly affluent but devoted to the life of the mind and the arts. Politically they belonged to the Social Democratic Party but were not, as far as I can remember, particularly active in it. However, it was difficult not to become aware of political and public events during the 1930s, even if these did not affect one directly and if, as a child, one could see little or no connection between them. I remember, in chronological order, the brief civil war in Vienna in February 1934, when there was some shooting in the inner courtyard of the block of flats in which we lived and I could watch smoke rising from the Karl-Marx-Hof in the distance; the assassination – or rather, the funeral – of Chancellor Dollfuss, murdered by Nazis in June of that year; the abdication crisis in Britain, the topic of a number of disrespectful jokes; and the Spanish Civil War and the Sino-Japanese War, both recorded in the newsreels that I saw on my occasional visits to the cinema. These events evidently made an impression on me, but I connected them with an external world that made no difference to my own life.

All of this changed abruptly in March 1938, though even then the impact came by stages. I am pretty certain that I was unaware of the existence of Adolf Hitler until the day of the *Anschluss*. I did know of 'Nazis' in the preceding weeks, since the newspapers, the radio news and family conversation were full of little else as Austrian Nazis, though banned, became bolder and more violent, flaunting swastika armbands and flags in public. The *Anschluss* itself I experienced in peculiar circumstances. I was in bed with 'flu, puzzled by the constant drone of aircraft and heavier-than-usual traffic in the street. My mother explained that Austria had ceased to be an independent state, that the Nazis were now in control, that as a consequence life would become difficult for Jews and that I was to watch what I said to anyone, since no one could now be trusted. The illusion that public events affected only others was over. So was the assumption that being Jewish, of which I was only dimly aware, was marginal to one's existence.

In part, my early distance from Judaism was due to my parents' secularism, in part a consequence of where we lived. Our house was some way from the main concentration of the Jewish population of Vienna. There were only a handful of other Jewish boys at my elementary school. All that distinguished me from the other pupils was that I did not attend religious instruction on the grounds that I was 'konfessionslos'. Along with the few Protestant boys I was classified as non-Catholic. It was only after the *Anschluss* that I learnt how superficial our family's dissociation from organised Jewish life was. Most of our closer friends and acquaintances turned out to be Jews, as did the family doctor and the kindergarten I had attended. These links were not religious. They were social and ethno-cultural.

In this way I learnt (though not in so many words) how archaic forms of affinity and ascription could survive – or revive – in an allegedly modern society.

Step by step we were re-segregated. My father, a design engineer with a civil engineering firm, lost his job, but was fortunately able to freelance for them. Then I was obliged to change to a Jews-only school, a long way from home, but academically highly acceptable. Violence hit us at the time of 'Kristallnacht', when our flat was ransacked by the *SA* and my father and grandfather were – fortunately briefly – dragged off. After that we were evicted from our flat, because a local Nazi big-wig had his eye on it. Gradually I learnt that the world was full, if not of enemies, then at least of potential enemies. Re-segregation took other forms. My father re-registered with the *Israelitische Kultusgemeinde*, much against the grain, given his anti-clerical outlook. A friend of the family, greatly distressed at my lack of a Jewish upbringing, took me to the Great Synagogue in the Tempelgasse on Yom Kippur, my first visit to this or any other place of worship. At the age of nine-and-a-half I learnt what the torah was. He also taught me Hebrew, which my parents accepted, since Palestine (as it then was) was a possible destination for our emigration. Preparations for emigration now dominated our lives. Our preference was for an English-speaking country a safe distance from the continent of Europe: Britain, Australia or the United States. But we were not choosy. On his application form my father filled the destination space with the words, 'die ganze Welt'.

In the end we left for Britain in February 1939, having been sponsored by the family of a retired Anglican clergyman in Hertfordshire. They quite literally saved our lives and I am happy to say that we have maintained contact with their children and grand-children. For my parents the move to Britain was an upheaval, even a trauma, facing my father with the challenge of finding a job in a country he did not know and of whose language he had only a smat-tering. For me it was an adventure. I did not join my family in Hertfordshire, but spent the first few months in a small boarding school – or rather an intimate residential home – for a crash course in English. My father succeeded in finding a job within a few weeks and we moved to New Malden in South London, near his place of work. This move to a large extent determined the way I was to grow up, with one foot in the culture we had left behind and the other in that of our new host society – bi-culturally as I like to call it.

The aims of this bi-culturalism were not necessarily easily recon-ciled. On the one hand there was a consensus within our family that we had left Central Europe for good. Too much had happened, too much that did not bear dwelling on, for the migration to be reversed. We might, if the political climate changed, resume contact with acquaintances or visit relatives, but as a place in which to settle, as a place of permanent residence, Central Europe was out of the question. That meant that the first priority was to learn English, to acculturate to our new environment, to integrate into British society. For my father English was a professional necessity, for my mother an everyday social one, for me and for my younger sister an educational one. Fortunately my crash course stood me in good stead, and in the spring of 1940 I gained a place at the local grammar school. More by accident than by design we had settled in a part of London where there were very few refugees. While we established contact with those that lived in our neighbourhood, we lacked the support-network that we would have benefited from in North-West London, in Swiss Cottage or Golders Green. At both the schools I went to I was the only refugee pupil. What was initially a deprivation became a challenge: we were forced to adapt in a way that we might not have done had we been protected by the comfort of an immigrant ghetto. Thus the omens favoured relatively quick acculturation.

But what were we to do about the culture we had brought with us? Desirable as it was that I should command perfect English as soon as possible, it was equally desirable that I should not forget my German. What, therefore, was the family *lingua franca* to be? The answer was a compromise, which ensured that all of us remained bilingual. That meant not only that we occasionally conversed in German, but that one continued to read German books, of which we had managed to bring out quite a few. Given that at the age of ten I had hardly begun to learn any German literature, I therefore received at least some of the literary education that would have been mine had I grown up in Vienna.

This might be a point at which to digress from the autobiographical chronology and anticipate answers to the question that the editor of this book posed. How much of my cultural persona is attributable to my early history? How much of my literary and artistic tastes have their roots in German-speaking Central Europe? In music I lean heavily towards the Austro-German classics. But these are the mainstay of concert programmes and record collections everywhere, so perhaps that proves nothing. I love to hear Alfred Brendel play Schubert or Elisabeth Schwarzkopf sing Richard Strauss, but the same goes for millions of people who have never set foot in Vienna. I did acquire an early appreciation of Gustav Mahler, well before he achieved the popularity he now enjoys; that may be the only significant exception in my otherwise rather conventional tastes. But I also have a special love for the English Tudor and Jacobean polyphonists, and this I owe to a phase in my life I shall come to later. What goes for music goes for literature. When I find myself in a German city with a good theatre I try to go to performances of the great classics which are not often played in Britain. But equally I try to see Racine or Molière when I am in Paris. So here again, not too much should be read into my theatre-going habits, especially since I do not exactly ignore Shakespeare or Restoration comedy or modern British playwrights. However, when it comes to twentieth-century literature that specialises in the Viennese-Jewish love-hate relationship with the rest of the human race – epitomised by Arthur Schnitzler and Karl Kraus – I do feel a special resonance. No doubt the refugee emigration helped to popularise aspects of Central European creativity that had been previously neglected in Britain and America. But here, too, the impact should not be exaggerated. The greatest British advocate of Sigmund Freud in Britain was Ernest Jones; of Bertolt Brecht it was Kenneth Tynan; of Elias Canetti it is Iris Murdoch; of Karl Kraus it is Edward Timms. There is no one-to-one correlation here. In any case, the purpose of this digression is to make a point to which I shall return, namely that it is very difficult to disentangle the formative influences one has undergone.

I attended my grammar school until 1947: my days there covered the whole of the war. While its course was of universal interest, at school and outside it, my family had, of course, a special stake in its outcome. We shared with everyone the German air raids of 1940 and 1941, as well as the assaults with 'V' weapons in the summer of 1944, but we also knew that a successful German invasion of Britain would have more drastic consequences for us than for our neighbours, and that the elation we would feel at the defeat of Hitler would be more intense. Once more public events impacted on personal fate. My school presented, as I have indicated, an entirely English environment. The syllabus was rather narrow: it included Latin and French, but not (in contrast to my sister's school) German. To my astonishment and embarrassment, I was regarded as an expert on all things to do with Nazi Germany: where would Hitler attack next? How good was the German army? Above all, the constantly nagging question: how could the German people support someone as manifestly mad and wicked as Hitler? Why did they not rise in revolt against him? I coped with these questions as well as a teenager could. Perhaps my attempts in this respect served as an apprenticeship for my later career in punditry.

In 1947 I left school and went to King's College Cambridge to read history. After taking my BA in 1950 I did my military service in the Royal Air Force and then returned to Cambridge for graduate work. At this stage of my education the influences on my later career became much clearer. The Cambridge history syllabus was wide, and covered everything from ancient history and the medieval European economy to modern times. I took a fair spread of subjects, but concentrated as far as possible on the period that interested me most, the nineteenth and twentieth centuries. My special subject was the Third French Republic from Boulanger to Dreyfus, which involved an in-depth study of those 20-odd years with documentation and primary sources. I read, among others, the works of Edouard Drumont, Maurice Barrès, Charles Péguy and Léon Blum. This was the first time that I had had to come to grips at an academic level with a phenomenon that I had witnessed often enough at a personal level: the European Radical Right. I had to write essays, and pass an examination, that required me to understand and explain integral nationalism, religious and racial prejudice, blood-and-soil mystique and anti-Semitism. Above all, it confronted me with a paradox that has taken me the best part of a lifetime to try to resolve: Why was it that the century that I had always associated with the expansion of liberty, with reason, progress and respect for human dignity, with a repudiation of traditional authoritarianism and ancient prejudices, spawned, in its last decades, those irrationalities and superstitions that have haunted my century? Quite a lot of what I have written and lectured on in the past forty years constitutes an attempt to come to terms with that conundrum. My answers, like everyone else's, have been tentative, but I hope I have made my contribution.

So much for one part of my education and one part of my academic agenda, the part can be traced most directly to my own life-history. There were, however, others. Cambridge broadened my mind, as it is bound to do, and helped me to understand my own times better than I should otherwise have understood them. But it was also a further stage in my Anglicisation, as school had been before. In contrast with my school, King's and other colleges had undergraduates with backgrounds similar to mine, and this was naturally a bond between us. But the majority of my contemporaries and friends, including those with whom I have maintained lifelong contact, were British and, for the most part, not Jewish. Perhaps some of them found my company interesting and worthwhile because I was slightly different from them; if so, I hope I was able to reciprocate. As with my fellow-students, so with those who taught me, the influence was overwhelmingly British. Of those whose lectures I attended, only two had a Central European background: Nikolaus Pevsner and Eric Hobsbawm. Those who taught me in college were English to their marrows. Like the best Oxford and Cambridge tutors they treated me as an individual, but without flattery and without concessions. The two who influenced me most, Christopher Morris (now dead) and Noel Annan (still alive and vigorous), both imbued me with the gift of scepticism, a respect for empiricism and, more than anything else, the necessity of writing good, plain English. Both taught me, in a very English way, not to be solemn about my work. Their advice to me was full of common sense that disguised professionalism of a high order. When I asked Noel Annan what book would most help me to a better under-standing of Victorian England, he suggested *Middlemarch*. When Christopher Morris thought that I was overdoing the revision for my Part II Tripos, he firmly ordered me to the university cricket ground, where the West Indies were playing on their first post-war tour with such giants as Worrell, Walcott and Weekes. Relaxation, I learnt, was the key – or at any rate a key – to academic success. My six years in Cambridge undoubtedly formed me more strongly than any other period in my life. Sometimes when I listen to myself lecturing I think I can hear echoes of those who lectured to me.

My life at Cambridge was not exclusively academic. There was music (though I was never a performer). The services at King's College Chapel, which were attended mainly by non-believers, and the recitals by the University Madrigal Society opened the world of Tallis, Gibbons and Byrd to me, to take their place beside Haydn, Mozart and Schubert. There was also politics. For the reasons I have given, it was impossible for an adolescent of my circumstances to ignore politics, but until I went to university I had not been a participant. Now I joined the Labour Club and the debates of the Union Society. Though I never achieved high office, this heightened my interest in British politics, which also played a part in my academic career.

During my undergraduate years I had no clear notion of my professional future, and certainly no well-formed ambition for a university career. This became probable only when I got a First in both parts of the Historical Tripos and the college encouraged me to think I should get financial support if I wanted to return as a research student. Even that, however, provided no guarantee: not every author of a successful doctoral thesis climbs the academic ladder. Moreover, my time in the RAF would give me time to reflect further and to formulate my topic. When I did return to Cambridge in 1954 my plans had matured and clarified. I would once more take up the challenge posed by the Dreyfus affair: the apparent paradox of illiberalism in an age of liberalism, of persecution and discrimination in an age of emancipation. This time, however, I should tackle the question comparatively. I knew, or thought I knew, the background of the affair and the extent to which the literature of ideological anti-Semitism had flourished in nineteenth-century France – not only that of Edouard Drumont and Maurice Barrès, but before them of the Chevalier Gougenot des Mousseaux, Alphonse Toussenel and Pierre-Joseph Fourier. I was aware, as who could not be, of the stages by which the Nazis' racial fantasies had led to marginalisation of Jews, then their deportation and finally mass murder. As for Austria, I had witnessed with my own eyes what Karl Kraus had, in a different context, called the Austrian laboratory of the end of the world, and I knew enough Austrian history to have heard of Karl Lueger and Georg von Schönerer. What remained to be done? Quite simply, to synthesise the phenomenon of European anti-Semitism in the late nineteenth and early twentieth centuries and to provide a historical explanation of the disasters that had befallen my family, my generation, Europe and the world. Three years, I thought, would be adequate to the task.

My doctoral supervisor was Hugh Seton-Watson of the University of London, who combined no-nonsense Scottish scholarship with a deep, family-based understanding of Central and Eastern Europe. He was the ideal guide for my purposes. He introduced me to the existing literature, suggested lines of approach, let me get on with it and drew thick lines through all the passages in my draft chapters that he thought were rubbish. He was totally intolerant of any pretentiousness and superfluous theorising, of any conclusions not supported by the evidence. He cured me of any lingering tendency to use long, empty words, completing the purge begun by my undergraduate tutors. I spent six months in the archives and libraries of Vienna and three months in Berlin. Other than for brief tourist visits, these were my first extended stays in either country since 1939. I met fellow-students and younger historians, who were nevertheless still of a generation to have remembered the Third Reich and the war. Sometimes there were problems of communication. More than once, after I had explained to an archivist or librarian what materials I wanted, I would get the response, 'Ah, yes, you are interested in the Jewish Question'. 'No, no,' I would reply, 'the anti-Semitic question'. Puzzlement sat on their brows.

Though the purpose of my stay was research, its effect was also a re-immersion in the culture of my parents and grandparents. Given the rate of exchange in the 1950s, Austria and the Federal Republic were cheap for anyone coming from Britain. I exhausted the concert, opera and theatre repertoires of both cities, which gave me my first taste of Schiller, Goethe, Lessing, Grillparzer, Schnitzler and Nestroy on German-speaking stages. My only previous exposure to German theatre of that quality had been during the *Berliner Ensemble*'s memorable visit to Britain in 1956. I also spent my time doing what I most like doing, wandering around, discovering – or in the case of Vienna, renewing my acquaintance with – not only the Baroque of Schönbrunn and Charlottenburg, but the more characteristic town-scapes of Otto Wagner and Friedrich Schinkel some decades before they became as popular as they are now. Even as a child I had admired the 'Jugendstil' of the Viennese metropolitan railway that Wagner designed, though without knowing the name of the architect or anything about *fin-de-siècle* style. All these meanderings were a source of great pleasure, but they brought something else home to me. Though I think I understood what I saw better than if I had found myself in, say, Chicago or Leningrad, I did not feel at home in either Vienna or Berlin. I was a visitor – a visitor, no doubt, with special associations, but still someone whose real home was somewhere else. I had spent too long in Britain, undergone too many formative experiences, had become too accustomed to English as the language of daily use, to re-acclimatise myself to places in which I almost certainly did not want to be at home. Vienna, I realised, though the place of my birth, was not my 'Heimatstadt'.

I also made the discovery, in the course of my researches, that all thesis-writers make, namely that I had bitten off more than I could chew. I was collecting so much material on Germany and Austria before 1918 that any thought of including France soon turned out to be unrealistic. In any case, restricting the thesis to Germany and Austria made additional sense. I felt more confident in my judgement on them, even though my starting-point had been the Dreyfus affair, and the interaction between developments in the German-speaking areas was much clearer and much more in need of demonstration. I completed my thesis in 1960. It was published in 1964, translated into German in 1966, reissued in 1988, and is still in print.[1] I suppose that whatever professional reputation I have is based on it more than on anything else that I have written.

In choosing my research topic I had set myself a specific aim: to try to solve a problem that certainly related to my own life, but that I hoped was also of more general interest and concern. The book was reasonably well received, and quite widely adopted as a course text in the United States. On the other hand, it was not my intention to devote my life's work to this topic. I did not want to become a one-trick circus dog. By the time I finished my thesis, I had been appointed to a lectureship in politics at Oxford; by the time my book was published, I had become an Official Student (ie a Tutorial Fellow, a tenured position) in Politics and Modern History at Christ Church, Oxford. The syllabus that I was required to teach did not have all that much to do with my research preoccupations. Modern German history came into it, as did twentieth-century political movements. No one at this stage wanted to write any theses that I would have been qualified to supervise on anti-Semitism or modern Jewish political history, or even theories of nationalism. The subjects I mainly taught were comparative government, international relations and British government.

This change of tack did not disturb me. I had, after all, applied for these jobs, knowing what they would entail, and the responsibilities that went with them fitted some of my other interests. Growing up when I did, I had acquired a general interest in – one might almost say obsession with – politics. This was strengthened during my time at Cambridge, but did not originate there. I was particularly fascinated by the 1945 general election in Britain, which resulted in the defeat of Churchill and the election of a Labour Government. It was the first free election I had experienced. I kept a voluminous file of newspaper clippings on the campaign and its outcome which I still have. When, in 1995, the Fabian Society decided to organise a meeting and an exhibition on the fiftieth anniversary of this event, I was able to supply some material for it from this collection.

The early 1960s saw a sudden boom in the scientific study of electoral behaviour, which had originated in the United States and then spread first to Britain and then to Germany and elsewhere in continental Europe. Given my obsessions and my presence in Oxford, where David Butler of Nuffield College was the pioneer of the new science, I was well placed to take advantage of this boom. Over the next twenty years I wrote for various British newspapers on aspects of electoral analysis, as well as commenting on campaigns and popular votes for British and foreign broadcasting media. In 1967 I published a text book, *Political Representation and Elections in Britain*, which went through three editions and sold more copies than any of my other books. At the same time, given my continued interest in German politics, I also began to follow current West German party and electoral developments more closely. I took part in the first academic election study in the Federal Republic, organised by the Sociology Department of the University of Cologne in 1961. In fact, my first publications, which appeared before my book on anti-Semitism, were on West German party politics. Later in the 1960s I participated in a comparative study, initiated by Political and Economic Planning (PEP) of London, of West European party systems, contributing the section on Austria.

I hope that by now the nature of my bi-culturalism and its influence on my scholarly interests have become clearer. I had the major advantage of being bi-lingual and of being able to maintain an interest in German and Austrian affairs at least as great as that in British politics. On the one hand Britain was my home and I was a politically active citizen there. Much of my teaching related to current British issues and in so far as I was known to the British public at all it was in connection with my contribution to domestic topics. Similarly, what I wrote on post-1945 German and Austrian politics fell largely under the heading of my appointment as a Lecturer in Politics, informed though it was by my own historically-determined insights. It is fair to say that in the ten years after the publication of my book on anti-Semitism, my interest in German-related subjects took a subordinate place. After my 1961 election study I did not visit the Federal Republic again until 1969, again for an election study. I went to Vienna briefly in 1967 in connection with the PEP project, but that was my only visit to Austria between 1958 and 1984. My main foreign engagements were a series of visiting professorships in the USA, first at the University of Wisconsin, then at the Johns Hopkins Graduate School in Washington DC and at the University of Calilfornia in Los Angeles. I seemed to have attained one of my ambitions, that of not being a one-trick circus dog.

One's first trick, however, is never entirely forgotten. I had published my book on anti-Semitism at a low point of interest in that subject. Though I was asked to write a few reviews and give the odd lecture on related topics, there was not much demand for a follow-up. By the 1970s the situation began to change. Interest in German-Jewish history had revived, and the subject was beginning to flourish. In part that was undoubtedly due to the pioneering work of the Leo Baeck Institutue, founded in Jerusalem in 1955, and its increasingly scholarly and influential *Year Book*. In part it was also due to the broadening range of interest on the part of the German – and, somewhat later, Austrian – historical profession, which was a general phenomenon of the 1960s. The session on German-Jewish history at the *Historikertag* in Braunschweig in 1974, the first of its kind, was a significant symptom of this increased interest. This had two consequences. Though the *lingua franca* of German-Jewish studies continued to be English, since most of its practitioners were domiciled in English-speaking countries and the Leo Baeck Institute's *Year Book* was published in English, innovative works were once more appearing in German. In part the authors were German-born scholars living in the United States, Britain or Israel, like Ernest Hamburger, Hans Liebeschütz and Jacob Toury. The even more significant second consequence was that a generation of West German historians was emerging which devoted itself to researching and popularising the social, cultural and political history of the Jews of Germany. Those historians, in turn, have cultivated a successor generation of doctoral students and young academics, so that German-Jewish studies are now part of the mainstream of German historiography. This welcome development provided my own work with a new environment, and I was gradually drawn back to my original interest, first in Britain, then in the USA, then in Germany and Austria.

Let me mention a few instances of this development, in order to illustrate both the range of activities that arose out of this new level of interest and the way I was able to become involved in some of it. My entry into structured and organised German-Jewish history came, as for so many in both the English- and German-speaking worlds, through the Leo Baeck Institute, in my case that in London. The first invitation came in the 1960s with a request to contribute an essay on anti-Semitism in the Weimar Republic to the first of the Institute's now celebrated 'Sammelbände', *Entscheidungsjahr 1932*.[2] Unfortunately I could not accept that – I had too many other commitments – but I was able to participate in the third 'Sammelband', *Juden in Wilhelminischen Deutschland 1890-1914*, which came out in 1976. My essay in that dealt with the role of Jews in public life during the *Kaiserreich*.[3] Originally that chapter was to have been written by Ernest Hamburger, the author of the standard classic work, *Juden im öffentlichen Leben Deutschlands*,[4] but he was beginning to feel too old for this project, especially as he was also working on a sequel to his first volume to cover the Weimar Republic, a sequel that he was unfortunately unable to complete. This did mean, however, that I was able to seek his advice and draw on his unique store of personal knowledge and mature judgement. One could not have wished for a better apprenticeship.

There was another respect in which this particular approach suited me. I think of myself primarily as a historian of modern Germany and Austria. I have never been a specialist on the internal life of Jewish communities, on Jewish thought or on Jewish doctrinal or organisational controversies. Given my secular upbringing and my broad interests in political history, I approach German-Jewish topics under two headings: the German-Jewish experience as part of German (or Austrian) history, and the political developments of those two countries in their impact on modern Jewish history. It is the interaction that fascinates me, not the treatment of hermetically isolated topics. In this way I follow the tradition founded by Ernest Hamburger, and by Jacob Toury in Israel, with his *Die politischen Orientierungen der Juden in Deutschland*.[5] Later works, like Werner Mosse's two volumes on the German-Jewish economic élite,[6] follow a similar method. Looked at in this way, the study of anti-Semitism, and of Jewish and Gentile reactions to it, fits into a general consideration of modern mass movements and of nationalism, xenophobia and ethnic exclusiveness. The study of Jewish participation in business, politics or the media fits into a general consideration of the openness of particular societies and of the social mobility and career patterns that they permit. The study of Jewish family structures, fertility and marital stability can shed light on overall discussion of these subjects and of the degree to which particular moral traditions can survive in societies in which there is a general trend towards homogenised secularism. In this way the study of Jewish themes adds a dimension to the study of our own times and our forefathers'; it also makes it accessible and attractive to those who have no personal links with Jewish life.

I have no means of knowing whether I contributed, through my early writings, to the present level of interest in German- and Austrian-Jewish history. There is, however, no doubt that the growth of interest has brought me back to that subject more than would otherwise have been the case. In the last twenty years I have written ten papers on various aspects of it, published one major book, *Jews and the German State* (Oxford, 1992), and contributed to the four-volume *German-Jewish History in Modern Times*, edited by Michael A. Meyer of Hebrew Union College, Cincinnati, which is being published in English, German and Hebrew. I have lost count of the number of conferences that I have attended and at which I either read papers or acted as discussant. Most of these papers have been demanded, ie they were a response to requests from academic bodies in Britain, the USA, Germany, Austria and Italy. No doubt I should have continued to work on this and related topics in any case, but almost certainly not on this escalating and sometimes hectic scale.

The growth in demand has been gratifying in a number of ways. It is a recognition that my original choice of research, and the questions and answers it entailed, had some justification. It has enabled me to make contacts with a growing number of scholars in three continents, whose agenda coincides, or at least overlaps, with mine. Lastly, some of the occasions at which I have been present have given me particular satisfaction. The first conference of the Leo Baeck Institute on German soil took place in Berlin in 1985; the Institute's fortieth birthday was celebrated not only in London, New York and Jerusalem, the sites of the original centres, but in Bonn, where a public meeting attracted a large number of people who would otherwise not have given as much thought to the subject or heard of the organisations involved. It certainly gave me a feeling of something achieved that I was able to be present at both, and to act as something of a missionary for German-Jewish studies, given that these studies have a didactic as well as a purely scholarly aspect in the German-Austrian context. But the sweetest of all experiences occurred in Vienna in 1984. I was invited on the occasion of the magnificent exhibition 'Traum und Wirklichkeit' ('Dream and Reality') that dealt with *fin-de-siècle* Vienna. I not only took part in a long discussion on the Austrian-Jewish identity on the television talk-show 'Club 2', but was asked to lecture on the history of Austrian anti-Semitism in Karl Lueger's very own City Hall. That gave me quite a thrill.

In spite of these increasing demands, which will no doubt continue, I remain committed to having more than one trick in my repertoire. Though I have supervised a number of doctoral theses on modern Jewish topics, generally, though not always, with a German context, most of my teaching has been in comparative politics, with a German and occasionally Austrian bias. My most recent book, *German Politics 1945-1995* (Oxford, 1995), is the outcome of this teaching and my next two books will, if my plans materialise, also be on general German political history.

How, then, to answer the question of the influence of my personal background on my scholarly interests? The first thing to say is that I have two backgrounds, one Central European, the other English. Though born in Vienna, I have spent seven-eighths of my life in Britain. I have been a British citizen since 1947. My main language is English; it is the language in which I prefer to speak, teach and write and in which I communicate with my family. Though I have Central Europeans, or their descendants, among my close acquaintances, the vast majority of my social or intellectual circle is British. In so far as I have been politically active, that has been in Britain and in a British context. I suspect that my predominantly empirical ways of thought owe a great deal more to my English education then to any other factor. It may even be – and others can judge this better than I can – that the way I think and write about German-Jewish topics has been influenced by my English education and environment and by the model of Jewish-Gentile co-existence that I grew up with in Britain.

If I were asked to place myself socially – in itself no doubt a British preoccupation – it would be in the English professional middle class, which has shown itself accommodating and welcoming to many people like me. I move with ease in continental Europe and the fall of the Iron Curtain has enabled me to extend my repertoire. I can now go, with a minimum of bureaucratic hassle, to those parts of Central Europe that share a Habsburg or German heritage but were until recently closed off. I can relish the baroque, neo-classicism and *art nouveau* of Prague and Budapest, Riga and Cracow, even Lviv and Tchernisvsty (Czernowitz to my readers), as I have long relished them in Vienna, Munich and Berlin. But could I live in any of these cities?

I could if I had to. The practicalities would pose no problems. I speak the language, I know where to get a reasonably priced schnitzel and which tram to catch to which theatre. But I would not feel totally comfortable. There are too many ghosts. If I had to live outside Oxford and outside Britain, I might be better off somewhere totally neutral, like Zurich or Grenoble or Boston. I shall continue to write about modern Jewish history and the German-Jewish and Austrian-Jewish experience: it is part of my life, but not the whole of my life. I shall continue to observe and write about the politics of Germany and Central Europe. But I shall prefer to do so from the comfort and safety of this side of the Channel. I know where my roots are, but I also know where my home is. I do not want to change either of them.

**Notes**

1   *The Rise of Political Anti-Semitism in Germany and Austria* (New York, 1964); *Die Entstehung des politischen Antisemitismus in Deutschland und Österreich 1867 bis 1914* (Gütersloh, 1966).

2   See p 159.

3   Peter Pulzer, 'Die jüdische Beteiligung an der Politik', in Werner E. Mosse (ed.), *Juden im Wilhelminischen Deutschland 1890-1914* (Tübingen, 1976), pp 143-239.

4   Ernest Hamburger, *Juden im öffentlichen Leben Deutschlands: Regierungsmitglieder, Beamte und Parlamentarier in der monarchischen Zeit, 1848-1918* (Tübingen, 1968).

5   Jacob Toury, *Die politischen Orientierungen der Juden in Deutschland: Von Jena bis Weimar* (Tübingen, 1966).

6   See p 159.

## Selected Writings of Peter Pulzer

### Books

*The Rise of Political Anti-Semitism in Germany and Austria* (New York, 1964; revised edition: London/Cambridge, Mass., 1988; German edition: Gütersloh, 1966)

*Political Representation and Elections in Britain* (London, 1967)

*Jews and the German State: The Political History of a Minority, 1848-1933* (Oxford, 1992)

*German Politics 1945-1995* (Oxford, 1995)

### Articles

'Responsible Party Government and Stable Coalition: the Case of the German Federal Republic', *Political Studies*, June 1978, pp 181-208

'German Historians Debate the Holocaust', *Patterns of Prejudice*, Autumn 1987, pp 3-14

'Responsible Party Government: What Has Changed?', in Herbert Döring and Dieter Grosser (eds), *Grossbritannien: Ein Regierungssystem in der Belastungsprobe* (Opladen, 1987), pp 15-29

'Jews and Nation-Building in Germany', *Leo Baeck Institute Year Book* 41 (1996), pp 199-214

**Nicolai Rubinstein**

# Germany, Italy, and England[1]

I was born in 1911 in Berlin, where I spent my childhood. My father was a publisher. I was at first privately educated and then attended the *Mommsen-Gymnasium*. Later I transferred to the *Französische Gymnasium*, where nearly all the teaching was in French, which meant that I became virtually bilingual. When I was fourteen I left the *Französische Gymnasium* and spent two-and-a-half years, because of chest problems, first at Arosa and Montana in Switzerland and then in the Black Forest in Germany. After I returned to Berlin, I prepared myself with two teachers, one in Latin and Greek and one in mathematics, for the *Abitur*, which I passed in 1930. In the same year I began university studies in Berlin. My subjects were political economy and history, but after the first year I decided that statistics and business management were not for me, and consequently took history as my main and philosophy as my secondary subject. I first went to the introductory seminar of the medievalist Walter Holtzmann and then attended the seminar of the historian of the medieval Papacy Erich Caspar. He had a lasting influence on my formation as a historian. Other teachers who influenced me were the historian of Renaissance humanism Hans Baron and the philosopher Nicolai Hartmann, whose seminar on Plato I attended. I also went to lectures, among others, by the classical scholar Werner Jaeger, the historian Friedrich Meinecke and the art historian Hans Kauffmann.

When I left Germany in 1933 – my family emigrated to France – I was already working on my doctoral thesis on the Paduan humanist Pier Paolo Vergerio, under the supervision of Hans Baron. In Paris, I did research at the Bibliothèque Nationale; I was offered a place at the École Normale, which I turned down, because I decided to continue my university studies in Florence. I arrived in Florence on the last day of 1933. Florence appealed to me more than Padua, although in view of the subject of my thesis it would have been more sensible for me to go there. My supervisor at the university was the outstanding historian Nicola Ottokar, a Russian émigré who held the chair of medieval history. I took my doctorate at the University of Florence in 1935, with high marks, and as a result became the assistant to Ottokar, who put me in charge of some of his undergraduate teaching.

I continued to work in this capacity until 1938. After the conclusion of the Axis pact between Italy and Germany, Hitler persuaded Mussolini to introduce racial laws similar to those in Germany, and all foreign Jews were forced to leave Italy. I actually stayed longer than I should have done – I just did not feel like leaving Florence. This was risky, but friends of mine protected me. I finally left Italy in the spring of 1939, and returned briefly to Paris to see my family. At that time I was planning to go to the United States and had the affidavit which would have allowed me to do so. But I had a friend in London whom I had met in Florence, where he had told me that if ever I wanted to come and visit him, I would be welcome, so I decided to go first to London. I stayed with him for some months, and remain profoundly grateful to him for his introduction to English life. Then the war broke out, and I remained in England.

I had learnt Greek and Latin at school and through private tuition, French at home and at school, and had acquired, before I went to Florence, a fairly good reading knowledge of Italian (at one point, I decided that an excellent way to do so was to read the *Divina Commedia* from beginning to end); but I never had tuition in English. I had acquired colloquial English during my stay in Switzerland and had improved it in Florence. My problem was how to write in English. A few months after my arrival in England I got a grant from the Society for the Protection of Science and Learning. This grant was made dependent on my doing some academic teaching. It must have been owing to the support of the leading medieval historian F.M. Powicke that I was asked to give a course of lectures for the Faculty of Modern History at Christ Church in Oxford. I consequently moved to Oxford, where I also did tutorial work. I was not interned after the German invasion of Holland and Belgium in 1940 because, as my parents were of Hungarian nationality, I too had a Hungarian passport; and when in 1941 Hungary joined the alliance with Germany, the internment process had already been reversed. So I became a 'friendly enemy alien' and could go on with teaching until the end of the war. Like other refugees, I was subject to a number of restrictions, but these were very small inconveniences considering what many people had to endure during the war.

From January 1942 I taught history at Southampton University College, where I had been appointed to a temporary lectureship, but kept up my contacts with Oxford through tutorial teaching during weekends. When I arrived at Southampton, there were three of us in the history department of the University College. After one year, one of the three left, and from then onwards there were just two of us; my colleague, Alwyn Ruddock, taught all of English history, and I European history from 476 to 1914. As a result, I had little time for research. The first longer piece I published was 'The beginnings of political thought in Florence', an article on which I had been working even before I left Florence and which came out in 1942 in the *Journal of the Warburg and Courtauld Institutes.*

In 1945 I applied for a vacant lectureship at Westfield College, which formed part of the University of London, and was appointed to it. I remained at Westfield until my retirement in 1978. I taught medieval European history and the history of political ideas from Plato to Machiavelli, and the special subject on Florence during the Renaissance. The main differences, in the London history syllabus, between special subjects and the main papers is that the former are based on study of primary sources. In those days, these had to be in the original language; today, owing to the general decline in the linguistic abilities of undergraduates, they are translated into English. At Westfield College I had more time for research, although the teaching schedule was fairly heavy; and we had sabbatical leave every seven years. It was a small college (it is now merged with Queen Mary College) and I was at different times Head of Department, Dean and Vice-Principal. One of my colleagues in the history department was Francis Carsten; other eminent scholars included May McKisack, Christopher Brooke and Henry Loyn.

In 1947 I returned to Italy for the first time after the war, and from then on went there every year, often more than once, because Italy, and Florence in particular, remained at the centre of my research. In 1983 I taught for one semester at the University of Florence. In London I had a seminar on medieval Italian history at the Institute of Historical Research, which I began in 1949. A number of my postgraduate students, among them Roslyn Pesman Cooper, Dale and F.W. Kent, Robert Black, Lorenzo Polizzotto,

Diana Webb, Paula Clarke, Kate Lowe and John Henderson, have become distinguished historians and university teachers; and in general I could probably say that I have helped to produce a school of historians in the field of the Italian Renaissance in the English-speaking world.

Looking back on my academic career, I must emphasise that there is an important difference between me and the other historians who emigrated from Germany to Britain. Almost all of these continued to work on German history or went back to it, whereas I continued to work on Italian history; and as a result, after the war, had at first practically no contact with German historians. While German intellectual life in general had suffered profoundly from the emigration of writers, artists, and scholars, the impact of that emigration was particularly destructive in the field of Renaissance history, in which German and Austrian scholars had been playing a leading role since the days of Jacob Burckhardt. In 1933 a very large number of these scholars were Jewish, and as a result of their emigration there were hardly any historians in my field left in Germany after the war. This has gradually changed, but there are still considerable lacunae in German research on Renaissance Italy. My academic contacts outside England were, after the war, and have been ever since, predominantly with Italy and with America, where Renaissance studies have been flourishing.

One of my first visits to Germany after the war took place in 1981, when I was invited to read a paper at a conference in Berlin. I was also invited, on similar occasions, to Würzburg, Göttingen, Wolfenbüttel and Bonn, as well as in 1986 to the meeting of the Association of German Historians at Trier. For many years, until 1991, I was a member of the *Kuratorium* of the German *Kunsthistorische Institut* in Florence, most of whose annual meetings took place in Munich.

It goes without saying that my German background had a profound influence on my intellectual development, my scholarly work and my academic career. Even now, Goethe means much to me, as did for many years Stefan George. Although of Hungarian nationality, I always considered myself to be German by culture, even after I came to live in Italy, where I had many German friends, among them Wolfgang Frommel and Karl Wolfskehl, and the eminent German historian of Florence, Robert Davidsohn, to whom I owe a great deal in more ways than one. On an academic level, my training at the Friedrich-Wilhelms University in Berlin, though lasting only three years, had an enduring influence on my development as a scholar and teacher. I have mentioned Erich Caspar: his teaching of the techniques of historical research have left a permanent mark on my work as a historian, and when I began to have my own seminar in London, his seminar served me as a model of postgraduate teaching. I am afraid I also inherited some of the sense of scholarly superiority which formed part of German historical culture in the nineteenth and early twentieth centuries, and it took me some time to shed this legacy. I gradually learned from and adopted English traditions of historical research and writing, yet the earlier German influence certainly retained a great deal of its importance for my work in later life, when it was reinforced and broadened in significant ways through my long association with the Warburg Institute, of which I am now an Honorary Fellow.

I am one of those scholars who write articles rather than books. I think my most important book is *The Government of Florence under the Medici*, of which I have just completed a revised edition. I have also published two volumes of the edition of the letters of Lorenzo de' Medici. I am the general editor of this edition.

Since 1947, I have been a British subject. In belonging to a political community, much depends on how exclusive this bond is meant to be. As a citizen, I belong to England; as a member of a cultural community, I consider myself European. I love Italy, and feel half Florentine: in fact, I am an honorary citizen of Florence. I am deeply attached to England; I lived here during the war, and this has been an indelible experience for me.

## Note

1    This essay is based on an interview given by Nicolai Rubinstein to the editor on 1 June 1996 in London.

## Selected Writings of Nicolai Rubinstein

Books

*The Government of Florence under the Medici (1434 to 1494)* (Oxford, 1966)

(ed.), *Lorenzo de' Medici, Lettere*, volume 3 (Florence, 1977), volume 4 (Florence, 1981)

*The Palazzo Vecchio 1298-1532: Government, Architecture, and Imagery in the Civic Palace of the Florentine Republic* (Oxford, 1995)

Articles

'The Beginnings of Political Thought in Florence', *Journal of the Warburg and Courtauld Institutes* 5 (1942), pp 198-227

'I primi anni del Consiglio Maggiore di Firenze (1494-98)', *Archivio Storico Italiano* 112 (1954), pp 151-94, 321-47

'The Beginnings of Niccolò Machiavelli's Career in the Florentine Chancery', *Italian Studies* 11 (1956), pp 72-91

'Some Ideas on Municipal Progress and Decline in the Italy of the Communes', in D.J. Gordon (ed.), *Fritz Saxl: A Volume of Memorial Essays* (Edinburgh, 1957), pp 165-83

'Firenze e il problema della politica imperiale al tempo di Massimiliano I', *Archivio Storico Italiano* 116 (1958), pp 5-35, 147-77

'Political Ideas in Sienese Art: the Frescoes by Ambrogio Lorenzetti and Taddeo di Bartolo in the Palazzo Pubblico', *Journal of the Warburg and Courtauld Institutes* 21 (1958), pp 179-207

'Marsilius of Padua and Italian Political Thought of his Time', in J.R. Hale, J.R.L. Highfield and B. Smalley (eds), *Europe in the Late Middle Ages* (London, 1965), pp 44-75

'Florentine Constitutionalism and Medici Ascendancy in the Fifteenth Century', in N. Rubinstein (ed.), *Florentine Studies* (London, 1968), pp 442-62

'Machiavelli and the World of Florentine Politics', in M. Gilmore (ed.), *Studies on Machiavelli* (Florence, 1972), pp 5-28

'Lorenzo de' Medici: the Formation of his Statecraft', *Proceedings of the British Academy* 63 (1977), pp 73-94

'Le dottrine politiche nel Rinascimento', in *Il Rinascimento: Interpretazioni e problemi* (Bari, 1979), pp 183-237

'Il regime politico di Firenze dopo il Tumulto dei Ciompi', in *Il Tumulto dei Ciompi: Un momento di storia fiorentina ed europea* (Florence, 1981), pp 105-24

'The *de optimo cive* and the *de principe* by Bartolomeo Platina', in R. Cardini, E. Garin, L. Cesarini Martelli and G. Pascucci (eds), *Tradizione classica e letteratura umanistica: Per Alessandro Perosa* (Rome, 1985), pp 375-89

'Florentina Libertas', *Rinascimento* 26 (1986), pp 3-26

'The History of the Word *politicus* in Early-Modern Europe', in A. Pagden (ed.), *Ideas in Context: The Language of Political Theory in*

*Early-Modern Europe* (Cambridge, 1987), pp 41-56

'Machiavelli storico', *Annali della Scuola Normale di Pisa: Classe di lettere e filosofia*, series 3, 17, 3 (1987), pp 695-733

'Das politische System Italiens in der zweiten Hälfte des 15. Jahrhunderts', in *'Bündnissysteme' und 'Aussenpolitik' im späten Mittelalter* (*Zeitschrift für Historische Forschung*, Beiheft 5, 1988), pp 105-19

**Walter Ullmann**

# A Tale of

# Two Cultures[1]

I was born in Pulkau, Lower Austria, on 29 November 1910, the son of Dr Rudolf Ullmann, a general practitioner, and Leopoldine Ullmann, in a house where my mother's ancestors had lived since the seventeenth century. My father was a Sudeten German. I attended the local primary school, and then the *Gymnasium* in Horn, from which I graduated in 1929. My parents had intended to send me to the *Gymnasium* in Kremsmünster, but the inflation of those years meant that they could not afford to. So I had to go to Horn, and I commuted there daily by train for eight years. It was a hard training, but one that toughened me up. I started each day at 5.30 in the morning, walked about three kilometres to the station, and when I returned from Horn in the evening, I had to do my homework in preparation for the next day at school. I owe an enormous amount to the teachers who taught me German, Latin, Greek and history there. They laid the foundations for my later career. At that time students had to write a small dissertation in one of their exam subjects for their school leaving certificate. I chose Greek, and wrote about Thucydides and the Athenian expedition to Sicily. The subjects that attracted me most at school were Greek constitutional history, law and philosophy. In my second year at secondary school Solon's constitutional reforms were my special interest. From that time on, an interest in political science, political thought and law never left me.

The choice of what to study at university was not easy for me – for a long time I could not decide between classical philology and law. Finally I opted for law because it seemed to have a connection with the ancient world while also being orientated towards the present. At that time Leopold Wenger from Munich was giving a short introductory course in Roman law at Vienna. Later he was replaced by Friedrich von Woess. Both made a deep impression on me, Wenger because of his charming, witty, almost playful way of lecturing which revealed much wisdom and good sense, and Woess because of his strikingly polished, precise and clear-cut explanation of the institutions. Even after so many years, I can still hear the opening words of his first lecture: 'The institutions of Roman law do not lead an imaginary existence above the clouds'. Woess was the most full-blooded lawyer I have ever met. I later attended a seminar by Ernst Schoenbauer, who came from my part of the country. The information about Roman law which these two professors imparted long formed most of my basic stock of legal knowledge. (Many years later, at the Accursius celebrations held in Bologna in 1963,[2] I met Schoenbauer again. He was representing the Austrian Academy, and seemed to remember me. At the time he took a lively part in the Caracalla discussions.) I was less impressed by Rudolf Koestler, Hans Voltelini and Alfons Dopsch, because it seemed to me that they lacked a classical background. I found Emil Goldmann's classes on German legal history pedantic. Although I made good progress in my subject, I thought it was a great pity that the students were left so much to their own devices. One had no contact with the professors, only at best with young assistants, and they were extremely sparing with advice and help concerning literature and sources. How was a student who had just left school meant to find his way through the literature? I had many questions, but the only people I could discuss them with were the other students in the student home in the Porzellangasse, and that did not bring me much profit. I hated big-city life in Vienna. The hustle and bustle, the pace and the undeniable superficiality of Viennese life at that time disgusted me. Among my relatives in Vienna I was close only to the Engelhart family – Josef Engelhart, a well-known painter and sculptor, and his son Michel, later to become a professor at the *Technische Hochschule* in Vienna and the architect of the reconstructed *Burgtheater*. But even they could only temporarily alleviate my uneasiness. After taking the first state exam in April 1931, I considered whether to switch to a German university or a different one in Austria. In the summer I decided to go to Innsbruck.

This step was a turning point in my life. There I immediately felt at home and among like-minded people; there it was possible to get advice from a professor, and to discuss problems that were addressed in the lectures. In a word, students were guided in their study of law.

Written work was marked and commented on by the professor himself. In Innsbruck I attended lectures by Theodor Rittler who, next to Woess, was the scholar who made the most lasting impression on me. He was a brilliant teacher who could awaken a thirst for knowledge and a feeling for academic work among his students, and was able to give a young lawyer scholarly tools. To him I owe a scholarly way of thinking and a passion for research and knowledge. I considered it a great honour that he later entrusted me with the task of compiling and correcting the index to the second volume of his *Strafrecht* (1937). I remain very fond of Franz Gschnitzer, who died prematurely. His lectures on civil law were incomparably better than those given by Pisek in Vienna. Gschnitzer's openness was impressive. If he did not know a verdict or the answer to a question, he admitted it quite frankly. His modesty and helpfulness were no less 'instructive' than his spoken commentaries. Karl Wolff, on the other hand, the second lecturer on civil law in Innsbruck, was entirely uninteresting and uninterested. The other teachers were thorough, especially Paul Kretschmar, but not inspiring. They were all overshadowed by Rittler and Gschnitzer. My student years at the *Oenipontana*[3] were the happiest years of my life. I had many friends, and the incomparable natural beauty of the mountains combined with my personal and intellectual circumstances to create a unique harmony. In Innsbruck I met the men who, a few years later, were to play a fateful role in my life. Dr Hans Werder, one of the most brilliant men one could ever meet, was at that time the librarian of the Law Department library and he gave me an enormous amount of encouragement and advice. He had been a student of Ernst Beling's in Munich (with whom I had established contact myself). The other was Johannes Count Sarnthein, member of an old Tyrolean aristocratic family.

I began my legal career in the *Landesgericht* (district court) of Innsbruck in January 1934, after having received my PhD on 13 December 1933. My mother wanted me to be near home (my father had died in 1932). I therefore applied for a transfer as soon as 1934, first to the *Bezirksgericht* (county court) in Retz, and a little later to the district court in Korneuburg, where I stayed until I was appointed to the *Zivillandesgericht* (district civil court) in Vienna in February 1938. In Korneuburg there were excellent lawyers. Fellner, for example, later achieved a high position in the *Oberlandesgericht* (supreme court) in Vienna, and Pallin obtained a high position (*Generalprokurator*) there after the war. On Rittler's recommendation I became an (unpaid) assistant to Ferdinand Kadecka, professor of criminal law. At the same time I was also working, mostly in criminal departments, and generally in the court of appeal for criminal matters decided by the lower courts of the district, but also in pre-trial preparations, where I unfortunately had to deal with a number of political cases. However, these practical activities were extraordinarily fruitful for my academic work.

To begin with I concentrated on the essence of the criminal offence, and read voraciously. I lived in Vienna in order to be able to work in the National Library or University Library after office hours, when I was not required to teach at the university. I also gave lectures on criminal procedure at the *Oberlandesgericht*, whose President Leonhard organized regular sessions for trainee lawyers. Kadecka explained that there was much useful work to be done in legal history, and drew my attention to recently published works such as those by G. Dahm, Friedrich Schaffstein etc. The subject of criminal offence had expanded enormously. I found the literature which Kadecka had mentioned extremely interesting, and I began to study the postglossators[4] in earnest. As there was nobody who could help me in Vienna, the above-mentioned Hans Werder, who had in the meantime become Kadecka's full-time assistant, advised me to contact Woldemar Engelmann in Marburg, at that time the leading authority on the postglossators in the field of criminal justice. He did, indeed, turn out to be extremely helpful. My *habilitation* thesis was to be on the doctrine of the criminal attempt among the postglossators. I gave a number of reports on my work in the seminar. By the time of the *Anschluss*, my thesis was progressing quite well.

By virtue of my professional activities and my official work I soon recognised the true nature of the new regime. I had earned the merciless hatred of the Schuschnigg regime's so-called victims of justice, and had thus attracted the attention of the *Gestapo*. Moreover, I thought that the crisis of May 1938[5] would inevitably lead to war (my confidence in the great powers proved to be misplaced). Like many others, I believed that the imminent war would put an end to the Nazi nightmare by autumn 1938 at the latest, and I was determined not to serve the villains now in power under any circumstances. I accepted Werder's advice to disappear and go to England for a while. Count Sarnthein, who had settled in Vienna shortly after his marriage, gave me the same advice. Both had connections in England. Sarnthein was mainly responsible for getting me out of the clutches of the *Gestapo*. Added to all this it came as an unpleasant surprise that my grandparents on my father's side were not of the right racial origins (something of which I had been unaware). But in order to leave the country legally, I needed the permission of the military authorities, and I was granted four weeks' 'study leave'. I told my landlady that I had to go away for a while and, equipped with a return ticket, went to England to continue my studies in Cambridge, which had the best library of medieval legal literature. The Society for the Protection of Science and Learning arranged all this for me. I hoped to finish my research by the autumn, that is, at the same time as the end of the Nazi regime. 'Munich',[6] however, destroyed all my hopes. As a refugee, and not even an Austrian any more, but a German from the Third Reich, and legally classed as a deserter, I found myself totally uprooted in a foreign country, although I had such strong roots in my native soil. In Cambridge I was even suspected of being a Nazi spy. I had never, however, been active politically. My opinions were conservative-Catholic. The times that followed were hard, depressing, wearing and full of cares. I came to know bitter poverty, need, deprivation, social uncertainty and anxiety about the future. I was totally without means, and my possessions were limited to the contents of the suitcase with which I had arrived. I was constantly plagued by doubts about the correctness of my decision. Added to this were worries about my mother, who had to collect my things from my lodgings in the Langegasse and take them home. After the war she told me that she had felt as if she were collecting the possessions of someone who had died. She survived the war in Pulkau, but died in 1949, just as she was preparing to visit us in England. Shortly after Germany's invasion of the Sudeten areas of Czechoslovakia, Dr Werder himself came to stay with his friends in England to escape the war. He remained in England, dying many years after the war from the effects of a heart attack (his brother had been in the *SS* in Germany).

In Cambridge I enjoyed the goodwill of many scholars, foremost among them H.D. Hazeltine, the legal historian, W.W. Buckland, the Roman law jurist, and Robin Laffan, the historian. I lived on the funds I received from a refugee committee and the Society already mentioned. High-minded, understanding people put me up, always of course for limited periods. It was a restless and insecure existence. However, from time to time I could forget my cares as I immersed myself in my work. The libraries in Cambridge are indeed unique, and especially that of Trinity College, where I worked most of the time. A highly condensed summary of my (intended) *habilitation* thesis was published just before the outbreak of the war in the *Revue d'histoire du droit*, which at that time was edited by E.M. Meijers in

Leiden. After a year during which the hardship and distress I suffered can be appreciated only by those who have gone through a similar experience, friends helped me to find a job at Ratcliffe College, a Catholic boarding school in Leicestershire, in the summer of 1939. I had a heavy teaching load, but could also continue my work. Life became bearable, and I found myself among like-minded people. I shall always remember with affection the school, run by the order founded by Antonio Rosmini, for the salvation it offered me. A close relationship persists to the present day. Even if my salary was rather meagre – I earned £50 per year, that is, the same as the housemaids – at least I was 'independent'. After a few months, my salary was increased to £70. I felt like Croesus, and could even afford to buy books.

In the winter of 1939-40 I began to publish in English, in the field of legal history. My position was made inconceivably more difficult by the fact that all my legal training, practical experience and love for the subject were of no use to me in England because the English legal system, the common law, is so completely different. What seemed like a serious disadvantage, however, was to turn into a great advantage because I was able to explain medieval legal sources which nobody in this country had yet studied in depth, although libraries hold vast amounts in this field. I was able to become something like a bridge-builder. Scholars in England had only a vague notion of the medieval *ius commune* and ecclesiastical law. It also gradually became clear to me that medieval jurisprudence and the law had played a much larger part in the historical process than medievalists at the time were prepared to admit. The sources are rich in both quantity and quality, and excellently preserved. It was the concept of law as such, the idea of the law and the related problem of generating law that on closer analysis had a lasting impact on developments in the Middle Ages and shaped the history of the period. We cannot understand the Middle Ages without looking at law and history equally. Law without history, and history without law both represent mere patchwork in medieval studies. During the Middle Ages law and history were more intimately connected than perhaps at any other time before or after. The no-man's-land between law and history was largely neglected territory, not only in England, but also in Germany, France and Italy. My researches, however, were rudely interrupted by the collapse of France in June 1940. It now became my duty to join the British Army as a volunteer. I was assigned to the Pioneer Corps, which contained a large number of Austrians, including men from

Innsbruck and the Burgenland, mostly from the former 'Fatherland Front' founded by the Chancellor Dollfuss, and many Jews. But after three years I was discharged from the army on health grounds. In the autumn of 1943 I returned to the school that had already once thrown me a lifeline. After the end of the war I offered my modest talents to Austrian academia, but the response was by no means encouraging.

I used every opportunity to continue my researches in Cambridge, which was only about 150 kilometres from the school, and in cathedral libraries. At that time I was mainly engaged in collecting material. The result was my first book, *The Medieval Idea of Law*, published in 1946, preceded by a number of articles. The book was unexpectedly well received, seeming to have opened up previously unknown perspectives. The topic had suggested a comparative analysis between ecclesiastical law and the canonists. In the process I had 'discovered' a report by Baldus on the election of Urban VI. This is what encouraged me to come to grips with the problems this raised, and explains the genesis of my second book, published in 1948, about the great Western schism. I soon realised that studying medieval civilians and canonists opened up extremely wide perspectives. In 1946, while still a school teacher, I was completely unexpectedly named Maitland Memorial Lecturer in Cambridge for the academic year 1947/48. This was an exceptional honour because previously only established scholars had been appointed to this position. The endowment is dedicated to the memory of the great legal historian Maitland, who died in 1906. I resolved to discuss the political ideas of the medieval canonists before a select audience. I believed that this would be fully in accord with Maitland's ideas, for he had put forward a view which I heartily agreed with: 'Law was the point, in the Middle Ages, where life and logic met.'

In the summer of 1947 I received, also unexpectedly, an invitation to take up a teaching post that had suddenly become vacant at the University of Leeds. At last I was able to work as a full-time academic teacher. A great deal of enthusiasm went into my lectures, although I had never been a student at an English university in the usual way, and did not know what level of knowledge I could assume among my students. My teaching experience at Ratcliffe College stood me in good stead. I spent two very happy years at the University of Leeds. Library facilities there were astonishingly good. The great cathedral libraries of Lincoln, York and Durham were within easy reach. In May 1949, contrary to all expectations, I was appointed to a chair at Cambridge. My Maitland lectures of February-March 1948 had obviously made a good impression. They were published in book form in the summer of 1949.

My preoccupation with the papacy never left me. In its own eyes the institution of the papacy embodied the idea of law and its practical realisation within the historical framework. The connection between law and history seemed to have found its fullest expression in the medieval papacy. And Cambridge offered excellent libraries for researching the legal and historical aspects of the papacy. My teaching commitments also furthered this research project. In Oxford and Cambridge the teaching of students is divided between university lectures and individual tutoring in college. This type of teaching is not only advantageous for the students – I had sorely missed this sort of contact in Vienna – but also extremely worthwhile for the teacher, because he is forced to remain up to date with the most recent literature, and to adapt to the individual needs of each student in their weekly sessions. I found the intellectual climate of Cambridge highly stimulating; this is one of the oldest universities in Europe. Among academics, it is said that one does not move on from Oxford or Cambridge. Indeed, I refused very tempting offers from other universities, especially in America. I was to remain the only Austrian to hold a chair in the History Faculty. My teaching in the field of legal history, especially my lectures, broke new ground. From the start, my lectures were always highly popular. But it was also hard work because my students had no legal training. I therefore decided to give lectures and seminars on Roman law and ecclesiastical law in the Middle Ages. Since Henry VIII's ban, I was the first person for exactly 400 years to teach ecclesiastical law at an English university. I always endeavoured to show how fruitful it can be to combine a legal and a historical analysis. The students were bright and interested. Many of those who wrote PhDs with me after doing their undergraduate studies in my seminar today hold important academic positions. Brian Tierney, for example, went to Cornell University in the USA and is the leading medievalist there today; M.J. Wilks is Professor of Medieval History at the University of London. Charles Duggan, a specialist on canon law, and Janet Nelson, who works on ecclesiastical history, are also at the University of London. Jack Watt is Professor of Medieval History in Newcastle, A.B. Cobban, whose specialism is the history of universities, teaches at the University of Liverpool, while P.D. King teaches early medieval history at the University of Lancaster. Black is at the University of Dundee and is a specialist on conciliar theory and the late medieval papacy. John Gilchrist, who works on canon law, is Professor at Trent University in Canada, while P.A. Linehan, a Spanish specialist, has developed a rich programme of teaching and research at Cambridge and Arthur S. McGrade is a professor teaching late medieval political philosophy at the University of Connecticut in the USA. In addition, a number became librarians or archivists, such as Christopher Ligota, who is a librarian at the Warburg Institute of the University of London. My students themselves in turn produced students, so that I am told I now preside over a large family of children and grandchildren.

I frequently represented my university at congresses and academic ceremonies where I met many famous foreign colleagues and learned to move on the international stage, so to speak, something which did not come naturally to me with my rural background. I also took part in many international conferences, and gave lectures at numerous European and American universities, and to learned societies. I was Guest Professor at Johns Hopkins University in the USA in 1964/65, and in Tübingen and Munich in 1973. I was especially honoured by invitations to lecture at Innsbruck and Salzburg. The fact that Innsbruck conferred on me an Honorary Doctorate in political sciences I consider an unearned distinction. Of my other academic activities I should perhaps mention that I am editor of the 'Cambridge Studies in Medieval Life and Thought', a series which has so far grown to encompass twelve volumes, co-editor of the *Journal of Ecclesiastical History*, and a contributor to the series 'Päpste und Papsttum'. In 1968 I became a Fellow of the British Academy, and an Honorary Fellow of St Edmund's House, Cambridge, one of the colleges, in 1976. I have been a Fellow of Trinity College since 1959, where I had taught between 1949 and 1959. In February 1977 I was elected a Corresponding Member of the Bavarian Academy of Sciences...[7]

I do not want to conceal the fact that some purist historians opposed the connections I made between law and history. I have two things to say on this subject. Although a number of my books went into a third and fourth edition, almost all were reprinted (some several times), and several were translated into German, Italian, Spanish and Japanese, with reprints, the reception of my integrative method by scholars was only partly positive. Some reacted coolly, or even rejected it. There is, I believe, at least a partial explanation for these differing reactions. It is certainly regrettable to observe how infrequently one encounters independent judgement nowadays, and how often one finds an obvious inability to combine ideas, to grasp them in their entirety and variety, to recognise their origins and assess the widely spread areas which they have influenced. Added to this is the fact that the conclusions to which the 'new' method (which should, really, be the old one) necessarily gave rise created uneasiness because there was no space for them in the way of thinking which had become habitual among medievalists. Surprisingly enough, however, the very same conclusions were recognised and accepted by historians of the modern period, social scientists, and political scientists. A number of medievalists objected to the legal basis of the principles but after all, principles can only be expressed and interpreted in precise terms. Combining law and history effectively prevents historians from projecting back modern values and using modern concepts and ideas which jeopardise the acquisition of historical knowledge. The integrative method immunises historians against influences which could distort the historical picture. The historian must arrive at the knowledge that despite all continuity, homogeneous medieval society and modern pluralist society rest on entirely different premises. Those who object to the integrative method overlook this fundamental insight, and thus prevent themselves from fulfilling the basic demand made of the historian, namely to explain how, why and when we became what we are today.

Secondly, neither excited and emotionally charged bad temper, nor the volume at which criticism is expressed, nor deliberate mis-understanding, not to mention wilful distortion, can do away with the new knowledge because it more or less springs from the sources if they are examined with an open mind and the integrative method. To gain knowledge from sources requires reflective understanding, and this excludes the projection backwards of modern ideas and principles. Understanding in this context signifies thinking and experiencing in a contemporary way, in other words, participating in the historical process. And this participation can only take place on the basis of an intimate knowledge of the sources.

This outline of a career which is perhaps unusual would be incomplete without some mention of my loyal wife, an Englishwoman and scholar of English literature in her own right. Since we first met when she was a student, she has stood by me with untiring encouragement, and sensitive, intelligent and constructive criticism, always selfless and never despairing even during the most difficult days. We got married during the invasion scare of 1940 when I was a soldier; if we were to perish, then it would be together. However bitter and frequent the disappointments I suffered during the early years, she always gave me new heart, looked with confidence to the future, and gave me endless strength through her faith. Without her I would have failed.

## Notes

1   Walter Ullmann died in 1983. The essay published here is the translation of a paper which Ullmann wrote in September 1977 in Cambridge, when he was elected a Corresponding Fellow of the Austrian Academy of Sciences. The original was entitled 'Autobiographische Darstellung des Lebenslaufs des korrespondierenden Mitglieds Walter Ullmann'. The biography of Ullmann by Elizabeth Ullmann, *Walter Ullmann: A Tale of Two Cultures* (Cambridge, 1990) is based on the 'Autobiographische Darstellung'. The subtitle of this publication was adopted for the present translation.

I should like to thank the Austrian Academy of Sciences in Vienna and Trinity College Cambridge for their help, and for granting permission to print a shortened English version of the 'Autobiographische Darstellung' in the present volume. Translated by Angela Davies, German Historical Institute London.

2   Franciscus Accursius (1185-1263), Italian jurist.

3   Universitas Oenipontana = University of Innsbruck.

4   Fourteenth- and fifteenth-century successors to the medieval glossators, who annotated Roman legal texts and adapted Roman law to the practical needs of the day. The post-glossators, mainly Italians, are the founders of modern European jurisprudence.

5   On 20 May 1938 the Czechoslovak government mobilised its forces, pointing to an imminent military intervention by Nazi Germany. France and Britain assured Prague of their support in the case of a German invasion.

6   The Munich Conference of 29-30 September 1938. At the conference Britain, France, Italy and Germany agreed to the cession of the Sudetenland from Czechoslovakia and its annexation by the Third Reich.

7   Three pages of the 'Autobiographische Darstellung' have been omitted from the translation at this point. In the passage omitted Ullmann provides more information about his integrative approach, the significance of Bible studies for medievalists, the legal force of baptism, and feudalism.

## Selected Writings of Walter Ullmann

*The Medieval Idea of the Law as Represented by Lucas de Penna: A Study in Fourteenth-Century Legal Scholarship* (London, 1946)

*The Origins of the Great Schism: A Study in Fourteenth-Century Ecclesiastical History* (London, 1948)

*Medieval Papalism: The Political Theories of the Medieval Canonists* (Maitland Memorial Lectures 1947-48, London 1949)

*The Growth of Papal Government in the Middle Ages: A Study in the Ideological Relation of Clerical to Lay Power* (London 1955; German edition: Graz, 1961)

*Principles of Government and Politics in the Middle Ages* (London, 1961)

*A History of Political Thought: The Middle Ages* (Harmondsworth, 1965)

*The Relevance of Medieval Ecclesiastical History: An Inaugural Lecture* (London, 1966)

*The Individual and Society in the Middle Ages* (Baltimore, 1966; German edition: Göttingen, 1974)

*The Carolingian Renaissance and the Idea of Kingship* (London, 1969)

*A Short History of the Papacy in the Middle Ages* (London, 1972; German edition: Berlin, 1978)

*The Church and Law in the Earlier Middle Ages: Collected Studies,* volume 1 (London, 1975)

*Law and Politics in the Middle Ages: Introduction to the Sources of Medieval Political Ideas* (Cambridge, 1975)

*The Papacy and Political Ideas in the Middle Ages: Collected Studies,* volume 2 (London, 1976)

*Medieval Foundations of Renaissance Humanism* (London, 1977)

*Scholarship and Politics in the Middle Ages: Collected Studies,* volume 3 (London, 1978)

*Jurisprudence in the Middle Ages: Collected Studies,* volume 4 (London, 1980)

*Gelasius I (492-496): Das Papsttum an der Wende der Spätantike zum Mittelalter* (Stuttgart, 1981)

# Index